saturday kitchen
cooking bible

Madhur Jaffrey Tom Kerridge Thomas Keller Lawrence Keogh Tom Kime T
Nathan Outlaw José Pizarro Arthur Potts Dawson Glynn Purnell Tana Ramsay
Michel Roux Jr Silvena Rowe Mark Sargeant Vivek Singh Clare Smyth Ric
Matt Tebbutt Cass Titcombe Marcus Wareing Nic Watt Tristan Welch Bryn Willia
ampbell Antonio Carluccio Richard Corrigan Gennaro Contaldo Anthony Dem
Harris Angela Hartnett Donna Hay Will Holland Ken Hom Madhur Jaffrey Tom
Martin Francesco Mazzei Danny Millar Nick Nairn Nathan Outlaw José Pizarr
ankin Stéphane Reynaud Alain Roux Michel Roux Michel Roux Jr Silvena Rowe
anaka Cyrus Todiwala Andrew Turner Matt Tebbutt Cass Titcombe Marcus W
lackiston Adam Byatt Michael Caines John Campbell Antonio Carluccio Richar
illies Bill Granger Anna Hansen Henry Harris Angela Hartnett Donna Hay Wil
ime Tom Kitchin Atul Kochhar James Martin Francesco Mazzei Danny Millar Nick
andall Paul Rankin Shaun Rankin Stéphane Reynaud Alain Roux Michel Roux M
tovell James Tanner Jun Tanaka Cyrus Todiwala Andrew Turner Matt Tebbutt Cas
ertinet Galton Blackiston Adam Byatt Michael Caines John Campbell Antonio
almiche Stuart Gillies Bill Granger Anna Hansen Henry Harris Angela Hartnett
eogh Tom Kime Tom Kitchin Atul Kochhar James Martin Francesco Mazzei Dann
amsay Theo Randall Paul Rankin Shaun Rankin Stéphane Reynaud Alain Roux
tein Fernando Stovell James Tanner Jun Tanaka Cyrus Todiwala Andrew Turner N
therton Richard Bertinet Galton Blackiston Adam Byatt Michael Caines John C
imbleby Daniel Galmiche Stuart Gillies Bill Granger Anna Hansen Henry Harris A
eller Lawrence Keogh Tom Kime Tom Kitchin Atul Kochhar James Martin F
awson Glynn Purnell Tana Ramsay Theo Randall Paul Rankin Shaun Rankin Stép
ingh Clare Smyth Rick Stein Fernando Stovell James Tanner Jun Tanaka Cyrus
Velch Bryn Williams Jason Atherton Richard Bertinet Galton Blackiston Adar
ontaldo Anthony Demetre Henry Dimbleby Daniel Galmiche Stuart Gillies Bi
om Madhur Jaffrey Tom Kerridge Thomas Keller Lawrence Keogh Tom Kime Tc
utlaw José Pizarro Arthur Potts Dawson Glynn Purnell Tana Ramsay Theo Ran
Silvena Rowe Mark Sargeant Vivek Singh Clare Smyth Rick Stein Fernando
itcombe Marcus Wareing Nic Watt Tristan Welch Bryn Williams Jason Atherton
arluccio Richard Corrigan Gennaro Contaldo Anthony Demetre Henry Dimb
artnett Donna Hay Will Holland Ken Hom Madhur Jaffrey Tom Kerridge Thom
Mazzei Danny Millar Nick Nairn Nathan Outlaw José Pizarro Arthur Potts Da
eynaud Alain Roux Michel Roux Michel Roux Jr Silvena Rowe Mark Sargeant
odiwala Andrew Turner Matt Tebbutt Cass Titcombe Marcus Wareing Nic Wat

chin Atul Kochhar James Martin Francesco Mazzei Danny Millar Nick Nair
Randall Paul Rankin Shaun Rankin Stéphane Reynaud Alain Roux Michel Rou
Fernando Stovell James Tanner Jun Tanaka Cyrus Todiwala Andrew Turne
on Atherton Richard Bertinet Galton Blackiston Adam Byatt Michael Caines Joh
nry Dimbleby Daniel Galmiche Stuart Gillies Bill Granger Anna Hansen Henr
ge Thomas Keller Lawrence Keogh Tom Kime Tom Kitchin Atul Kochhar Jame
r Potts Dawson Glynn Purnell Tana Ramsay Theo Randall Paul Rankin Shau
argeant Vivek Singh Clare Smyth Rick Stein Fernando Stovell James Tanner Ju
Nic Watt Tristan Welch Bryn Williams Jason Atherton Richard Bertinet Galto
n Gennaro Contaldo Anthony Demetre Henry Dimbleby Daniel Galmiche Stua
d Ken Hom Madhur Jaffrey Tom Kerridge Thomas Keller Lawrence Keogh Tor
Nathan Outlaw José Pizarro Arthur Potts Dawson Glynn Purnell Tana Ramsay The
ux Jr Silvena Rowe Mark Sargeant Vivek Singh Clare Smyth Rick Stein Fernand
be Marcus Wareing Nic Watt Tristan Welch Bryn Williams Jason Atherton Richar
o Richard Corrigan Gennaro Contaldo Anthony Demetre Henry Dimbleby Danie
lay Will Holland Ken Hom Madhur Jaffrey Tom Kerridge Thomas Keller Lawrenc
Nick Nairn Nathan Outlaw José Pizarro Arthur Potts Dawson Glynn Purnell Tan
Roux Michel Roux Jr Silvena Rowe Mark Sargeant Vivek Singh Clare Smyth Ric
butt Cass Titcombe Marcus Wareing Nic Watt Tristan Welch Bryn Williams Jaso
Antonio Carluccio Richard Corrigan Gennaro Contaldo Anthony Demetre Henr
Hartnett Donna Hay Will Holland Ken Hom Madhur Jaffrey Tom Kerridge Thoma
o Mazzei Danny Millar Nick Nairn Nathan Outlaw José Pizarro Arthur Pott
ynaud Alain Roux Michel Roux Michel Roux Jr Silvena Rowe Mark Sargeant Vive
a Andrew Turner Matt Tebbutt Cass Titcombe Marcus Wareing Nic Watt Trista
t Michael Caines John Campbell Antonio Carluccio Richard Corrigan Gennar
ger Anna Hansen Henry Harris Angela Hartnett Donna Hay Will Holland Ke
in Atul Kochhar James Martin Francesco Mazzei Danny Millar Nick Nairn Natha
ul Rankin Shaun Rankin Stéphane Reynaud Alain Roux Michel Roux Michel Rou
l James Tanner Jun Tanaka Cyrus Todiwala Andrew Turner Matt Tebbutt Cas
d Bertinet Galton Blackiston Adam Byatt Michael Caines John Campbell Antoni
aniel Galmiche Stuart Gillies Bill Granger Anna Hansen Henry Harris Ange
r Lawrence Keogh Tom Kime Tom Kitchin Atul Kochhar James Martin Francesc
Glynn Purnell Tana Ramsay Theo Randall Paul Rankin Shaun Rankin Stéphan
Singh Clare Smyth Rick Stein Fernando Stovell James Tanner Jun Tanaka Cyru
Welch Bryn Williams Jason Atherton Richard Bertinet Galton Blackiston Ada

saturday kitchen

cooking bible

200 delicious recipes cooked in
the nation's favourite kitchen

WEIDENFELD & NICOLSON

First published in Great Britain in 2013
by Weidenfeld & Nicolson
an imprint of The Orion Publishing Group Ltd
Orion House
5 Upper St Martin's Lane
London WC2H 9EA

An Hachette UK Company

10 9 8 7 6 5 4 3 2 1

ISBN: 9780297869108

Recipes and text © Cactus TV Limited 2013
Design and layout © Weidenfeld & Nicolson 2013
Project edit by Zelda Turner
Design and art direction by Loulou Clark
Photography by Andrew Hayes-Watkins
Food styling by Anna Burges-Lumsden
and Lisa Harrison
Props by Giuliana Casarotti
Food assistant: Katy Ross and Phil Wells
Photography assistant: Zoe Russell

A CIP catalogue record for this book
is available from the British Library.

Printed and bound in China

The Orion Publishing Group's policy is to use papers
that are natural, renewable and recyclable products
and made from wood grown in sustainable forests.
The logging and manufacturing processes are
expected to conform to the environmental regulations
of the country of origin.

www.orionbooks.co.uk

Contents

Foreword 9

Introduction 10

Breakfast & brunch 14

Small dishes 38

30-minute meals 74

Weekend lunch..............................106

Salads 146

Family feasts 176

Planning ahead.............................216

Friends for dinner 254

Puddings 294

Best bits 330

The golden rules for wine & food 332

What's in season 336

How to shop... 340

Index...343

Foreword

Welcome to the *Saturday Kitchen Cooking Bible*! In these pages you will find over 200 mouth-watering recipes from the last few years that have featured on the show.

I have been lucky enough to present *Saturday Kitchen* since 2006 and in that time I have shared the hobs with hundreds of great chefs and even managed to meet some of my all-time cooking heroes along the way. The dishes in this book will give you a good flavour of the kinds of dishes we have been able to share with the viewers and their style and content should allow you to understand the passion for cooking that all of us involved in the show feel.

A television show is never the work of just one man and I am merely the driver of a very well-oiled television machine. Behind the scenes there are lots of other people working hard to make the magic happen. From our incredible team of home economists, to the camera operators all the way to our egg-pun obsessed production staff. We are a team and it is an honour and a privilege to work amongst such dedicated people.

There have been so many highlights on the show but my birthday programme comes pretty close to perfection. Cooking with Alain Roux, Nathan Outlaw and Marcus Wareing with their seven Michelin stars between them made for a spectacular morning, which even ended with a car-shaped cake fresh from the kitchen at The Waterside Inn. It doesn't come any better than that!

The ethos of the show is simple: the food is the star. It is this mantra that has allowed us access to some of the greatest culinary talent on the planet. Each week we aim to cook the best possible food we can while always keeping the dishes accessible and attainable to all. This book is testament to that. The recipes in here can all be cooked at home and although some may require a little more planning than others, they all are worth the effort.

People assume that I don't get nervous anymore on the show and generally that's true but there are times when even I get the odd butterfly or two, especially if I am stood next to the likes of Thomas Keller, Pierre Koffmann, Alain Roux or his dad Michel Roux Sr. I have been a fan of Thomas Keller's, in particular, since I was a student. His books and restaurants have provided me with so much inspiration over the years and when we finally convinced him to join us it was something very special indeed. I shall never forget the way he made his omelette and it has nothing to do with the fact that the show nearly crashed off the air because he took so long!

Getting up close to these great chefs is one of the best bits of the show and this book is packed full of top tips and techniques from lots of our *Saturday Kitchen* regulars. We have even asked everyone for their perfect five minute dessert! There are so many delicious things to try from so many top top chefs that it's tricky to know where to begin, so just flick to any page and dive in.

This book is very much a team effort and just like the show it is a coming together of loads of ideas and recipes from the whole culinary world. By tucking into its pages and having a go, you too can join our merry band of food heroes and put a smile on your or someone else's face when you sit down to the results.

Happy cooking!

James Martin

Introduction

Wherever possible on *Saturday Kitchen*, we use free-range organic chicken and eggs, higher welfare fish and meat, and the freshest seasonal ingredients (page 336). You'll find a fantastic variety of locally caught fish and seafood recipes in this book, from the great-tasting gurnard in Cass Tiscombe's summer stew (page 84) to Gennaro Contaldo's tagliatelle with mussels (page 78). As Rick Stein reminds us, 'There are enough fish species caught around the coasts of Britain for us to eat a different kind every week of the year.' And, of course, the more we experiment with new types of fish, the more sustainable our fish eating becomes.

When it comes to cooking meat, there's something for every occasion, from Thomas Keller's extraordinary roast chicken (page 236) to Michel Roux's veal blanquette (page 243) and Tana Ramsay's easy homemade sausages (page 208). Whatever you choose, make sure you buy the best meat you can afford, from a trusted source. As James Martin explains: 'It helps to make friends with your butcher as it is he who decides where your meat comes from, how it was reared and slaughtered, how long it was hung for and what cuts to select: and all those things add up to good-quality meat.'

With beef especially you get what you pay for. British-reared breeds such as Aberdeen Angus, Longhorn and Hereford are considered to be among the best in the world. And wagyu beef (page 284), which originated in Japan, has become the last word in luxury. Don't be afraid to use cheaper cuts of meat for stews, soups or curries – thigh, belly, tongue, cheek and oxtail all make for an excellent flavoured dish when they are cooked slow and long.

Store cupboard secrets

Cunning store cupboard standbys mean you can throw together a feast at a moment's notice. And you don't have to go shopping for every meal. With this in mind, we asked the Saturday Kitchen *brigade for the food products they're never without. Included in this list are all the good, basic ingredients that pop up throughout this book, alongside some guilty pleasures, like Rick Stein's instant Aromat seasoning and Michel Roux's shop-bought pastry. Happily, it turns out, even top chefs cheat when cooking at home!*

Dried pasta The ultimate store cupboard staple. Barilla and De Cecco are good brands, says Angela Hartnett, offering a whole range of pasta shapes and flours (for when you fancy making your own pasta).

Fish sauce 'It works with everything,' according to Ken Hom.

Fresh herbs Basil, mint, chives and flat-leaf parsley can all be grown from seed in a windowbox and harvested as and when they are needed. For a homemade high-end garnish 'you can grow coriander cress very easily,' says Vivek Singh. 'Simply soak coriander seeds overnight, lay them on a kitchen towel and allow to sprout. As tender green shoots begin to come out, they become coriander cress.'

Japanese panko breadcrumbs Low cal, low salt, lighter than traditional Western breadcrumbs, they coat food in a delicate, crispy sheath, while allowing the flavours within to shine.

Ketchup 'Great to use as a seasoning,' suggests Michel Roux Jr.

Knorr Aromat Seasoning 'This is what I call a proper cheat ingredient,' declares Rick Stein of Knorr's bright yellow, powdered blend of herbs and spices.

Lea & Perrins Worcestershire Sauce 'A British culinary classic that gives a brilliant lift to leftovers, stocks, sauces and cocktails,' Tom Kitchin

Miso paste 'Wonderful as part of a marinade for meat, good in dressings and to add umami base flavours to soups and stews,' Henry Dimbleby.

Mustard 'Colman's is best in sauces, or fantastic smeared on top of a pork pie or sausage roll,' Tom Kerridge.

Sea salt and whole black peppercorns Judicious seasoning will make a dish. The chefs' favourite is Maldon sea salt, which has a wonderful texture and taste.

Shop-bought pastry Perfect for stress-free, speedy desserts. As Michel Roux puts it: 'Entertaining at home is not a competition!'

Spices When it comes to adding flavour, colour and aroma, spices are the easiest way to make food exciting. Vivek Singh has the following tips for spicing up your kitchen:

1. *Don't buy spices in bulk; buy what you can use in 2 or 3 months, no more.*

2. *Buy your spices whole – roast and grind them as needed.*

3. *Store ground spices in airtight containers away from sunlight and use within 2 weeks of grinding: if you don't, all or most of the flavour will be lost.*

4. *When using both whole and ground spices in a dish, remember whole spices go at the beginning of the dish and ground spices go towards the end.*

5. *The more expensive the spice, the smaller the quantity you need to add to the dish. Additionally, more expensive spices are mostly added later into the cooking.*

Stock cubes Everyone from Antonio Carluccio to Silvena Rowe uses stock cubes at home. Nathan Outlaw recommends Bisto 'as a quick and easy way to thicken homemade sauces.' And Nick Nairn 'adds a tiny amount of good-quality gravy granules at the end of gravy making, to give gloss and a bit of starchy thickness.'

Tabasco 'For its combination of sweet, sour and heat that can lift many a sauce, dish or simple preparation without overpowering anything.' Bjorn van der Horst reckons Tabasco is 'perfect for those moments of doubt when you taste a dish and say to yourself, "mmm, it's just not there yet, something's missing".'

Tinned food Stock up on tinned Italian tomatoes, tinned fish (mackerel, anchovies and sardines) and tinned pulses,which you can whiz up into flavoursome dips, pasta sauces, soup and salads.

White truffle oil Prized by Shaun Rankin 'for its amazing flavour; it can help to season and gives such a different taste to soups and purées.'

Kitchen essentials

The right kitchen equipment can transform anyone into a happy and efficient home cook. Here are ten everyday basics the Saturday Kitchen *team couldn't live without:*

A good set of knives Ideally you need an all-purpose chef's knife, a bread knife and a paring knife for more intricate work. Michel Roux Jr recommends the Japanese Global brand. Bryn Williams likes Victorinox, which are 'light, hardwearing and perfectly balanced'. Tom Kerridge favours 'very sharp Robert Welch knives'. No gadget is as important as a good quality chef's knife. Spend a little more and it will last forever.

Dough scraper 'Not only is it useful for mixing and scraping out bowls,' explains expert baker Richard Bertinet, 'but it means I can keep my hands clean for longer in case the phone rings. It also doubles as a windscreen scraper in the winter!'

Electronic kitchen scales Brilliant for baking, where you weigh things down to the last gram. That said, Gennaro Contaldo claims to seldom use any kitchen scales!

Food processor A good processor will save you so much time and energy in the kitchen: chopping, slicing, mixing, whisking, beating, kneading and doing all the prep work for you. Buy the best you can afford – generally speaking, the bigger, the better.

Good-quality wooden chopping board 'A great investment,' according to James.

Japanese mandoline Unbeatable for quick fine slicing. As Bill Granger says, 'It not only saves time, but requires much less effort than agonisingly trying to create uniform slices with a knife. It also gives your dishes that polished, cheffy appearance.'

Quality cookware On the show we use a range of ovenproof non-stick frying pans and lidded pans, sturdy high-sided roasting trays and flameproof baking dishes, which can be used on the hob as well as in the oven. They make the cooking process easier and save on washing up.

Silicone spatulas and wooden spoons For stirring, scraping, mixing, flipping … Buy a few: you'll use them all the time!

Spice grinder For amazing, freshly ground spices, invest in a spice grinder or recycle an old coffee grinder – it will do the job perfectly. For pounding and crushing herbs, salts and spices, a pestle and mortar is also highly recommended.

Wok Great for cooking all kinds of fast, healthy food. Look for one that's fairly hefty rather than anything too lightweight.

Don't buy anything until you're sure you need it.

New equipment can be seductive. As Rick Stein warns, 'A short tour around my garage (and it would be short, because my garage is tiny, unlike James Martin's!) will reveal a cornucopia of little used gadgets. Don't speak too loudly because I should say never used. Things like a sandwich toaster, a meat slicer with a very small blade and a George Forman grill – given to me, honest!' Fortunately, you don't need a lot of kit to cook the majority of dishes in this book. So once you've got the essentials covered, pick a recipe you like and just start cooking!

Cook's notes

Eggs/butter
All eggs are medium and butter is unsalted unless otherwise stated.

Oven temperatures
We use fan-assisted Fahrenheit ovens on the show. If you are cooking with a conventional oven (without fan assistance), follow the temperature guidelines in this book but increase the cooking time slightly.

Conversion table
Recipes are given in metric measurements. Strictly speaking, 1 ounce equals 28 grams: in practice, we express an ounce as 25 grams. This is to make your sums a little easier: with most recipes a few grams here or there won't make any difference.

Measurements
1 tsp is the equivalent of 5ml
1 tbsp is the equivalent of 15ml

breakfast & brunch

Weekends start early for a chef and nobody gets a lie-in with *Saturday Kitchen Live*. For the foodie team, preparations begin at 5 a.m. and by the time us guest chefs arrive, an hour or so later, the smell of bacon butties is amazing. (Though if you ask James Martin, over the six years of filming and the 8,000 bacon butties that have been made, he's never even been offered one!)

On busy mornings, breakfast has to be quick and easy. It's something to grab in a rush because you're trying to get the children to school and yourself off to work. Antonio Carluccio's staple is biscuits and coffee (the classic Italian). Ken Hom survives on green tea. Mark Sargeant grabs some yoghurt with honey.

But give a good chef half an hour in the kitchen in the morning and things start to get a lot more exciting …

From a speedy homemade jam and crumpets to James Martin's waffly good breakfast, from tattie scones to kipper cakes, this chapter has everything you need to break your fast in style.

Take inspiration from Ireland, Scotland or Mexico. Try an Anglo-Indian brunch with Madhur Jaffrey. Compete with the world's fastest chefs or take your time over the perfect omelette, Thomas Keller style.

Finally, there's the full English: the ultimate big breakfast. It's an English staple that has stood the test of time. Men went to war on this breakfast – and it's so nutritious when using fresh, seasonal ingredients. Check out my haute cuisine twist on tradition (page 22). It's enough to keep you satisfied all day!

Jason Atherton

A speedy strawberry jam

by James Martin

This fresh-tasting jam is high on fruit, low on sugar, which means it should be eaten the week, if not the day it is made. It's best served at the table, still warm, with toast, crumpets, hot scones or swirled into fresh Greek yoghurt. Yum!

Rinse and hull the strawberries. Halve or even quarter the large ones and check for soft spots, which must be removed.

Add the fruit to a stainless steel or enamel pan and cook for 1 minute, then add the sugar, lemon zest and juice and cook for 5–6 minutes until the sugar has dissolved and the mixture has thickened slightly. Stir occasionally and spoon off any of the pink froth that may come to the surface as you go.

Remove half of the mixture from the pan, place into a blender and blend to a purée. Spoon off a little of the strawberry juice if it is too runny.

Return the purée to the pan with the remaining cooked strawberries, stir well and cook for a further 3–5 minutes until thick.

Serves 8–10

700g strawberries
300g caster sugar
½ lemon, zest and juice

Buttermilk crumpets

by James Martin

You can make these crumpets in advance and lightly toast them just before serving. Serve warm with butter and fresh jam. Or add a poached egg (page 21), fried black pudding, hollandaise (page 52) and crispy bacon to kick off your weekend in style.

Sift the flour and salt into a large mixing bowl and stir in the yeast. Make a well in the centre, then pour in the buttermilk and 175ml warm water and mix well to form a smooth thick batter. Cover the bowl tightly with cling film and allow to prove in a warm place for about an hour, until doubled in size.

Preheat the oven to 170°C/325°F/Gas 3. Grease the insides of the metal rings well and brush a non-stick frying pan with oil before placing it over a medium heat.

To cook the crumpets, half fill each crumpet ring with batter. Let them cook gently until the top has completely set then use a couple of large forks to lift off the rings and flip the crumpets over. Cook the other side for 1 minute only. Move to the oven and bake for 10 minutes until cooked through.

Serves 4

You'll need 4 crumpet rings or egg cooking rings

225g strong flour
7g salt
7g quick action dried yeast
150ml buttermilk
1–2 tbsp light olive oil

A very slow omelette

by Thomas Keller

Thomas Keller is one of the most highly-skilled chefs in the world and the owner of not one, but two 3-Michelin star restaurants in the US. His perfectionist approach may have cost him the Saturday Kitchen omelette challenge (with a staggering 2 minutes, 47 seconds), but his slow-cooked, soft-centred omelette is worth trying at home.

Crack the eggs into a bowl and whisk till the yolks and whites are mixed to a completely uniform state and no streaks of white can be seen. Vigorous whisking will work here, but a blender is the easiest and most efficient way to do this. Season with a good pinch of sea salt and freshly ground black pepper.

Heat a large non-stick pan over a medium-low heat, add a good knob of butter and swirl to coat. When the butter starts to bubble and foam, pour in the egg.

Rather than frying the omelette over a high heat, the way to get your eggs nice and creamy is to cook the omelette very slowly. The aim is to create a perfectly smooth, creamy texture, without tough spots or air holes. An alternative to frying is to put the pan in the oven for 4–5 minutes on a very low temperature so that the top of the omelette cooks at the same time as the bottom.

As the omelette starts to set, carefully lift the edges upwards with a spatula, allowing the uncooked egg to run underneath. What we're after here is a yellow, uniform exterior without browning or air pockets and a creamy, just-cooked interior. Practice will teach you when it's perfect.

Remove from the heat. Use your spatula to fold 2 edges inwards, shake so that they roll together, then tilt your pan slightly and tip the whole lot onto a plate, with the fold at the bottom. Season, to taste, and eat immediately.

Serves 1–2

3 fresh eggs, preferably organic
generous knob of butter (about a tablespoon)
sea salt and freshly ground black pepper

....

Tip: More interested in racing against the clock? The secret to topping the leader board is to forget about taste: 'You'd think on a show like this chefs would know how to make a good omelette,' says James, 'but after six years on *Saturday Kitchen* I have yet to try one!' Going to press, the top three chefs to beat are Paul Rankin: 17.52 seconds, Lawrence Keogh: 17.74 seconds, and Gennaro Contaldo: 18.16 seconds.

Perfect poached eggs
by James Martin

Ever wondered how chefs get perfect poached eggs, every time? If you don't have a 100 per cent success rate with yours, give the Saturday Kitchen *method a whirl.*

Half fill a medium saucepan with water and wait until it is bubbling away furiously. Add a hefty pinch of salt and the white wine vinegar.

Using the handle of a slotted spoon, whisk the water to create a whirlpool (this will help the eggs to hold their shape). Crack the eggs into the centre of the vortex, one or two at a time. Use the freshest eggs you possibly can – they'll hold together better. As the eggs cook, use the spoon to keep the water moving and ensure that that the egg whites wrap around the yolks. Take care, as you don't want to break the eggs.

Simmer for 2–3 minutes, or until the egg white is cooked. Remove the eggs carefully with the slotted spoon and place on kitchen paper to drain. Repeat the process with the remaining eggs.

pinch salt
a splash of white wine
   vinegar (optional)
very fresh eggs, preferably
   organic

....

Tip: If you have other bits of a dish to prepare, place the poached eggs into a bowl of iced water to stop them overcooking. They can be stored like this for up to a day. When ready to serve, reheat the eggs by warming them through in a pan of gently simmering water.

A fancy fry-up

by Jason Atherton

Once you've mastered the basics, try Jason's twist on the traditional full English breakfast – a playful haute cuisine dish of crispy bacon, tomato fondue, croutons, mushroom velouté and poached eggs.

Preheat the oven to 170°C/325°F/Gas 3. Lay the bacon between 2 heavy baking trays and bake for around 12 minutes or until crisp. Keep warm until ready to serve.

To make the croutons, add half the butter to a hot frying pan and heat until foaming. Add the diced bread and cook until golden-brown all over. Drain on kitchen paper.

Add the remaining butter to the pan with the trompettes de mort and cook until just tender, about 2 minutes. Drain on kitchen paper.

For the tomato fondue, heat a large frying pan until hot, add 3 tablespoons olive oil, shallot, garlic, thyme and bay leaf and cook gently until everything has softened. Add the tomato purée and cook for 2–3 minutes.

Reserve one third of the chopped tomatoes. Add the remaining tomatoes to the pan and cook for 6–7 minutes until the tomatoes have broken down and are nearly dry. Place the mixture into a food processor and blend to a fine purée then strain through a sieve into a clean pan and stir in the reserved tomatoes over a low heat. Whisk the mustard, vinegar and the remaining olive oil together then stir into the tomatoes.

For the mushroom velouté, heat a sauté pan until hot, add the butter and heat until foaming. Add the mushrooms, thyme and garlic and cook until golden-brown. Add the cream and cook until reduced and thickened. Place into a food processor, blend until smooth then strain through a sieve into a clean pan. Season, to taste, with sea salt and freshly ground black pepper.

Half fill a medium saucepan with water and bring to the boil. Poach the eggs for 3 minutes each (see page 21 for method).

To serve, place a spoonful of the tomato fondue on one side of each soup plate, and a spoonful of the mushroom velouté on the other side. Pile the trompettes de mort in the centre and scatter croutons and parsley around the plate. Place the egg on top of the mushrooms and finish with a couple of pieces of crispy bacon.

Serves 4

8 thin slices bacon
50g butter
2 slices white bread, diced
120g trompettes de mort
4 eggs
2 tbsp flat-leaf parsley,
  leaves only

for the tomato fondue

4 tbsp olive oil
1 large shallot, finely
  chopped
3 garlic cloves
1 thyme sprig, leaves picked
1 bay leaf
1 tsp tomato purée
1kg vine-ripened tomatoes,
  skinned, deseeded, roughly
  chopped
1 tsp mustard
1 tsp vinegar

for the mushroom velouté

115g butter
500g flat mushrooms, peeled
2 sprigs thyme, leaves picked
2 garlic cloves
150ml double cream
sea salt and freshly ground
  black pepper

Vuelve a la vida

by Fernando Stovell

Vuelve a la vida means 'return to life' in Spanish. Half Bloody Mary, half seafood cocktail, Fernando's recipe makes an incredible brunch and quite possibly the most delicious hangover cure ever invented – cool, spicy, zesty, and singing with flavour.

Mix the shallots, chilli, oregano, tomatoes, ketchup, orange juice, lime juice, Tabasco sauce and Worcestershire sauce together in a bowl until well combined. Stir in the prawns followed by the avocado, then season to taste.

Spoon the cocktail into margarita glasses – or whatever goblets you fancy – and sprinkle with the chopped coriander.

....

Tip: Serve alongside Fernando's hearts of palm salad (page 161), bowls of guacamole, salsa and salted crackers for a Mexican-style tapas lunch.

Serves 4

2 shallots, finely chopped
1½ jalapeño or green chillies, finely chopped
1–2 tsp fresh oregano
2 tomatoes, peeled, seeds removed, chopped
6 tbsp tomato ketchup
110ml orange juice
2 limes, juiced
Tabasco sauce, to taste
dash Worcestershire sauce
400g cooked Atlantic prawns, peeled
200g cooked tiger prawns, peeled
1 avocado, peeled, diced
6 tbsp chopped coriander
sea salt and freshly ground black pepper

Salmon, eggs and Irish potato bread
by Danny Millar

*Salmon and eggs is a match made in heaven. Add some Irish potato bread and a
luxurious green butter sauce and you have something approaching perfection.*

To make the potato bread, mix the mashed potato, flour and egg yolk together to
form a dough, then season to taste. Roll to a thickness of 5mm and cut into discs.
With a 9cm pastry cutter you should get 7 cakes.

Heat a non-stick pan over a medium heat and cook the cakes for 1½ minutes on each
side. Remove from the pan and set to one side. If you are preparing the potato bread
in advance, once cool, wrap the discs in cling film and chill in the fridge for 2–3 days,
or freeze for up to a month.

To make the green butter sauce, add the shallot, white wine and white wine vinegar
to a pan and reduce until a tablespoon of liquid remains. Whisk in the butter, one
piece at a time. Remove from the heat, then add the capers, anchovy and parsley and
check for seasoning.

Meanwhile, soft boil 4 eggs by placing in boiling water for 4–5 minutes, then chill in
iced water for 1 minute to stop them cooking. Peel the eggs, taking care not to break
them, and keep warm.

Place the salmon in a hot pan with a little oil. Cook for 1 minute on either side; the
salmon has already been cured so it won't take long.

At the same time, melt a good knob of butter in a clean pan and fry the potato bread
until crisp on either side.

When you are ready to serve, place the potato bread on the plate with the salmon on
top. Gently break the salmon open to expose its gorgeous pink inside. Place an egg on
top of the salmon then crack it open so that the yolk oozes out. Add a little seasoning,
pile on the watercress then spoon over plenty of buttery sauce.

Serves 4

**You'll need a 9cm
pastry cutter**

250g classic mash (page 214)
60g plain flour
4 whole eggs and 1 egg yolk
4 x 160g fillets cured organic
    salmon (trout or mackerel)
25g butter
a handful of watercress
sea salt and freshly ground
    black pepper

for the green butter sauce
1 shallot, finely chopped
4 tbsp white wine
2 tbsp white wine vinegar
110g unsalted butter, cold
    and diced
2 tbsp capers
1 anchovy, finely chopped
½ bunch flat-leaf parsley,
    finely chopped

Tip: Danny made this on the show with cured
Glenarm organic salmon, reared off the coast of
Northern Ireland (see page 340), but any sustainably
caught, cured salmon, trout or mackerel would
work beautifully here.

Welsh rarebit

by James Martin

Cheese on toast, deluxe-style. If you don't have Ogleshield, any hard English cheese will do here, so experiment with double Gloucester, Cheshire, Lancashire or whatever else you have in the fridge.

Preheat the grill to high.

Heat the cheese and milk in a saucepan, stirring regularly, until the cheese has melted. Add the flour and breadcrumbs and cook for a further 2–3 minutes, stirring continuously. Remove the pan from the heat and set aside to cool.

Whisk in the Worcestershire sauce, egg, egg yolk and mustard. Season, to taste, with salt and freshly ground black pepper.

Meanwhile, lightly toast the bread on one side. Spread the cheese mixture onto the untoasted side of the bread and grill for 1–2 minutes, or until the cheese is bubbling and golden-brown. Serve immediately.

....

Tip: Choose a thick, crusty bread like ciabatta. You want something that's robust enough to take the weight of the topping.

Serves 4

110g Ogleshield cheese, grated
110g Cheddar cheese, grated
50ml whole milk
25g plain flour
25g fresh white breadcrumbs
dash Worcestershire sauce
1 egg, plus 1 egg yolk
½ tsp English mustard powder
4 slices of thick crusty white bread
sea salt and freshly ground black pepper

Tattie scones and a big breakfast

by Lawrence Keogh

Lawrence's Scottish-style potato cakes are a beautiful thing to make with leftover mash. Served with roasted tomatoes, streaky bacon and fried egg, they turn breakfast into a grand event.

Preheat the oven to 200°C/400°F/Gas 6.

Pour the Worcestershire sauce into a pan and place over a medium heat. Bring to the boil, then reduce the heat and simmer until reduced by just over a third.

Place the tomatoes on a roasting tray, dot with half the butter and season well. Bake for 20–25 minutes, then tip into the pan with the reduced Worcestershire sauce and set aside.

Meanwhile, lay the rashers of bacon on a baking tray and place in the oven for 5–6 minutes, until crisp and golden-brown.

Heat a frying pan until hot, add the other 25g butter and the mushrooms and fry for 2–3 minutes, season well.

Meanwhile, mix the warm mashed potato with the butter, flour, mace and salt to form a soft dough. Roll the dough on a lightly floured surface to the thickness of a pound coin and cut into 8 rectangles, about 10 x 6cm.

Heat a griddle pan until very hot then rub lightly with oil and add the tattie scones. Cook for about half a minute on each side, until crisp and golden all over, then remove.

Heat some more oil in a frying pan and fry the eggs over a gentle heat, in order to avoid crisp egg white. Season with salt and pepper.

Place a tattie scone on each plate, then place some of the mushrooms on top. Spoon the tomatoes over the mushrooms, place 3 rashers of bacon on top, followed by the eggs. Place the remaining tattie scones on top as lids, drizzle over any excess Worcestershire sauce and serve.

Serves 4

150ml Worcestershire sauce
4 plum tomatoes, halved
    lengthways, seeds and
    core removed
50g butter
12 rashers streaky bacon
8 field mushrooms, peeled
    and thickly sliced
50ml sunflower oil
4 eggs
sea salt and freshly ground
    black pepper

for the tattie scones

300g warm classic mash
    (page 214)
25g butter
75g plain flour
pinch ground mace
pinch salt

A waffly good breakfast
by James Martin

James's crispy waffles with hollandaise, poached eggs and streaky bacon is a brunch to satisfy the heartiest of appetites. Serve with strong coffee or a spicy Bloody Mary.

Preheat a waffle maker to a medium setting. Preheat the oven to 140°C/275°F/Gas 1. Place a baking sheet onto a large wire rack in the oven to keep warm.

Mix the flour, baking powder, salt and sugar in a large mixing bowl. Whisk in the eggs, milk and butter until well combined, taking care not to over mix.

Ladle some of the batter into each well of the waffle maker, close the lid and cook for 5 minutes, or until golden-brown and crispy.

Repeat the process until the batter is used up. Keep the waffles warm on the baking sheet in the oven.

Meanwhile, half fill a medium saucepan with water and bring to the boil. Poach the eggs for 3 minutes each (see page 21 for method).

Fry the bacon in a hot pan until crisp on both sides, then drain on kitchen paper.

To serve, place the waffles onto 4 serving plates, top with the poached eggs and bacon and finish with a drizzle of hollandaise sauce and the chopped chives.

Serves 4

250g plain flour
1 tbsp baking powder
1 tsp salt
1 tbsp caster sugar
3 eggs, lightly beaten
425ml whole milk
115g unsalted butter, melted
4 eggs
12 slices streaky bacon
1 quantity hollandaise sauce
  (page 52)
2–3 tbsp chives, finely
  chopped

Pancetta-baked eggs

by Donna Hay

A luxurious twist on the classic combo of bacon and eggs. Serve with hot buttered toast for breakfast or with Donna Hay's minted pea and feta salad (page 160) for a delicious light lunch.

Preheat the oven to 180°C/350°F/Gas 4.

Grease 4 holes of a deep-cup muffin tray. Line each hole with 2–3 slices of pancetta, covering the base and the sides.

Whisk the eggs, cream, Parmesan and basil leaves together in a bowl until well combined. Season, to taste, then divide the mixture among the muffin holes and bake in the oven for 12–15 minutes, or until the eggs are golden on top and just set.

Serves 4

sunflower oil, for greasing
12 slices of pancetta
3 eggs
125ml double cream
20g freshly grated Parmesan
a small handful basil
   leaves, torn
sea salt and freshly ground
   black pepper

....

Tip: Once home, store your feta in the original brine and it will keep in the fridge for up to three months. Fresh pancetta should look pink and damp – avoid anything that's discoloured or dry. The fat should be white or creamy coloured, never yellow, and the rind should be thin and elastic.

Kipper cakes with tartare sauce

by James Martin

Kippers were the quintessential British breakfast food of the Victorian and Edwardian eras, and they're enjoying a foodie revival today. James Martin's soft little cakes make a change from the traditional haddock version and are lovely in winter when smoky flavours work best.

For the fishcakes, place the kippers and milk into a saucepan and bring to the boil. Remove from the heat and set aside to cool. Once cool, drain and flake the fish, removing as many bones as possible, and set aside. (You can discard the milk.)

Mash the cooked potatoes in a large bowl until smooth, then add the parsley, egg yolk and kippers. Stir until well combined and add seasoning.

Shape the mixture into 4 equal-sized patties, then chill in the fridge for at least 2 hours. (You can make these the night before and refrigerate, if you prefer.)

Sprinkle the flour onto a plate. Beat the eggs in a bowl. Sprinkle the breadcrumbs onto a separate plate. Once the fishcakes have chilled, dredge each in the flour, then dip in the egg and finally roll in the breadcrumbs.

Heat the olive oil in a frying pan over a medium heat and fry the fishcakes for 3 minutes on each side, or until golden-brown. Keep warm in a low oven.

For the tartare sauce, place the egg yolks, white wine vinegar, mustard and salt in a food processor and start the motor. Through the feeder tube, add the oil in a thin steady stream, pouring it as slowly as you can. When the oil has been incorporated, the sauce will have thickened.

Pour the sauce into a medium-size bowl and then mix in the cornichons, capers, parsley and chives. Add a good squeeze of lemon juice and check the seasoning – you want it to be piquant but not too harsh.

Serve the fishcakes with lemon wedges, little bowls of tartare sauce and some watercress scattered over.

Tip: Keep your watercress in a jar of water, like a bunch of flowers, and place in the fridge. With the leaves covered with a perforated plastic bag, it will stay fresh for a few days longer this way.

Serves 4

for the kipper cakes
4 smoked kippers
400ml whole milk
450g floury potatoes, peeled, cut into equal-sized chunks, boiled until tender
2 tbsp chopped parsley
1 egg yolk and 3 eggs
200g plain flour
200g flaky breadcrumbs
2 tbsp olive oil
lemon wedges, to serve
1 bunch watercress, to serve
sea salt and freshly ground black pepper

for the tartare sauce
2 large egg yolks
1 tsp white wine vinegar
½ tsp Dijon mustard
1 tsp sea salt
1 lemon, juiced
275ml rapeseed oil
2 cornichons, finely chopped
2 tsp capers, finely chopped
1 tbsp roughly chopped parsley
1 tsp chopped chives
lemon juice, to taste
black pepper

An Anglo-Indian brunch

by Madhur Jaffrey

Madhur Jaffrey's meal of jhal faraizi, karhai broccoli and sweet and sour squash can be eaten at any time of the day, and is a tasty way to spice up leftover meat. If a curry in the morning isn't your thing, the sweet and sour squash alone makes a great breakfast hash, served with ketchup on the side and a fried egg on top.

For the jhal faraizi, boil the potatoes in a pan of salted water and set aside to cool. Peel and cut into 7mm cubes.

Heat the oil in a large non-stick frying pan over a medium-high heat. Add the cumin seeds and let them sizzle for 5 seconds, then add the onion, cooked potatoes and chillies. Lower the heat to medium and stir-fry the mixture for 4–5 minutes, or until the onion has softened and is somewhat translucent. Add the beef, salt and lots of freshly ground black pepper, then stir and mix for 1 minute more.

Reduce the heat to medium-low. Press down on all the ingredients in the pan with a spatula to form a flat cake that fills the pan. Continue to cook for 12–15 minutes, turning the pan so that the bottom of the 'cake' browns evenly. Keep warm.

Meanwhile, for the karhai broccoli, heat the oil in a lidded wok or frying pan over a medium-high heat. When the oil is hot, add the asafoetida, cumin and mustard seeds (be aware of mustard seeds popping out of the pan into your eyes). As soon as the mustard seeds begin to pop, add the broccoli. Stir-fry for 1 minute, then add the salt and cayenne pepper.

Serves 4

for the jhal faraizi
340g small floury potatoes, unpeeled
2 tbsp olive or rapeseed oil
½ tsp whole cumin seeds
1 medium onion, cut into 7mm cubes
2–3 green bird's eye chillies, chopped
340g roast beef (or lamb), cut into 7mm cubes
1 tsp salt
freshly ground black pepper

for the karhai broccoli
3 tbsp olive or rapeseed oil
pinch ground asafoetida
¼ tsp whole cumin seeds
¼ tsp whole mustard seeds
400g trimmed broccoli florets
½ tsp salt
¼ tsp cayenne pepper

Pour in 4 tablespoons of water and bring the mixture to a simmer. Cover the pan with a lid, lower the heat until the mixture is simmering gently and cook for 7–8 minutes, or until the broccoli is just tender, stirring now and then.

To make the butternut squash, heat the oil in a lidded pan over a medium heat. When hot, add the asafoetida and mustard seeds. As soon as the seeds start to pop – a matter of seconds – add the squash. Stir-fry the butternut squash for 2–3 minutes, or until the pieces just start to brown. Add 50ml water, cover the pan with a lid, lower the heat and cook for 8–10 minutes, or until the squash is tender. Add the salt, sugar, cayenne pepper and yoghurt. Stir until well combined and cook, uncovered, over a medium heat, until the yoghurt is no longer visible. Stir in the chopped coriander.

To serve, spoon the butternut squash onto each plate, pile the broccoli alongside and finish with a generous spoonful of jhal faraizi.

....

Tip: When you're in the mood for something warm and savoury (and packed full of antioxidants), butternut squash is hard to beat. Shop for bulbs that feel heavy for their size. Squash gradually lose water after harvesting, so the higher the moisture content, the sweeter and more nutritious the fruit.

for the sweet and sour butternut squash
3 tbsp mustard or olive oil
generous pinch ground asafoetida
½ tsp whole brown or yellow mustard seeds
560g peeled and deseeded butternut squash, cut into 2.5cm pieces
a scant tsp salt
1½ tsp caster sugar
¼ tsp cayenne pepper
1 tbsp plain yoghurt
2 tbsp chopped coriander

small dishes

There is something very satisfying about eating a selection of small dishes as it keeps your palate interested and means that you get to sample a whole range of different flavours and textures.

For me, sharing small plates with friends and family is a brilliant way to eat. It instantly gets the conversation sparked up as you will find yourself passing dishes around the table and discussing which you like the best, probably even arguing over the last mouthful of Angela Hartnett's spiced aubergine or James's stuffed peppers!

The birthplace of small plates is Spain, which is very famous for the tapas style of eating, and in most of the bars the food may even be free, just to entice you in to drink more. In most cases these tiny morsels are absolutely delicious, and in places such as San Sebastian the tapas has become something of an art form with each bar specialising in their own tapas or 'pintxos' as they are called over there.

Don't think this idea is solely Spanish though. In the times of classic British dining in the grand hotels and gentleman's clubs you would have found an hors d'oeuvre section on the menu and the guest would choose a few items to eat as their starter or just something to nibble on while they waited for their meal to be cooked.

The following chapter is a selection of small and delicious dishes from across the globe, which are great for all occasions. A few of them together will make a great snack, a light lunch or even a brilliant way to start a dinner party, but be careful as they can be so delicious that you may not have room left for the main course!

Mark Sargeant

Fougasse (French flatbread)

by Richard Bertinet

If you like Italian focaccia bread, then you must try its French cousin fougasse. It's the ideal loaf for the novice baker. Simple and fun to make – you can even rope in family and friends to help with the kneading – and so impressive looking, with a texture that is crunchy on the outside and soft on the inside. Rip it to bits and eat it straight from the oven, dunked into soup, or with Richard's delicious dips (overleaf) before a meal.

Preheat the oven to 240°C/475°F/Gas 8 and pop a baking stone or tray in to warm up.

Mix the yeast and flour in a large bowl (or rub the yeast into the flour, if using fresh yeast). Add the salt and water. Holding the bowl with one hand, mix the ingredients with your other hand for 2–3 minutes, or until the dough starts to form.

Transfer the dough onto an unfloured work surface and continue to knead, flinging, stretching and folding the dough over on itself until it becomes soft, smooth and elastic. Place the dough into the bowl, cover with cling film and set aside for at least an hour, or until the dough has doubled in size.

Use a plastic spatula to release the dough from the bowl – you should be able to scoop it out easily in one piece – and transfer it to the work surface without stretching it. Be careful not to deflate the dough when handling it, but let it spread out to cover a square of your work surface. Generously flour the top of the dough, cover with a clean tea towel and rest for 5 minutes.

Using a plastic scraper (or a thin wooden spatula), divide the dough into 2 rectangles, then cut each piece again into 3 roughly triangular strips. Handle the dough as gently as you can so that it stays as light and full of air as possible, and keep the pieces well floured.

Serves 6

10g fresh yeast or 5g dry
500g strong white flour
10g sea salt
350ml water

Cut a large diagonal across the centre of each piece of dough, making sure that you don't go right to the edges of the dough, but cut all the way through the dough to the work surface.

Make 3 smaller diagonal cuts fanning out on each side of the central one. Put your fingers into the slits and gently open them out to form holes. Be bold – it is better to make fewer cuts and really open out the holes.

Lift the pieces of dough onto a lightly floured wooden peel (a board for sliding bread into the oven) or flat-edged baking tray, then slide them onto the preheated baking stone.

Spray water into the inside of the oven and close the door. Reduce the heat to 230°C/450°F/Gas 8 and bake for 10–12 minutes, or until golden brown. If you like, bake the last 3–4 minutes with the oven door open a fraction to give a crisper crust.

Richard's top tips

- Give the dough time. The quicker you make it, the quicker it will go stale.

- To get a really good crust, where all the flavour is, preheat the oven and spray water very finely inside, with 15–20 squirts to create steam. When you load the oven, finish with 5 more squirts and close the door.

- Remove any shelves you don't plan to bake on so that you can slide the bread freely in and out of the oven.

- If you want to freeze your fougasse, part bake them for 6–7 mins, then remove the bread from the oven, cool, wrap in freezer bags and freeze. When you're ready to use, bake from frozen at around 190°C for 12 minutes.

Three classic dips
by Richard Bertinet

Chickpea and olive oil

Fragrant with fresh lemon juice and garlic, this is the easiest dip in the world to make.

Pulse the chickpeas and garlic in a blender or food processor until smooth. Add the lemon juice and pulse until smooth, then add the olive oil, a little at a time and pulse until the mixture is a fairly loose, but not too runny paste (you may not need all of the olive oil). Season to taste.

Serves 6

1 x 400g tin chickpeas, drained and rinsed
2 garlic cloves, roughly chopped
1 lemon, juiced
100–150ml extra virgin olive oil
sea salt and freshly ground black pepper

Tuna tapenade

A classic appetiser that can be knocked up in five minutes. Buy olives with their stones intact for a superior flavour.

Blend the olives in a food processor until roughly chopped. Add the remaining ingredients and keep pulsing in short bursts until you have a coarse paste.

for the tapenade
300g black olives, stones removed
75g tinned tuna packed in olive oil, drained
150g capers, drained
½ lemon, juiced
5 tbsp extra virgin olive oil

Pesto

Richard adds a little lemon juice to his pesto for extra zing and freshness. Great as a dip or an easy pasta sauce.

Put the pine nuts, garlic and Parmesan into your food processor and pulse to a coarse paste. Add the basil and pulse again, then add the lemon juice and the olive oil, a little at a time.

The secret to a great pesto is not to overwork the ingredients, otherwise the basil bruises and you lose its fresh flavour. Using the pulse button on a food processor enables you to work it as little as possible and keep the pesto nice and coarse. When you have the texture you want, taste and season with a little salt if you like – but remember that Parmesan is quite salty anyway.

for the pesto
110g pine nuts
3 garlic cloves, roughly chopped
110g freshly grated Parmesan
1 large bunch basil (enough to fill the bowl of your food processor loosely)
1 lemon, juiced
about 4 tbsp extra virgin olive oil
sea salt, to taste

Green pea and potato cakes

by Vivek Singh

Vivek warms up our taste buds with these spicy potato cakes. 'This is entertaining Indian-style,' he says: 'Rustle up some cold canapés and nibbles with drinks, followed by a large one-pot dish or an easy curry (page 182). With a minimum of prep, you'll enjoy maximum time with your guests and the least cleaning afterwards. A complete win win!'

Place the green peas, ginger, green chillies and coriander stalk into a blender and blitz to a coarse paste. Place the grated potatoes in a mixing bowl, add the green pea mixture, the cumin seeds, cornflour, peanuts and salt, and mix evenly. Using your hands, shape the mixture into patties.

Heat a large non-stick frying pan over a medium heat. Add the cakes and sear until they turn golden-brown on both sides.

Serves 4

300g green peas,
  fresh or frozen
4cm piece fresh ginger,
  peeled, chopped
4 green chillies, chopped
¼ bunch coriander stalks,
  washed, roughly chopped
5 medium-size potatoes,
  peeled, boiled and grated
2 tsp roasted cumin seeds,
  crushed
75g cornflour
35g roasted peanuts,
  crushed coarsely
1½ tsp salt

Sag aloo

by Will Holland

Will's take on the classic spiced spinach (sag) and potato (aloo) side. Delicious with a selection of other Indian-style dishes, or simply piled onto naan.

Cut the potatoes into quarters and boil for 8–10 minutes, until just tender.

Heat a large frying pan and when it's nice and hot, add the vegetable oil and the shallot and cook for 2–3 minutes, until softened. Add the garlic and spices and fry for 1–2 more minutes, or until fragrant. Add the cooked new potatoes and cook for a minute to two, until warmed through.

Remove the pan from the heat and toss in the baby spinach. Let the residual heat wilt the baby spinach then season to taste with salt, and garnish with coriander.

Serves 4

500g new potatoes
2 tbsp vegetable oil
1 banana shallot, finely sliced
1 garlic clove, grated
1 heaped tsp garam masala
1 heaped tsp mild Madras
  curry powder
¼ tsp ground turmeric
250g baby spinach leaves
salt, to taste
1 tbsp finely chopped
  coriander

Indian-style chip and dip

Naan bread by Cyrus Todiwala

Deliciously doughy naan: simple to make, perfect with a selection of raitas, a hot curry or a full-on Indian feast (page 193).

Preheat the oven and the heaviest baking tray you own to 230°C/450°F/Gas 8.

Mix the sugar, eggs and milk together in a bowl. Mix the baking powder, salt and flour together, and stir this in to form a dough. Knead briefly, taking care not to work the dough too much, otherwise it will become too stretchy. Once soft and smooth, place the dough in a bowl with the vegetable oil over it. Cover with a damp cloth and set aside for 15 minutes.

Divide the dough into 16 portions, then roll out each piece into a 20cm circle (you can use a plate for guidance) and brush with the melted butter.

Remove the hot baking tray from the oven and bake the first batch of naans for 5 minutes, until puffed up and slightly browned. Wrap the first naan breads in a clean tea towel to keep warm and repeat for the rest of the naans. Serve immediately.

Serves 4–6

35g sugar
2 eggs
400ml whole milk
1½ tsp baking powder
1 tbsp salt
750g plain flour
50ml vegetable oil
3 tbsp melted butter

Cucumber and mint raita by Cyrus Todiwala

A cool fresh raita that takes minutes to make. Use it to top fiery curries or as an easy dip.

Cut the cucumber in half lengthways, remove and discard the seeds, chop it up and add to a mixing bowl along with the rest of the ingredients. Mix everything together and serve in a small bowl for dipping.

Serves 4

1 cucumber
200g Greek-style yoghurt
3–4 mint leaves, finely
   shredded
½ tsp red chilli powder
1 tbsp cumin seeds, toasted,
   lightly crushed
1 sprig dill, roughly chopped
1–2 tbsp whole milk
pinch salt

Apple and fennel raita by Vivek Singh

This raita has very little yoghurt, so it's lovely and thick, with a lot of texture and flavour. If you can't get hold of Granny Smith, any sharp green eating apple will do.

Core the apple and cut into small dice. Finely chop the fennel heads and the fresh coriander. Lightly roast the fennel seeds in a dry pan.

Mix all the ingredients together, seasoning to taste. Serve in a small bowl for dipping.

Serves 4

1 Granny Smith apple
2 heads baby fennel
handful coriander
1 tsp fennel seeds
200g Greek-style yoghurt
½ tsp salt
1 tsp sugar

Tomato and onion seed chutney by Vivek Singh

A fresh, spicy chutney that goes well with most Indian snacks.

Heat the oil in a pan, add the black onion seeds, bay leaf and the whole red chillies until they start to crackle, then add the chopped tomatoes and raisins and bring the mixture to the boil. Reduce the heat and cook for 30 minutes, or until soft.

Add the ground chilli and the sugar and simmer for 15 minutes or until the chutney has thickened. Leave to cool and serve straightaway, or keep in sterilised jars in the fridge for up to a week.

Makes 700ml

30ml vegetable or
  sunflower oil
½ tsp black onion
  (nigella) seeds
1 bay leaf
2 dry red chillies
500g tomatoes,
  deseeded, chopped
1 tbsp raisins
1 tsp ground red chilli
200g sugar

Patatas fritas

by José Pizarro

One in every four British potatoes is made into chips – that's approximately 1.5 million tonnes every year. Or to put it another way, if you laid all the British potatoes that are turned into chips every year end to end they would stretch around the world 76 times. Here's how to make yours...

Heat a deep-fat fryer to 120°C/250°F. Cook the potatoes for 2 minutes, then remove them from the oil with a slotted spatula. Increase the temperature to 180°C/350°F and cook the potatoes for a further 4–5 minutes, or until pale golden-brown. Remove the patatas fritas from the fryer and set aside to drain on kitchen paper. Season, to taste, with salt.

Serves 4

vegetable oil, for frying
3 large potatoes, peeled, very finely julienned
sea salt

Herby chips

by Gennaro Contaldo

Serve a big bowl of these with drinks and dips. They're the perfect party chips.

Make sure the potatoes are clean and dry, then cut them into strips of 3 or 4 lengthways – you're after proper chunky chips.

Heat the oil in a deep, heavy-bottomed saucepan or a deep-fat fryer. Mix the herbs and breadcrumbs together on a plate. Dip the potatoes into the egg whites and then into the herb mixture until thoroughly coated. Set the potatoes aside for 1–2 minutes.

Fry the chips in the hot oil for 5–6 minutes, or until golden-brown and tender. Remove the chips with a slotted spoon and set aside to drain on kitchen paper. Season, to taste, with salt.

Serves 4

750g large new potatoes, washed
vegetable oil, for frying
5 tbsp chopped fresh mixed herbs (such as rosemary, sage and chives)
5 tbsp fresh breadcrumbs (preferably homemade)
2 egg whites, lightly beaten
sea salt

Asparagus with hollandaise sauce

by James Martin

A spring time classic. Freshness is everything with asparagus, so grab bundles of the sweet, tender stalks while you can (the British asparagus season runs from late April to mid June) and enjoy with a good hollandaise. James's sauce recipe is quick and easy, relying on a food processor rather than strong arm muscles for the whisking.

To make the hollandaise, place the butter in a small saucepan over a medium heat and bring to a simmer. In a second small pan, heat the lemon juice with the vinegar until just boiling.

Drop the egg yolks into a food processor with a pinch of salt and blend briefly. With the motor still running add the hot lemon and vinegar. Then slowly add the melted butter until incorporated to a thick, creamy, smooth sauce. Season with a little salt and black pepper.

While the hollandaise is cooling, bring a pan of salted water to the boil, add the asparagus spears and blanch for 1–2 minutes. Drain well, return the asparagus spears to the pan, off the heat, and drizzle over the olive oil. Shake the pan to coat the asparagus spears, then season to taste with salt and freshly ground black pepper.

Meanwhile, heat a griddle pan over a medium–high heat. When the pan is smoking, add the seasoned, blanched asparagus and griddle for 3–4 minutes, or until tender. You will need to turn them occasionally, to ensure even cooking, but you want them to be just cooked, with a nice 'bite'. Add the butter to the pan and, when foaming, shake the pan to coat the asparagus spears in the butter, season to taste.

To serve, divide the asparagus spears equally among 4 serving plates. Drizzle over the hollandaise sauce and serve immediately.

Serves 4

for the hollandaise
125g butter
2 tsp lemon juice
2 tsp white wine vinegar
2 large egg yolks
sea salt and freshly ground
   black pepper

for the asparagus
16 asparagus spears, woody
   ends trimmed
2 tbsp olive oil
25g butter
sea salt and freshly ground
   black pepper

Tip: Once picked, asparagus loses its flavour by the hour, so anything that has travelled from overseas is likely to disappoint. If you are not cooking them straight away, store the asparagus in the fridge with a damp paper towel wrapped around the bottom of the stalks and you can get away with keeping them for a couple of days.

Spiced aubergine
by Angela Hartnett

Angela's sweet-sour stew is so versatile and can be served cold as an antipasto or warm as a side. It's also fantastic spread onto crostini, or as a sauce with pasta or couscous.

Put the aubergines into a colander, add about half a teaspoon of salt and drain for half an hour.

Heat 25ml of the olive oil in a pan and fry the red onions for 5 minutes, or until softened. Add the tomatoes and cook until the tomatoes have broken down into a thick sauce and you have a nice little tomato and onion stew. Season with sea salt and freshly ground black pepper, then remove from the pan and set aside.

Add half of the remaining olive oil to the pan and fry half the aubergines for 4–5 minutes, or until tender. Remove the aubergine pieces and set aside to drain on kitchen paper. Add the rest of the olive oil to the pan and fry the remaining aubergine chunks.

Return the aubergine, tomato and onion mixture to the pan and stir in the red wine vinegar, cumin, basil and coriander. Sprinkle over the pine nuts and taste for seasoning again.

Serves 4

2 large firm aubergines,
   cut into 2.5cm chunks
½ tsp salt
110ml olive oil
2 red onions, finely chopped
4 plum tomatoes, seeded
   and diced
2 tbsp red wine vinegar
a good pinch cumin seeds
a handful basil leaves, torn
a handful coriander leaves
1 tbsp pine nuts, lightly
   toasted in a pan
sea salt and freshly ground
   black pepper

Tip: Be careful not to cut the aubergine chunks too small or they will absorb too much oil and become heavy and very greasy.

Slow-roasted tomatoes

by James Martin

Since there isn't much sun in the UK, James does 'sun-dried tomatoes' at home. Serve as a warm vegetable side, stirred into pasta, or cold with a selection of other dishes.

Preheat the oven to 150°C/300°F/Gas 2.

Place the tomatoes, cut-side up, onto a roasting tray just big enough to accommodate them.

Drizzle over the olive oil and sprinkle with the thyme, sea salt and freshly ground black pepper. Place in the oven and slowly roast for 3–5 hours until the moisture has mainly evaporated and the tomatoes have dried out. How long you cook them for is up to you: the longer they are roasted, the drier they get, and the more intense the flavour. Here the aim is for tomatoes that are still a bit sweet and juicy.

Remove the tomatoes from the oven and serve immediately. Alternatively, turn the oven off and leave to cool, preferably overnight, in the oven.

....

Tip: Get more flavour from tomatoes by removing the plastic packaging and leaving them in a fruit bowl in a sunny spot to breathe and ripen. If stored in an airtight jar covered in olive oil, the slow-roasted tomatoes can last for a couple of months.

Serves 4

6 tomatoes on the vine,
  halved widthways
4 tbsp olive oil
4 sprigs thyme
sea salt and freshly ground
  black pepper

Beetroot and goat's curd tart
by Stuart Gillies

This warm tart is so simple with bought puff pastry. Cut into triangles and topped with luscious goat's curd, salt and vinegar caramel, and toasted pine nuts it will keep a small crowd happy.

Preheat the oven to 200°C/400°F/Gas 6.

Place the beetroot onto a tray with the garlic, thyme and 50g of the sugar and roast in the oven for 1–1½ hours, or until tender. Once cooked allow the beetroot to cool before peeling. Cut into very thin slices using a mandoline or a very sharp knife.

Roll the pastry out to a rectangle the thickness of a pound coin and prick with a fork. Place onto a flat baking sheet and cover with a second tray to stop the pastry rising. Bake in the oven for 15–20 minutes or until the pastry is golden-brown.

Heat the butter in a small saucepan and fry the onion for 3–4 minutes, or until just softened. Add the port and red wine vinegar and cook until reduced by half. Blend the mixture in a food processor until smooth.

Meanwhile, heat the remaining sugar in a small saucepan with 2 tablespoons of water. Once the sugar has dissoved, increase the temperature so that the mixture browns and caramelises. Once the mixture is dark brown in colour, remove the saucepan from the heat and add 20ml water to stop the caramel from setting hard. Allow the caramel to cool slightly, then add the salt and sherry vinegar.

Spread the red onion purée over the cooked pastry, then lay the beetroot on top in a fish scale pattern. Drizzle with two-thirds of the caramel and place in the oven for 2–3 minutes, or until hot.

Remove the pastry from the oven, trim the ends and cut into triangle shapes. To serve, place a scoop of goat's curd on top of each triangle. Sprinkle over the pine nuts and drizzle generously with the remaining caramel.

Serves 4

2 large beetroot
1 garlic bulb, cut in half,
   skin left on
2 sprigs thyme
150g caster sugar
300g ready-roll all-butter
   puff pastry
50g butter
1 red onion, finely sliced
50ml port
25ml red wine vinegar
large pinch salt
25ml sherry vinegar
150g goat's curd or soft
   goat's cheese
50g pine nuts, toasted in
   a dry frying pan

....

Tip: To preserve the beetroot's rich ruby colour and fantastic nutrients, rinse and brush clean but do not remove the skin or root until after cooking.

Easy stuffed peppers

by James Martin

These couldn't be simpler. Serve as part of a platter of antipasti or alongside James's sticky lamb chops (page 101) for a crowd-pleasing lunch.

Preheat the oven to 180°C/350°F/Gas 4.

Place the peppers, cut-sides facing upwards, into a roasting tray. Add an onion eighth and a tomato quarter and a sprig of rosemary to each pepper. Season, to taste, with sea salt and freshly ground black pepper, then drizzle over the olive oil.

Transfer the peppers to the oven and roast for 30–40 minutes, until the peppers are tender and slightly blackened. Remove and serve hot, warm or at room temperature.

Serves 4

1 yellow pepper, cut in half, seeds removed
2 red peppers, cut in half, seeds removed
1 orange pepper, cut in half, seeds removed
1 red onion, cut into eighths
2 tomatoes, cut into quarters
8 small sprigs rosemary
2 tbsp extra virgin olive oil
sea salt and freshly ground black pepper

Artichokes à la barigoule

by Clare Smyth

Clare's simple recipe for artichoke hearts simmered in olive oil is a hearty Provençal stew, yet it takes only 15 minutes to cook. It's light and tasty and great for sharing, piled on hunks of crusty bread. Barigoule also goes deliciously with seafood. Try it alongside some succulent pan-fried or poached fish, or toss with steamed mussels.

Heat a small lidded pan over a medium heat and add the olive oil. Gently fry the shallots and bacon for 2–3 minutes, until they're just beginning to colour.

Add the carrots, artichokes, turnips, mushrooms and radishes and gently fry for 1–2 minutes, then add the garlic. Increase the heat, add the wine and cook for a couple more minutes, until the liquid has reduced by half. Add the stock and reduce the heat to a simmer.

Cover the pan with the lid and cook for 3–4 minutes, or until the vegetables are tender. Remove the lid, increase the heat to high and cook for a further 3–4 minutes, or until the liquid has reduced to a thick glaze.

Stir in the chopped parsley and add some sea salt and freshly ground black pepper.

Serves 4

25ml good olive oil
2 shallots, peeled but left whole (you can drop them briefly in boiling water first to loosen the skin)
15g smoked bacon lardons
1 carrot, peeled and sliced
3 baby artichokes, outer leaves removed, trimmed
4 baby turnips
4 button mushrooms
4 long baby radishes
1 garlic clove, thinly sliced
75ml dry white wine
225ml chicken stock
1 tbsp chopped flat-leaf parsley
sea salt and freshly ground black pepper

A quick salmon terrine

by James Martin

This smoked and confit salmon terrine can be put together in no time at all. It makes the perfect party appetiser or a lovely lunch, sliced into pieces and served with a light salad.

Preheat the oven to 220°C/425°F/Gas 7.

Line the loaf tin with cling film, leaving enough extra to hang over the edges. Slice the salmon into 3 thick slices that will fit snugly into the tin.

Place the salmon onto a baking tray and spoon over the goose fat. Transfer to the oven to cook for 5 minutes. Remove from the oven and leave to cool.

Beat the butter and chives together, season with salt and freshly ground black pepper.

Lay a quarter of the smoked salmon in the cling film-lined loaf tin, covering the base and sides. Place a piece of cooked salmon into the tin, completely covering the base. Spoon over a third of the chive butter, neatly spreading it to the edges. Add a layer of the smoked salmon, covering to the edges. Repeat in layers until you use up all the ingredients, finishing with a layer of smoked salmon. Press down firmly. Cover with cling film.

Place the terrine in the fridge and chill for at least 1 hour before serving.

....

Tip: Look out for farmed organic salmon. Ordinary salmon farms rely on wild feed, whereas the organic sector feeds their salmon with the offcuts and trimmings of fish that was already destined for our plates, which makes better environmental sense. Choose salmon with firm flesh that bounces back when pressed gently, leaving no mark. The skin should be clean and slimy, with a nice shine.

Serves 6–8

You'll need a 1kg loaf tin (1.3 litre capacity)

750g salmon fillet, skin removed
225g goose or duck fat, or olive oil, if you prefer
250g butter, softened
8 tbsp roughly chopped chives
400g sliced smoked salmon
sea salt and freshly ground

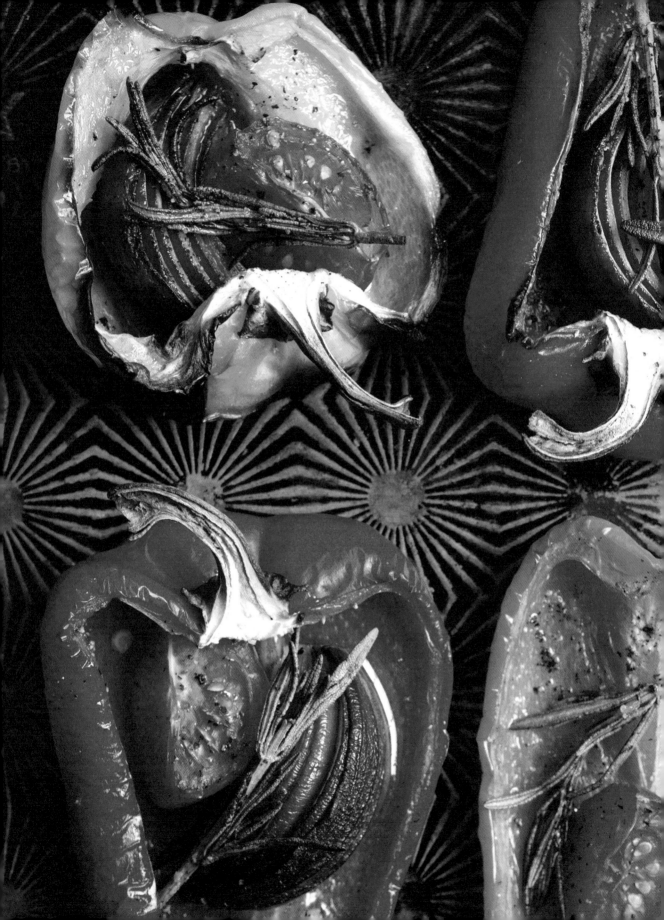

Prawn and spring onion fritters
with aioli and pimientos de Padrón
by Rick Stein

Rick's Andalucian fritters are easy to assemble, and make an expensive ingredient like prawns go a long way. On Saturday Kitchen, *Rick served these with the aioli and pimientos de Padrón (page 64), to make a lively tapas spread.*

Sift the flour, baking powder and a pinch of salt into a mixing bowl. Make a well in the centre and add 300ml water and the wine.

Gradually mix the dry ingredients into the liquid to make a batter, then whisk until you have a thick cream. Fold in the prawns, spring onions and parsley.

Pour ½cm oil into a large frying pan and place over a high heat. Leave until hot but not smoking, or until a drop of the batter sizzles immediately. Take care, as hot oil can be very dangerous.

Carefully drop large spoonfuls of the batter into the pan and spread each one out a little with the back of the spoon so they develop lovely thin, crispy edges as they cook. Don't be tempted to overcrowd the pan – only cook 2–3 at a time.

Cook, turning the fritters over every now and then, for about 2 minutes or until puffed up and golden brown on both sides. Remove with a slotted spoon and drain on a tray lined with plenty of kitchen paper. Eat straight away while they are still hot and crispy.

Continued overleaf

Serves 4

175g plain flour
½ tsp baking powder
pinch salt
1 tbsp dry white wine
175g raw prawns, cut into
    small pieces
2 spring onions, thinly sliced
1 tbsp chopped flat-leaf
    parsley
olive oil, for shallow frying

Aioli

Quick, easy and very tasty, Rick Stein's garlic mayonnaise is excellent with his prawn and spring onion fritters but also goes well with rice dishes, grilled lamb and vegetables.

Put the garlic cloves onto a chopping board and crush them under the blade of a large knife. Discard the papery skins, sprinkle the garlic with the salt and work into a smooth paste using the knife blade.

Scrape the garlic paste into a bowl and add the egg yolk. Whisk together, then very gradually whisk in the olive oil to make a thick sauce.

for the aioli

4 garlic cloves, unpeeled
½ tsp salt
1 egg yolk
175ml extra virgin olive oil

Pimientos de Padrón

Pimientos de Padrón are small green Spanish peppers, roughly the size of your thumb. Fried in olive oil and salted, they're popular in tapas bars throughout Spain. Some are sweet, but about one in every ten peppers is hot, which makes the experience of eating them a kind of culinary Russian roulette. Great for entertaining!

Heat a medium frying pan over a high heat. When the pan is hot, add the olive oil and the peppers and toss well. Sauté the peppers for 2–3 minutes, until they blister and begin to turn brown. Transfer to a plate lined with kitchen paper, then sprinkle with salt.

for the pimientos de Padrón

2 tbsp olive oil
200g Padrón peppers, stems on
1 tbsp sea salt

Crisp shrimp risotto cakes

by Galton Blackiston

Galton's stuffed rice balls can be made well in advance then taken out of the fridge and fried at the last minute. They make great appetisers, or serve with Galton's tomato and radish salad (page 153) for an elegant sit-down lunch.

Pour the stock into a pan. Heat to barely simmering, then keep warm over a low heat.

Heat the butter in a large frying pan over a medium heat. When the butter is foaming, add the shallots and garlic and fry for 2–3 minutes, or until softened. Add the rice and cook for 1–2 minutes, stirring continuously, until the grains are translucent and coated in the butter. Add the white wine and simmer, stirring continuously, until most of it has evaporated.

Add a ladleful of the warm stock and stir it into the rice. Simmer gently, stirring regularly, until all of the liquid has been absorbed by the rice, then add another ladleful of stock. Continue ladling the stock in, and stirring, until the rice is just tender and the mixture is creamy. You may not need to use all the stock.

Stir in the brown shrimps and peas and continue to cook until completely warmed through. Stir in the Parmesan and chopped chives, then season, to taste, with sea salt and freshly ground black pepper.

Remove the risotto from the heat and set aside to cool, then chill in the fridge for at least 30 minutes, but preferably overnight. This is to enable the risotto to thicken up.

Pour the egg and milk mixture into a bowl and sprinkle the breadcrumbs onto a plate. Line a baking tray with greaseproof paper.

Divide the chilled risotto into 12 equal portions – loosen the mixture with a little hot water before dividing, if necessary. Using wet hands, roll the risotto portions into balls, then flatten them slightly with the palms of your hands to form patties about 2cm thick.

Dip each risotto cake first into the egg and milk mixture, then dredge in the breadcrumbs until completely coated. Transfer to the prepared baking tray. When all the risotto cakes have been coated and placed onto the baking tray, cover the tray with cling film and chill in the fridge until needed.

Heat a large, heavy-based frying pan over a medium heat and add a tablespoon of olive oil. When the oil is smoking, add the risotto cakes in batches and fry for 4–5 minutes on each side, or until crisp and golden-brown on both sides and completely warmed through. Drain on kitchen paper.

Serves 6

1.2 litres chicken stock or vegetable stock
50g salted butter
2 shallots, peeled, finely chopped
2 garlic cloves, chopped
250g risotto rice
4 tbsp white wine
250g peeled shrimps, preferably brown
75g petits pois
25g freshly grated Parmesan
3 tbsp finely snipped chives
1 egg, whisked with 6 tbsp whole milk
150g breadcrumbs
1 tbsp olive oil
sea salt and freshly ground black pepper

Octopus, cannellini beans and smoked ricotta

by Francesco Mazzei

This is something to wolf down. Francesco uses a fantastic salty charred ricotta 'mustia' in his recipe, but if your Italian deli doesn't have any, a decent crumbly ricotta or smoked mozzarella will taste very good instead.

If using fresh cannellini beans, bring a pan of water to the boil, add the fresh beans, garlic and 2 thyme sprigs and simmer for 1 hour, or until tender. Drain the cooked beans well, then sprinkle over the thyme leaves from the 2 remaining sprigs, and season to taste with sea salt and freshly ground black pepper.

Meanwhile, bring a saucepan of water to a simmer, add the octopus pieces and simmer for 35–40 minutes, or until tender. Remove from the heat and set aside to cool.

Meanwhile, in a bowl, whisk together the red wine vinegar, honey, olive oil and oregano leaves until well combined. Season to taste with salt and freshly ground black pepper.

In a serving bowl, mix together the watercress and basil until well combined. Drizzle over the dressing and toss to coat the leaves.

When the octopus has cooled, drain well, then cut the tentacles into 2cm pieces. Heat a frying pan until hot, add a little oil, then add the octopus pieces and fry until golden-brown on all sides. Remove and set aside. Add the ricotta slices and fry for 2 minutes each side.

To serve, spoon the seasoned cannellini beans into the centre of each serving plate. Arrange the thicker pieces of octopus tentacles on top. Top the octopus with the sliced ricotta and then arrange the thinner pieces of octopus on top. Finish with the dressed watercress and basil. Drizzle any remaining dressing around the edge of the plate.

Serves 4

400g fresh cannellini beans, (or 1 x 400g tin cannellini beans, drained and rinsed)
1 garlic bulb, cut in half horizontally
4 sprigs thyme
600g octopus tentacles, cleaned
1 tbsp red wine vinegar
1 tsp acacia honey
4 tbsp extra virgin olive oil
2 sprigs oregano, leaves only
75g watercress leaves
4 sprigs purple basil, leaves only
160g ricotta mustia, or any crumbly ricotta, sliced
sea salt and freshly ground black pepper

Sesame chicken kebabs and mango salsa

by Nick Nairn

If you've got friends coming over and are looking for an easy chicken recipe, Nick's kebabs will do the trick. Crunchy on the outside and full of hot, sweet flavour, they're great thrown on the barbecue – or fried if the weather lets you down.

If you are using bamboo skewers, soak the skewers in cold water for 20 minutes before using.

Put the pancetta (or bacon) and the chicken cubes into a food processor and blend to a very smooth paste. In a small bowl, whisk the egg white with the salt, sugar, cornflour and sesame oil. Blitz the lot in a food processor until you have a smooth, slightly rubbery mixture. Transfer to a bowl, and stir in the water chestnuts, spring onions and chilli (if using).

Take one heaped teaspoon of the mixture at a time and squeeze it around one end of a skewer, extending the kebab halfway down. Repeat until all the mixture is used up – you'll make around 24 kebabs.

Sprinkle the sesame seeds on a small flat tray and roll the kebabs to cover.

Heat a frying pan containing 1cm of oil, until just starting to smoke, then add the kebabs and cook on each side for about 1½ minutes, or until cooked through and golden. Drain on kitchen paper.

Meanwhile, to make the mango salsa, peel and finely dice the mango, onion and chilli, and place in a bowl. Add the mint and coriander leaves, lime juice and olive oil and toss lightly to combine. Season to taste with a little salt and pepper.

To serve, place the skewers on a plate in the centre of your table and eat at once with the mango salsa.

....

Tip: Alongside the mango salsa, bowls of soy sauce and sweet chilli sauce are great for dipping.

Serves 6

You'll need 24 small skewers for the kebabs

for the kebabs
50g pancetta or dry cured streaky bacon, finely chopped
450g boneless, skinless chicken breasts, roughly cubed
½ egg white
1 tsp salt
½ tsp sugar
2-3 tsp cornflour
2 tsp sesame oil
6 canned water chestnuts, drained and finely chopped
2 spring onions, finely chopped
1 red chilli, finely chopped (optional)
small handful sesame seeds
vegetable or groundnut oil, for deep frying (optional)

for the mango salsa
1 mango
1 small red onion
1 red chilli
2 tbsp finely sliced mint leaves
2 tbsp chopped coriander leaves
1 lime, juiced
2 tbsp olive oil
sea salt and freshly ground black pepper

Chorizo tapas

by Mark Sargeant

Mark's simple tapas recipes make the most of chorizo's smoky flavour. Serve with bread, slices of Manchego cheese and, if you like, a glass or two of sherry.

Chorizo in red wine

Heat a frying pan until medium hot, add the olive oil, shallot and garlic and fry for 2–3 minutes, or until softened. Add the chorizo to the pan and fry for 1–2 minutes, or until crisp and the oil is released. Add the bay leaves and red wine, and cook until the volume of wine has reduced to just coat the chorizo.

Serves 4

2 tbsp olive oil
1 banana shallot, sliced
1 garlic clove, finely chopped
300g cooking chorizo, cut
   diagonally into 2.5cm
   chunks
2 bay leaves
200ml red wine
   (Rioja works well)

Prawns with chorizo

Heat a frying pan until medium hot, add the olive oil and garlic and fry for 1–2 minutes. Add the chorizo and fry for a further 1–2 minutes. Add the sea salt and prawns and cook for 2–3 minutes, or until the prawns are just pink. Add the dry sherry and stir with a wooden spatula to deglaze the pan.

Tip the chorizo, prawns and all their lovely juices into a serving dish and sprinkle over the parsley.

for the prawns with chorizo

2 tbsp olive oil
2 garlic cloves, sliced
300g cooking chorizo,
   cut diagonally into ½cm
   thick slices
a pinch sea salt
8 medium-sized prawns,
   shell on
50ml dry sherry
2–3 tbsp chopped flat-leaf
   parsley

Spicy lamb meatballs

by José Pizarro

These saucy meatballs (or 'albondigas') are a popular snack in tapas bars all over Madrid. Served with a bowl of crispy patatas fritas (page 50), they make a stunning value dinner.

To make the meatballs, soak the bread in the milk for 5 minutes, then squeeze out the excess milk. Place the bread into a bowl with the ham, lamb mince, garlic, spices, parsley and seasoning and mix until well combined. Shape the mixture into approximately 40 meatballs (each weighing about 20g).

Heat 2 tablespoons oil in a frying pan and fry the meatballs for 4–5 minutes, or until crispy and golden-brown all over. You will need to do this in batches.

For the sauce, heat the olive oil in a frying pan and fry the shallots, garlic and chilli for 8–10 minutes, or until softened. Add the tomatoes, sherry, stock, bay leaves, salt and pepper and simmer gently, stirring now and then, for 1 hour, or until the sauce has reduced and thickened.

Add the meatballs and simmer gently for 5 minutes or until heated through. Discard the bay leaves.

To serve, spoon the meatballs into a bowl, or onto serving plates, scatter with the chopped parsley and drizzle with a little more olive oil.

....

Tip: For perfect, crispy meatballs, always fry them in a little oil before adding to the sauce.

Serves 4

for the meatballs
40g thinly sliced crustless
   white bread
3 tbsp whole milk
125g thinly sliced Serrano
   ham, finely chopped
600g lamb mince
2 garlic cloves, crushed
1½ tsp cumin seeds,
   freshly ground
1½ tsp coriander seeds,
   freshly ground
¾ tsp hot paprika
handful chopped flat-leaf
   parsley
3–4 tbsp olive oil, for frying
sea salt and freshly ground
   black pepper

for the sauce
3 tbsp olive oil
150g shallot, finely chopped
3 garlic cloves, crushed
½ tsp crushed dried chillies
2 x 400g tins of tomatoes,
   or 800g fresh tomatoes,
   peeled, chopped
200ml good-quality
   fino sherry
200ml homemade
   chicken stock
2 bay leaves
½ tsp salt
freshly ground black pepper

30-minute meals

Thirty years ago when I was much younger and more naive, I used to complicate my life by preparing elaborate, obscure Chinese dishes for supper. I had much more time in those days and actually took great pleasure preparing those meals. Lately however, with a heavy travel schedule and the pressures of a modern busy life, my style of cooking has changed radically.

Now, when I cook for family or even when I entertain, I keep it simple. I love the thought of Francesco Mazzei's fish stew with Sardinian fregola, which is full of rich satisfying taste and perfect for a cool autumn evening. And what can be quicker and tastier than all the wonderful pasta or noodle ideas in this chapter?

Whatever appeals, the key to enjoying a quick meal is not to skimp. Buy the best ingredients you can, and open a good bottle of wine. Just because you're after something quick and easy doesn't mean you can't make it a special occasion. Buy a bottle of champagne if you like. Bubbles make any meal festive, even a fast one!

Avoid trying to impress. I always think it is grander to make delicious simple food than to present fancy but mediocre-tasting dishes. Make dishes within the realm of home cooks. If you are preparing a Chinese meal, don't attempt more than one stir-fry dish. There is such a diversity of recipes in the Chinese repertoire and many braised, steamed or roast dishes can be prepared ahead of time.

In my opinion, light meals are usually the best remembered ones. Nothing is worse than a heavy meal that stays with you for the whole evening. What we are after is simple fare, like Gennaro Contaldo's griddled swordfish or Atul Kochhar's tandoori grey mullet. You can always count on fish and seafood as one of the quickest, lightest and healthiest foods to cook.

This chapter is packed with recipes that are easy to prepare, and do not compromise on flavours or good health. If you decide to try something new, have fun with it. And never panic. If something doesn't turn out the way you thought it should, just don't mention it. I am sure it will taste even better the next time around!

Ken Hom

Tagliatelle with mussels

by Gennaro Contaldo

Juicy sweet mussels are cheap and plentiful in UK coastal waters and the rope-grown method of rearing them is as eco-friendly as seafood gets. Avoid the green-lip mussels from New Zealand, which are already dead and have had half the shell removed, and look for large, farmed Scottish mussels instead.

Heat the olive oil in a large lidded frying pan, add the anchovy, capers and garlic and fry for 2–3 minutes. Add the chopped tomatoes, oregano, chilli and mussels. Stir well then partially cover with the lid and cook on a medium heat for 4–6 minutes, or until most of the mussels have opened (discard any mussels that have not opened).

Remove most of the mussels from their shells and discard the shells, keeping some aside to garnish. Return the mussels to the sauce. Meanwhile, cook the pasta in a large pan of boiling water according to packet instructions (or for 2–3 minutes for homemade pasta).

Drain the pasta, reserving a little of the cooking water. Tip the pasta into the sauce and stir until well combined. If necessary, loosen the sauce with a little reserved pasta water.

To serve, spoon the pasta into bowls, sprinkle over the parsley and the mussels in their shells and eat at once.

....

Tip: To clean the mussels, plunge them in a basin of cold, running water, scrubbing the shells well or rubbing them briskly against each other to get them nice and clean. Pull off the hairy 'beards'. Discard any that have broken shells, or that do not close tightly when tapped. Don't let them stand in water – they will open and lose their natural juices.

Serves 4

800g fresh mussels, cleaned and debearded (see tip)
90ml extra virgin olive oil
1 fillet of anchovy, finely chopped
1 tbsp capers, finely chopped
3 garlic cloves, finely chopped
1 x 400g tin of plum tomatoes, chopped
½ tsp chopped oregano leaves
¼ red chilli, finely chopped
300–400g tagliatelle (see page 224 for Gennaro's fresh pasta dough)
handful of flat-leaf parsley, finely chopped

Penne with halloumi and cherry tomatoes

by Matt Tebbutt

A simple pasta dish that everyone loves. Dry roasting the tomatoes will intensify their naturally sweet flavour, balancing out the rich saltiness of the halloumi cheese.

Dry roast the fresh cherry tomatoes (that is, cook them without any oil) in a hot frying pan over a medium heat for 4–5 minutes, or until just softened. Remove from the pan and set aside.

Add the olive oil, onion, garlic and chilli to the pan the tomatoes were cooked in and fry for 2–3 minutes.

Add the halloumi and cook for 1–2 minutes on each side, until pale golden-brown on both sides. Add the tinned cherry tomatoes and bring to the boil, then reduce the heat and simmer for a few more minutes. Add the dry-roasted tomatoes and oregano and cook for a further minute. Season, to taste, with sea salt and freshly ground black pepper.

Meanwhile, bring a large pan of salted water to the boil, add the penne pasta and cook according to packet instructions. Add the cooked pasta to the pan holding the sauce and mix gently until well combined. Serve with the grated Parmesan.

Serves 4

250g cherry tomatoes,
   on the vine
1 tbsp olive oil
1 red onion, finely chopped
2 garlic cloves, peeled,
   finely chopped
1 red chilli, finely chopped
250g halloumi cheese,
   cut into 1cm cubes
1 x 400g tin cherry tomatoes
1 tbsp chopped oregano
   leaves
400g penne pasta
150g grated Parmesan
sea salt and freshly ground
   black pepper

....

Tip: There's no need to put olive oil in the pasta pan to prevent it from sticking: most chefs don't regard it as necessary and it can also stop the sauce clinging to the pasta when serving.

Pasta con sarde

by Arthur Potts Dawson

A Sicilian masterclass in balancing sweet and sour flavours, this classic dish with fresh sardines, fennel, raisins and pine nuts is very pretty and wonderful tasting too. The cooking time is slightly over 30 minutes, but this dish takes no time at all to prepare!

Heat 6 tablespoons of the oil in a large frying pan over a low to medium heat. Add the fennel, onions, fennel seeds and chillies, then half-cover the pan with a lid. Fry gently for 18–20 minutes, or until the vegetables have softened but not coloured.

Add half of the sardines and all the raisins and pine nuts and stir until well combined. Remove the lid from the pan, then continue to cook over a low heat for a further 8–10 minutes, stirring and mashing up the ingredients with a wooden spoon every now and then, until the sardines have fallen apart, giving you a rich base.

Increase the heat, add the white wine and 175ml water and bring the mixture to a simmer, stirring well. Continue to simmer until the volume of liquid has reduced by half, then return the heat to low and simmer the sauce very slowly for a further 4–5 minutes, or until it has thickened. Taste and season with salt if necessary – it will not need any pepper due to the chilli.

Arrange the remaining sardine fillets, skin-side up, side by side, on top of the sarde sauce, then drizzle over 2 tablespoons of the extra virgin olive oil. Cover the pan again and cook the sardines and sauce over a low heat for 7–10 minutes. There's no need to stir anything at this stage, just let the fish continue cooking.

Meanwhile, bring a large pan of salted water to the boil and cook the linguine according to packet instructions. When the pasta is al dente, drain well, and return to the pan.

Add the sarde sauce, cooked fillets and 2 tablespoons of olive oil to the pan with the cooked pasta in it and toss well, then add a good squeeze of lemon juice. Serve piping hot, garnished with the reserved fennel fronds and lemon zest.

Serves 4

10 tbsp extra virgin olive oil
1 large bulb of fennel, trimmed, finely sliced, fronds reserved and finely chopped
2 small onions, finely chopped
1 heaped tsp fennel seeds, crushed
2–3 small fresh red chillies, finely chopped
600g sardines, filleted (you can ask your fishmonger to do this for you)
75g raisins
50g pine nuts
175ml white wine
450g dried linguine
1–2 lemons, zest and juice
salt, to taste

Fish stew with Sardinian fregola

by Francesco Mazzei

Made from durum wheat that is rolled into small balls then toasted to give it a nutty bite, fregola is a really versatile pasta that can be used in salads, much like couscous, or thrown into one-pot dishes like this, where the pasta absorbs the rich seafood flavours. Don't be put off by the long list of ingredients here. This is simple cooking and mouthwateringly good to eat.

For the squid, heat a frying pan until medium hot, add the olive oil, thyme and shallots and cook gently for a couple of minutes until the shallot is soft and golden. Add the garlic and cook for a minute more.

Add the squid and as soon as they start to give off their juices add the white wine. Once the alcohol has evaporated, add the tomato purée and simmer for approximately 4 minutes until the squid is tender. Season to taste with salt and remove the pan from the heat.

For the fregola, heat a sauté pan until medium hot, add half the olive oil and the garlic, shallots, chilli, thyme and cook gently for 1 minute. Add the stewed squid, fregola and stock, bring to a simmer then cook for about 10 minutes, adding extra stock or water if necessary to keep the fregola covered.

Add the clams and the mussels and cook for 2–3 minutes, or until they open, then add the tomato sauce, cherry tomatoes, basil and prawns.

Heat a separate frying pan until hot, add the remaining oil and fry the red mullet fillets on each side until golden then remove from the pan and set aside. Return the pan to the heat and fry the scallops for 1 minute on each side.

To serve, stir half the herbs through the fregola then ladle it into bowls. Place the red mullet and scallops on top of the fregola then garnish, to taste, with the remaining herbs.

....

Tip: Eating species that are at low levels of the food chain is a responsible option. When buying scallops, look for those that have been hand-dived as this method has far less of an impact on the marine environment than dredging does.

Serves 2

for the stewed squid
1 tbsp olive oil
1 sprig thyme
50g shallots, finely sliced
1 garlic clove, finely diced
200g squid, cleaned and cut into small squares
50ml white wine
1 tbsp tomato purée
fine sea salt

for the fregola
3 tbsp olive oil
1 garlic clove, finely chopped
1 tbsp shallots, finely chopped
½ red chilli, finely chopped
1 sprig thyme
110g fregola
300ml fish stock
125g clams, cleaned and soaked (discard any clams that remain open after rinsing)
175g fresh mussels, cleaned and debearded (page 78)
60ml tomato sauce
60g cherry tomatoes, halved
1 small bunch basil, leaves only
125g large prawns, raw, shelled
2 small red mullet fillets, skin scored with a sharp knife
2 scallops, cleaned
1 tsp finely chopped chives
1 tsp finely chopped dill
1 tsp finely chopped tarragon

Gurnard with broad bean, spinach and mint stew

by Cass Titcombe

Once used as lobster bait, the gurnard may still be one of the ugliest fish in the sea, but these days it's championed by celebrity chefs for its stunning flavour, sustainable status and excellent meaty flesh. Try it for yourself in Cass's fabulous summer stew.

Heat 2 tablespoons of the olive oil in a large saucepan and fry the onion and potatoes for about 10 minutes, or until the vegetables are softened but not brown.

Add the garlic and cook for a further minute.

Add the stock and season with salt, to taste. Bring the stew to the boil, then cover and simmer for about 10 minutes or until the potatoes are tender.

Add the broad beans and cook for a further minute. Stir in the chopped spinach and cook for 1–2 minutes until wilted. Finally, stir in the mint and season with pepper, to taste.

Heat a frying pan until hot, add the remaining olive oil and fry the gurnard fillets, skin side down for 2–3 minutes until just crisp. Flip the fillets over and continue to cook for another 2 minutes, or until the fish is cooked through.

Remove the gurnard from the pan and set aside to rest for a couple of minutes.

Meanwhile, heat a separate frying pan and fry the bacon lardons for 2–3 minutes until golden and crispy.

To serve, spoon the stew between 2 bowls, top each with a gurnard fillet and sprinkle over the bacon lardons.

Serves 2

4 tbsp olive oil
½ onion, sliced finely
200g new potatoes, lightly scraped then quartered lengthways
1 garlic clove, finely chopped
40ml chicken stock
200g frozen shelled and podded broad beans, thawed
250g spinach, chopped
10g mint leaves, sliced finely
4 x 175g gurnard or monkfish fillets, pin boned, skin scored
110g streaky bacon, cut into lardons
sea salt and freshly ground black pepper

Tip: Gurnard are tricky to fillet at home, due to their highly armoured bodies, so it's best to ask your fishmonger to fillet the fish for you. And don't forget to cook the fillets skin side down to ensure a crispy skin – you only need to flip the fish for the last minute or two to finish the cooking.

Roast brill with scorched lettuce

by Glynn Purnell

Brill is a tasty flat white fish, similar to turbot but not as pricey and, for the moment at least, plentiful in our waters. It is best cooked simply, as here, with a light dusting of flour that caramelises in the pan, alongside some good seasonal vegetables.

Preheat the oven to 200°C/400°F/Gas 6.

Dust the brill fillet with flour and then rub with a tablespoon of olive oil. Heat a dry ovenproof frying pan until hot, add the oiled brill and fry on each side until golden-brown then place in the oven for 4–5 minutes.

Heat a separate frying pan until medium hot, add the butter and onion and cook until soft. Add the crème fraîche and spring onions and stir through. Season with freshly ground black pepper then add the chives. Remove from the heat and set aside.

Scorch the lettuce leaves with a blowtorch then season with sea salt and freshly ground black pepper. Mix together with the watercress and blanched baby leeks.

Whisk the white wine vinegar, half the lemon juice and the olive oil together in a bowl then season, to taste, with sea salt and freshly ground black pepper.

Remove the brill from the oven, add a knob of butter and the remaining lemon juice to the pan and baste the fish with the juices.

To serve, spoon some fondue of onion onto a plate and top with the brill fillet. Dress the scorched lettuce, watercress and baby leeks with the vinaigrette and place around the brill.

....

Tip: When sweating onions, or indeed any vegetables, put a lid over the pan so that they don't dry out but rather cook in their own juices, thereby intensifying their flavours.

Serves 4

You'll need a chef's blowtorch

for the brill
2 suprême of brill
   (fillet pieces)
50g plain flour
olive oil, for rubbing onto
   the fish
50g butter, plus extra
   for basting
1 medium large onion, sliced
250g crème fraîche
½ bunch spring onions,
   shredded
½ bunch chives, finely
   chopped
6 cos lettuce leaves
1 bunch watercress
8 whole baby leeks, blanched
1 tbsp white wine vinegar
½ lemon, juiced
4 tbsp olive oil
sea salt and freshly ground
   black pepper

Griddled swordfish with mint and marjoram

by Gennaro Contaldo

Gennaro's swordfish goes beautifully with the summer flavours of his fennel, radish and pepper salad (page 150), or serve with whatever fresh veg is in season.

Mix the oil and lemon juice in a bowl and season well with sea salt and freshly ground black pepper. Add the mint, marjoram and garlic and stir to combine.

Pour a little water into a large griddle pan with a lid, so the lines of the griddle pan are just above the water level. Place onto a high heat and bring to the boil, then turn the heat down to simmer gently.

Pat the swordfish dry with kitchen paper. Brush each slice with oil and season well. Place the swordfish steaks onto the griddle pan, cover with the lid and cook for a couple of minutes.

Remove the lid, brush each steak with a little more oil on both sides, then turn the fish over and return to the pan. Cover with the lid and cook for a further 2–3 minutes, or until the swordfish is cooked to your liking.

Serve the fish hot, with the sauce spooned around the steaks.

Serves 4

8 tbsp extra virgin olive oil, plus extra for brushing
2 tbsp lemon juice
1 small handful mint, finely chopped
1 small handful marjoram leaves, finely chopped
1 garlic clove, very finely chopped
4 x 200g swordfish steaks
sea salt and freshly ground black pepper

....

Tip: If you can't find swordfish, feel free to use tuna, John Dory or grey mullet instead.

Quick hot-smoked salmon paella
by Mark Sargeant

A delicious twist on the traditional paella, this one-pot dish is easy to make and ready in no time at all. Hot-smoked fish is actually cooked all the way through, so you only need to flake the salmon in large chunks over the finished rice and allow the heat to warm it gently.

Heat the oil in a heavy-based deep frying pan and cook the onion and garlic for 5 minutes, stirring regularly.

Add the chorizo and fry until it releases its oil, then stir in the smoked paprika and rice.

Keep stirring until the rice is coated in oil before pouring in the stock. Bring to the boil and simmer for 15 minutes, stirring occasionally.

Tip in the peas and clams and cook for about 5 minutes more, or until the rice is done and the clams open (discard any that don't open).

Check for seasoning, then stir through the parsley, flakes of salmon and lemon wedges. Serve immediately.

Serves 4

1 tbsp olive oil
1 onion, sliced
1 garlic clove, crushed
110g chorizo sausage
1 tsp smoked paprika
300g long grain rice
1 litre hot chicken stock
200g fresh or frozen peas
500g clams, cleaned and soaked (discard any clams that remain open after rinsing)
3 tbsp chopped flat-leaf parsley
250g hot-smoked salmon fillet, skinned and flaked
1 lemon, cut into wedges
sea salt and freshly ground black pepper

....

Tip: Though it's tempting to keep it in the packet you bought it in, rice lasts a lot longer when transferred to an airtight container and stored in a cool, dark place. Keep cooked rice in a sealed container in the fridge for no longer than one day.

Steamed Cantonese-style fish with spicy tofu

by Ken Hom

Ken's steamed fish is healthy and low fat without compromising on flavour. Use any firm white fish fillet, such as cod or sole, skinned, or a whole fish such as Dover sole or turbot. The spicy tofu can be made ahead of time and gently reheated.

Pat the fish dry with kitchen paper and evenly rub with salt, rubbing it inside the cavity as well if you are using a whole fish. Set aside for 30 minutes – this helps the flesh to firm up and draws out any excess moisture.

Prepare a steamer or put a rack into a wok or deep-sided pan. Fill with 5cm of water and bring to the boil over a high heat.

Rinse off any salt and pat dry, then transfer the fish to a heatproof plate and scatter the ginger over the top. Put the plate of fish into the steamer (or onto the rack). Cover tightly with a lid and steam the fish fillets for 4–5 minutes, or until just cooked through. Remove the plate from the steamer and sprinkle the spring onions and light and dark soy sauces over the fish.

Just before serving, heat the groundnut oil and sesame oil together over a high heat. When the oil is smoking, pour it over the steamed fish.

Meanwhile, for the tofu, heat a wok or large frying pan until hot. Add the oil and the yellow bean sauce and stir-fry for 30 seconds. Add the soy sauce and salt and continue to stir-fry for another minute. Finally, add the chilli powder and continue to stir-fry for 30 seconds.

Pour in the stock (it may spit when it comes into contact with the oil, so take care), then add the bean curd cubes and cook for 3 minutes. Stir in the garlic and the cornflour mixture and cook for a further 1–2 minutes, or until the sauce has thickened.

To serve, divide the fish equally between 4 serving plates and garnish with fresh coriander. Ladle the tofu alongside and garnish with the Sichuan peppercorns.

Tip: Instead of using a wok to steam the fish, try wrapping it in cling film and microwave over a high heat for 3–5 minutes.

Serves 4

for the fish
450g firm white fish
1 tsp coarse sea salt
   or plain salt
1½ tbsp finely shredded
   fresh ginger
3 tbsp finely shredded
   spring onions
2 tbsp light soy sauce
2 tbsp dark soy sauce
1 tbsp groundnut oil
2 tsp sesame oil
coriander sprigs, to garnish

for the spicy tofu
1 tablespoon groundnut oil
1 tbsp whole yellow
   bean sauce
1 tbsp dark soy sauce
½ tsp salt
1 tsp red chilli powder
   or cayenne pepper,
   depending on your taste
170ml chicken stock
450g fresh tofu, cut into
   3.5cm cubes
2 tbsp chopped garlic
2 tsp cornflour mixed with
   1 tbsp water
1 tsp Sichuan peppercorns,
   roasted and finely ground

Clams, smoked bacon and cider broth

by Mark Sargeant

With chargrilled garlic bruschetta lining the bottom of the soup bowls, this dish resembles an Italian bread soup, but the secret ingredient here is the English cider, which adds a subtle fruity note to the fantastic deep salty rich flavours of the broth.

Heat 1 tablespoon of the oil in a lidded frying pan over a medium heat. Fry the bacon and anchovy for 2–3 minutes, or until all the fat is released from the bacon.

Add the thyme, carrot, celery, leek and onion and cook for 2–3 minutes, or until softened. Stir in the clams and cider and cover the pan with a lid. Bring the mixture to a simmer, then steam the clams for 2–3 minutes, or until all of the clams have opened. Stir in the parsley.

Meanwhile, drizzle the remaining olive oil over the slices of bread and sprinkle with the sea salt. Heat a griddle pan until hot and grill the slices of bread for 1–2 minutes on each side, or until golden-brown char marks appear on both sides. Rub each slice of toast with the garlic – it's amazing how much impact this has on the flavour of the bread.

To serve, press a slice of charred bread into the bottom of each serving bowl and ladle over the clam broth.

....

Tip: Make sure you discard any clams that don't shut quickly when tapped and any that don't open after cooking.

Serves 4

3 tbsp olive oil
150g smoked bacon, chopped
1 anchovy fillet
1 sprig thyme
1 carrot, peeled, finely chopped
1 celery stick, trimmed, finely chopped
1 small leek, trimmed, finely chopped
1 onion, finely chopped
2kg medium clams, cleaned and soaked (discard any clams that remain open after rinsing)
300ml good-quality dry cider
handful of flat-leaf parsley, chopped
4 slices crusty white bread, plus extra bread for dunking
½ tsp sea salt
1 garlic clove, cut in half

Okra curry, couscous and flatbread
by Matt Tebbutt

Matt's simple curry and couscous proves just how delicious okra can be. Look for okra stems that snap cleanly and don't bend, and small young pods, which are tender and a lot better to cook with. The spicy flatbread makes an impressive side. And with unleavened bread there is no yeast involved, which means no waiting around for your dough to rise. Instant satisfaction!

Heat the oil in a frying pan over a medium heat, add the mustard and fennel seeds and fry until they start to pop. (You can cover the pan with a lid to protect your eyes and face.) Add the fresh and dried chillies and the curry leaves and cook for another 30 seconds, or until fragrant.

Add the onion to the frying pan and fry for 2–3 minutes, or until softened. Then add the ground turmeric and okra, stir until well combined and cook for 2–3 minutes, or until the okra has softened.

Add the crème fraîche and the stock and heat gently until the mixture is simmering. Season, to taste, with sea salt and freshly ground black pepper.

Meanwhile, place the couscous and olive oil into a bowl and pour over the boiling water. Cover the bowl with cling film and set aside for 4–5 minutes, or until all the water has been absorbed.

Place the sliced shallots into a bowl with the vinegar and sugar and mix until well combined. Set aside to marinate for 2–3 minutes.

Fluff the couscous grains with a fork. Add the marinated shallots and the flat-leaf parsley and season to taste with sea salt and freshly ground black pepper. Stir the mixture until well combined.

To serve, spoon the couscous into the centre of each plate and top with the curry.

Serves 4

1 tbsp olive oil
1 tsp yellow mustard seeds
1 tsp fennel seeds
1 red chilli, finely chopped
1 dried chilli, soaked in water for 10–20 minutes until softened, drained, finely chopped
10 curry leaves
1 onion, finely chopped
¼ tsp turmeric
400g okra, tops trimmed, sliced diagonally into 2cm pieces
50g crème fraîche
110ml vegetable stock
sea salt and freshly ground black pepper

for the couscous

200g couscous
3 tbsp extra virgin olive oil
275ml boiling water
2 banana shallots, peeled, finely sliced into rings
3 tbsp red wine vinegar
1 tbsp caster sugar
2 tbsp chopped flat-leaf parsley

Flatbread

Place all the ingredients into a bowl and mix together. Stir in enough water (approx 125ml) to form a firm dough.

Transfer the dough to a floured surface and knead for 2–3 minutes, or until smooth.

Cut the dough into 4 equal-sized portions and roll out into discs 1cm thick.

Heat a griddle pan over a high heat. Brush each flatbread disc with olive oil on each side and place onto the griddle pan. Cook on each side for 1–2 minutes, or until slightly risen and golden-brown.

Remove from the pan and set aside. Wrap in a tea towel to keep warm. Repeat with the remaining discs.

for the flatbread
300g plain flour
2 heaped tsp baking powder
1 tsp sea salt
1 tbsp black onion
   (nigella) seeds
1 tbsp chilli oil
olive oil, for brushing

Tandoori grey mullet with cep salad
by Atul Kochhar

The earthy flavour of the fish is perfectly balanced by Atul's cep salad and the delicate spices of his quick marinade. A simple dish that tastes anything but.

Mix all of the marinade ingredients together in a bowl until well combined. Place the grey mullet into a dish, pour over the marinade and rub it into the fish. Set aside to marinate for 30 minutes.

Preheat the grill to high. Mix the lemon juice, butter and chat masala together.

Grill the fish for 2–3 minutes on each side and baste with the lemon butter.

For the cep salad, heat 3 tablespoons olive oil in a frying pan, add the ceps, garlic, thyme and ajwain seeds (or a little more thyme) and fry for 2–3 minutes, or until cooked through.

Mix the remaining 3 tablespoons olive oil with the chopped curry leaves, pepper and sugar. Add the ceps to the bowl and stir until well combined.

To serve, place the fish onto serving plates and spoon the mushrooms alongside.

....

Tip: Avoid eating grey mullet during the January to April spawning season. The marinade is also nice with chicken or pork, if the fish is out of season.

Serves 4

for the marinade
1 ½ tbsp ginger and garlic paste (garlic, ginger and vegetable oil, blended to a paste)
1 tsp black pepper
½ tsp garam masala powder
1 tbsp ground coriander
½ tsp cumin powder
½ tsp red chilli powder
2 tbsp vegetable oil
salt, to taste
1 tbsp lemon juice
1 tbsp plain yoghurt

for the grey mullet
4 small grey mullets, cleaned, scaled, flesh scored
1 tbsp lemon juice
2 tbsp melted butter
1 tsp chat masala

for the cep salad
6 tbsp olive oil
300g ceps, cut in long pieces
1 tbsp chopped garlic
1 sprig lemon thyme
¼ tsp toasted ajwain seeds (optional)
5 curry leaves, chopped
½ tsp crushed black pepper
½ tsp sugar

Chicken on crispy noodles

by Ken Hom

Ken says, 'I love this dish as it was a childhood favourite when working in my uncle's restaurant. The crispy, crunchy noodles provide an unbeatable texture contrast to the soft chicken.'

For the chicken, place the chicken strips into a bowl and add the egg white, 2 teaspoons cornflour, salt and freshly ground white pepper. Mix well until the chicken is evenly coated, then cover the bowl with cling film and chill in the fridge for at least 20 minutes.

Meanwhile, blanch the fresh egg noodles for 2–3 minutes in a large pan of boiling salted water until just tender. (If using dried egg noodles, cook according to packet instructions.) Drain well and set aside.

Heat a frying pan over a high heat, then add 1½ tablespoons of the groundnut or peanut oil. Evenly spread the drained noodles over the base of the pan, then turn the heat to low and allow the noodles to gently fry for 4–5 minutes, until golden-brown and crisp on the bottom. Gently flip the noodles over, adding another 1½ tablespoons of the oil to the pan. Cook for a further 3–4 minutes, or until the noodles are golden-brown and crisp all over. Remove from the pan and drain on kitchen paper.

Heat a wok over a high heat and add the remaining groundnut oil. When the oil is very hot, remove the wok from the heat and immediately add the marinated chicken strips and stir-fry quickly for a couple of minutes, or until the chicken is sealed all over. Drain the chicken and set aside, discarding the oil.

Clean the wok and place back over a high heat. Add the rice wine, oyster sauce, soy sauce, chicken stock and the black pepper. Bring the mixture to the boil, reduce the heat, stir in the cornflour mixture and bring to a simmer. Return the chicken pieces to the wok and stir to coat in the sauce.

To serve, place the crispy noodles on a serving plate and spoon over the chicken and sauce. Garnish with the chopped spring onions.

Serves 4

- 250g boneless, skinless chicken breasts, cut into thin strips
- 1 egg white
- 2 tsp cornflour
- 1 tsp salt
- ½ tsp freshly ground white pepper
- 175g fresh thin egg noodles (substitute dried egg noodles if unavailable)
- 6 tbsp groundnut or peanut oil
- 2 tbsp Shaoxing rice wine or dry sherry
- 1½ tbsp oyster sauce
- 1 tbsp light soy sauce
- 300ml chicken stock
- ½ tsp freshly ground black pepper
- 1 tbsp cornflour mixed with 1½ tbsp water
- 3 tbsp finely chopped spring onions

Asian-style pasta

by Ken Hom

Ken mixes things up with his stir-fried pasta, with delicious results!

Cook the pasta in a large pan of boiling salted water until al dente (according to packet instructions) then drain well and set aside.

Heat the oil in a lidded wok (or saucepan) over a high heat until slightly smoking. Add the garlic, ginger, onion and orange zest and stir-fry for 1–2 minutes. Add the bacon and stir-fry for 3–4 minutes, until the bacon is golden-brown. Add the peppers, sugar, stock, chopped tomatoes, curry paste, tomato purée, then season to taste with salt and freshly ground pepper. Stir well.

Reduce the heat until the mixture is simmering, then cover the wok with a lid and continue to simmer for 30 minutes, or until the sauce is thick and the peppers are tender.

Add the drained pasta to the sauce, mix well and heat until the pasta is warmed through. Turn the mixture out onto a large warm platter, garnish generously with the basil and chives and serve at once.

....

Tip: This is a great recipe for leftover pasta and the dish will work best if the pasta is cold. Only add the pasta at the very end to coat the sauce and reheat, or the pasta will overcook and become mushy.

Serves 4

450g dried Italian pasta, such as farfalle
3 tbsp olive oil
3 tbsp finely chopped garlic
1 tbsp finely chopped fresh ginger
1 small onion, chopped
2 tbsp finely grated orange zest
6 bacon rashers, chopped
2 red peppers, cut into 1cm dice
2 yellow peppers, cut into 1cm dice
2 tsp sugar
300ml chicken stock
400g tin chopped tomatoes
3 tbsp Madras curry paste
2 tbsp tomato purée
½ tsp freshly ground black pepper
handful each chopped basil, snipped chives

Stir-fried chilli pork

by Bill Granger

Bill Granger is the master of quick and easy. Served with some steamed rice, this recipe is fantastic if you need a tasty dinner on the table in a matter of minutes.

Mix together the soy sauce, mirin, hoisin sauce, sesame oil and chilli flakes in a shallow dish until well combined. Add the pork, toss to coat and leave in the fridge to marinate for 15 minutes.

Heat a wok over a high heat and add 1 tablespoon of the oil. Once smoking, add half the pork and stir-fry for 1–2 minutes.

Remove from the wok with a slotted spoon and stir-fry the remaining pork. Remove the pork from the wok.

Heat the remaining tablespoon of oil and add the garlic, chillies, 1 tablespoon of water and the onions. Stir-fry for 1–2 minutes. Cover with a lid and cook for a further 1–2 minutes.

Add the soy sauce and sugar and return the pork to the wok. Cook for a final minute. Garnish with the roasted peanuts and serve with steamed rice.

....

Tip: Cook the pork in batches to ensure that each piece is nicely browned.

Serves 4

1 tbsp soy sauce
2 tbsp mirin or dry sherry
2 tbsp hoisin sauce
2 tbsp sesame oil
1 tsp dried chilli flakes
800g pork fillet, cut into
   thin slices
2 tbsp sunflower or
   vegetable oil
4 garlic cloves, crushed with
   the flat of a knife
3 red chillies, cut in half
   lengthways, stalks left on
   and deseeded
6 spring onion bulbs, halved,
   or 1 small red onion, cut
   into wedges
1 tbsp soy sauce
2 tbsp granulated sugar
2 tbsp roasted peanuts
350g Thai jasmine rice,
   steamed

Walnut-crusted pork

by Gennaro Contaldo

In Gennaro's words, 'this is a fantastic, quick dish to cook. Children will love it with my herby chips, as everything is coated in breadcrumbs!'

Mix the walnuts, breadcrumbs and thyme on a plate. Season with sea salt and freshly ground black pepper.

Sprinkle the flour onto a plate. Dredge the pork loin slices in the plain flour, shaking off the excess, then dip them into the beaten egg, followed by the walnut mix. Press the slices down well with your hands, to coat them in as much of the mixture as possible.

Heat the oil in a frying pan and fry the pork slices for 4–5 minutes on each side, or until cooked through.

For the salad, mix the salad leaves, olives, lemon juice and olive oil together in a bowl. Season to taste with sea salt and freshly ground black pepper.

To serve, place a pork slice onto each of the 4 serving plates, place some chips and a lemon wedge alongside and finish with some salad.

Tip: To check if the meat is cooked, insert a skewer in the thickest part: the juices that run out should be absolutely clear, without any trace of pinkness.

Serves 4

for the pork
50g shelled walnuts, very
    finely chopped (or blitzed
    in the food processor)
50g dried breadcrumbs
3 sprigs thyme, leaves only
3–4 tbsp plain flour,
    for dusting
4 slices pork loin, approx
    ½cm thick
2 eggs, beaten
5 tbsp olive oil
herby chips (page 50),
    to serve
1 lemon, cut into wedges
sea salt and freshly ground
    black pepper

for the salad
150g mixed salad leaves (red
    chard, chicory and rocket)
125g green olives
½ lemon, juiced
3 tbsp extra virgin olive oil
sea salt and freshly ground
    black pepper

Sticky chops

by James Martin

These spicy sticky chops are lip-smackingly good. You will need to marinate them for an hour, but once that's done they take a few minutes to cook. Serve with the stuffed peppers (page 58) a quick mash (page 214), or some crusty bread to mop up the juices.

Place the lamb chops in a large bowl. Drizzle over the olive oil and sprinkle over the fennel seeds and lemon juice. Turn the lamb chops until thoroughly coated in the mixture, then cover the bowl and chill in the fridge for 1 hour, to marinate.

Meanwhile, for the sticky sauce, heat the olive oil in a frying pan over a medium heat. Add the shallot, garlic and chilli and fry for 2–3 minutes, or until softened.

Add the star anise and fennel seeds and cook for a further minute, or until the spices are fragrant. Add the muscovado sugar, soy sauce and tomato ketchup, stir well, then bring the mixture to the boil. Reduce the heat until the mixture is simmering, then continue to simmer for 4–5 minutes, or until the sauce has thickened. Set aside.

Remove the chops from the marinade and scrape off any fennel seeds. Heat a griddle pan over a medium heat. Add the lamb and cook for 3–4 minutes, or until golden brown on one side.

Brush the tops of the lamb chops with some of the sticky sauce, then turn them over and brush the other side. Continue to cook for a further 2–3 minutes (for medium), or until cooked to your liking. Remove from the heat and set aside on a warm plate to rest.

Drizzle over the remaining sticky sauce and eat immediately.

Serves 4

8 medium-sized lamb chops
3 tbsp olive oil
1 tbsp whole fennel seeds
½ lemon, juiced

for the sticky sauce

1 tbsp olive oil
1 shallot, finely chopped
2 garlic cloves, finely
  chopped
1 red chilli, finely chopped
2 star anise
1 tsp ground fennel seeds
50g dark muscovado sugar
50ml soy sauce
300ml tomato ketchup

Beef slices with Oloroso sherry

by José Pizarro

This Spanish-flavoured dish is ready in less than 10 minutes, and makes a feast with José's olive oil mash (page 214). Fillet, sirloin or rump steak is ideal, but sliced beef escalopes – a cheaper cut from just below the rump – will also do.

Slice the steaks up into 2cm-wide strips and season with sea salt and freshly ground black pepper.

Heat the oil in a non-stick frying pan or wok over a high heat until it shimmers. Add the beef and rosemary and stir-fry for about 1 minute. When the meat starts to brown, add the garlic and pepper slices. Cook for 1 minute more and then pour in the sherry. Let it bubble furiously until the alcohol has evaporated – about 2 minutes.

Remove from the heat and stir in half of the chopped parsley and mint. Season to taste.

To serve, divide up the lettuce between 4 plates, followed by the beef mixture, making sure each serving gets some of the juices. Shake a few drops of extra virgin olive oil over the beef, and finish with a sprinkle of flaked almonds, the remaining parsley and mint and paprika.

Serves 4

4 slices beef steak, approx 200g each
2 tbsp extra virgin olive oil, plus extra for drizzling
1 rosemary sprig
1 garlic clove, finely diced
1 x 230g jar piquillo peppers, drained and sliced
6 tbsp dry Oloroso sherry
4 flat-leaf parsley sprigs, chopped
4 mint sprigs, chopped
2 cos lettuce, sliced
25g flaked toasted almonds (optional)
pinch hot-smoked paprika
sea salt and freshly ground black pepper

Beef in oyster sauce

by Ken Hom

Quicker and tastier than a takeaway and an absolute cinch to cook. Serve with Ken's spicy salad (page 156) for fresh flavour.

Put the beef, soy sauce, sesame oil, rice wine or dry sherry and cornflour into a bowl and mix together until well combined. Set aside to marinate for 20 minutes.

Heat a wok or large frying pan until it is very hot. Add the oil, and when it is very hot and slightly smoking, add the beef slices and stir-fry for 5 minutes or until they are lightly browned.

Remove the beef strips and set aside to drain in a colander over a bowl. Discard the drained oil.

Wipe the wok or pan clean and reheat it over a high heat. Add the oyster sauce and bring it to a simmer. Return the drained beef slices and toss them thoroughly with the sauce.

Turn the mixture onto a serving platter, garnish it with the spring onions, and serve at once.

Serves 4

450g beef fillet, cut into 5cm thin strips
1 tbsp light soy sauce
2 tsp sesame oil
1 tbsp Shaoxing rice wine or dry sherry
2 tsp cornflour
3 tbsp groundnut or vegetable oil
3 tbsp oyster sauce
1½ tbsp finely chopped spring onions

....

Tip: Feel free to substitute either chicken breasts or pork fillet for the beef, if you prefer.

Growing up in a large family, the youngest of six children, meal times were always fun. In particular, we always looked forward to the weekends and long Sunday lunches. Saturday mornings were spent baking with my mother and helping prep the food for our Sunday feast, while my father would dig up his carefully grown vegetables. The whole family would then come together around our large table to enjoy the fruits of our labour, some great conversation and, for my parents, a well-earned glass of wine.

It was here that I began my journey to become a chef. Weekends were truly memorable and made all the more so through the enjoyment of food glorious food. The dinner table is as relevant in today's busy world as it has ever been. Weekends still provide a fantastic opportunity to relax in one another's company and enjoy a proper meal together. It's surely one of life's great wonders!

After your weekly viewing of *Saturday Kitchen* I hope you're inspired to create some wonderful dishes of your own. This chapter features a selection from some great chefs. I love the sound of Nick Nairn's haddock ceviche, accompanied by a glass of chilled white wine on a hot summer's day. And Rick Stein's Malaccan black peppered crab with black beans, ginger and curry leaves makes a perfect light lunch. Angela's chicken with chorizo, peppers and sage is delicious to share with family and friends, or why not prepare a variety of dishes: serving Gennaro's aubergine 'parmigiana' with Silvena's octopus, chorizo and oregano, for example.

In the classic British tradition, Sundays are for lingering over long satisfying lunches. And on a cold winter's day, James Martin's hearty beef and ale pie or Paul Rankin's mixed game pie will take some beating. For lighter fare, have a go at Bryn's roasted salmon, gnocchi and chestnuts or Nathan's pollock, squid and mussel stew.

Whatever recipe you try for the weekend, give yourself the time to enjoy it, involve others in the prep and have fun establishing your own family traditions. I'm sure you will love them!

Michael Caines

Aubergine 'parmigiana' with roasted tomato

by Gennaro Contaldo

Every Italian cook has their own version of parmigiana: the classic aubergine dish from northern Italy. Gennaro's twist with stuffed tomatoes makes a moreish side or serve with some crusty bread for mopping, for a scrumptious meat-free meal.

Preheat the oven to 200°C/400°F/Gas 6.

Using a sharp knife, slice the tops off the tomatoes, about a quarter of the way down, to make the lids. With a small spoon or scoop, remove the seeds and pulp inside the tomatoes and reserve. Place the hollowed-out tomatoes onto a plate lined with kitchen paper. Add a pinch of salt to the cavity of each, then turn the tomatoes upside down and set aside for 10–15 minutes to allow any excess moisture to escape.

Meanwhile, heat 4 tablespoons of the extra virgin olive oil in a pan over a high heat. Fry the onion for 3–4 minutes, or until softened, then add the reserved tomato pulp and half of the basil leaves and season, to taste, with sea salt and freshly ground black pepper. Stir well.

Reduce the heat to medium, then half cover the pan with a lid and continue to cook the tomatoes for about 20 minutes, or until most of the moisture has evaporated and the mixture has thickened. Check and stir from time to time to prevent it from burning.

Heat 2 more tablespoons of olive oil in a separate frying pan over a medium–high heat. While the oil is heating up, sprinkle the flour onto a plate and dredge the aubergine rounds in it, shaking off any excess.

When the oil is hot, dip each round into the beaten egg. Add the coated aubergine to the hot oil, in batches if necessary, and fry for 3–4 minutes on each side, or until crisp and golden-brown on both sides. Remove from the pan using a slotted spoon. Drain on kitchen paper and sprinkle a little salt all over.

At this stage you are ready to assemble your ingredients in the cavity of each hollowed-out tomato. Begin with a slice of aubergine, then top with a spoonful of tomato sauce, followed by a basil leaf and then a slice of mozzarella. Repeat the layers until the tomato cavities are full and all the ingredients have been used up. (Reserve any leftover basil leaves for the garnish.) Put the lid on each tomato and transfer to an ovenproof dish. Season, to taste, with sea salt and freshly ground black pepper and drizzle over a little of the remaining olive oil.

Bake the stuffed tomatoes in the oven for about 25 minutes or until the tomatoes have softened and the cheese has melted. To serve, garnish with the remaining basil leaves, then drizzle over the remaining extra virgin olive oil and season again to taste.

Serves 6

- 6 beef tomatoes, ripe but firm (try to get ones that are all roughly the same size)
- 9 tbsp extra virgin olive oil
- 1 small onion, finely chopped
- 2 handfuls basil leaves
- 2–3 tbsp plain flour, for dredging
- 400g small aubergines, trimmed, thinly sliced into rounds
- 2 eggs, beaten with a large pinch salt
- 200g mozzarella
- sea salt and freshly ground black pepper

Dauphinoise and Taleggio pithivier
by Matt Tebbutt

These indulgent pies are carb heaven – puff pastry packed with rich earthy flavours and a gloriously melting Taleggio cheese. Served with a simple side of wilted spring greens, this is a weekend treat. (Though not one for veggies, as Taleggio is traditionally curdled with calf rennet.)

Preheat the oven to 180°C/350°F/Gas 4.

Place the potatoes into a bowl of cold water and swirl around to remove any excess starch. Drain well and pat dry.

Butter an ovenproof dish with about a teaspoon of the butter and place the potatoes in the dish in layers, overlapping a little, until the dish is just full. Season with sea salt, freshly ground black pepper and nutmeg between each layer.

Whisk the cream and milk in a bowl until well combined. Season with salt, pepper and nutmeg and pour the cream and milk over the potatoes. Dot with butter, then cover tightly with foil.

Bake the dauphinoise in the oven for 1 hour, or until the potatoes are just tender. After an hour, carefully remove the foil and return to the oven for a further 30 minutes, or until golden-brown on top. Remove from the oven and leave to cool, then stamp out four 7.5cm rounds. (The leftovers can be eaten at a later date.)

For the pithivier, increase the oven heat to 200°C/400°F/Gas 6.

Heat a frying pan until hot, add 25g of the butter and the wild mushrooms and fry for 2–3 minutes, or until just softened. Stir in the tarragon and season with salt and pepper. Remove the pan from the heat and set aside to cool slightly.

Roll the puff pastry out on a floured surface to a 5mm thickness. Cut out four 10cm circles and four 15cm circles. Place the small circles onto a baking tray and top with the rounds of dauphinoise. Add a spoonful of mushrooms and a slice of Taleggio cheese. Brush the edge of the pastry with the beaten egg.

Carefully lay the large circle of pastry over the top of each pile, press down lightly over the mound and around the edge to seal. Brush with the remaining egg and use the blunt edge of a small knife to create circular lines running from the top of the pithivier to the edge, just scoring the pastry but not cutting through it. Sprinkle with a little salt. Bake for 20–30 minutes, or until hot through with crisp, golden-brown pastry.

Heat a frying pan until hot, add the remaining butter, spring greens and 3 tablespoons of water and fry for 2–3 minutes, or until just wilted. Stir in the remaining mushrooms. To serve, spoon the spring greens onto plates with a pie alongside.

Serves 4

You'll need a 7.5cm, a 10cm and a 15cm pastry cutter

900g waxy potatoes, such as King Edward or Desiree, peeled and sliced thinly
125g butter
pinch freshly grated nutmeg
300ml double cream
300ml whole milk
200g mixed wild mushrooms, wiped clean
3 tbsp tarragon, roughly chopped
4 slices Taleggio cheese
500g ready-roll all-butter puff pastry
2 eggs, beaten
400g spring greens
sea salt and freshly ground black pepper

A splendid spud (with lobster)

by Nick Nairn

Nick's rich creamy version of lobster thermidor is chopped up and spooned into a jacket potato then baked until golden, bubbly and luscious. Served with a crunchy side salad, it makes the poshest baked potato lunch ever!

Preheat the oven to 200°C/400°F/Gas 6.

Bake the potato for 1–1¼ hours or until tender. Remove from the oven and set aside to cool slightly. Cut the potato in half and scoop out the flesh.

Heat the cream, mustard, lemon zest and juice together in a pan until boiling. Take it off the heat, whisk in the egg yolks until well combined, then stir in half the Parmesan and all of the basil. Season, to taste, with salt, sugar and freshly ground black pepper and continue to cook until the sauce thickens. Stir in the lobster meat.

Increase the oven to 230°C/450°F/Gas 8.

Spoon the lobster mixture into the potato shells, sprinkle over the remaining Parmesan and bake for 3–4 minutes.

Meanwhile, for the salad, toss all of the ingredients together in a bowl until well combined. Adjust seasoning to taste. Serve a spoonful of salad alongside the potato.

Tip: To achieve a really crisp skin on a baked potato, try washing the potatoes in cold water and then brushing with a little oil and dusting them with sea salt to draw the moisture out of the skin.

Serves 2

1 Red rooster, or other floury potato
1 tbsp olive oil
200ml single cream
1 heaped tsp Dijon mustard
½ lemon, zest and juice
2 egg yolks
35g grated Parmesan
2 tbsp chopped basil
pinch sugar
1 x 500g cooked lobster, meat removed, diced
sea salt and freshly ground black pepper

for the salad

1 cucumber, peeled, seeds removed, diced
2 tbsp chopped flat-leaf parsley
200g cherry tomatoes, quartered
1 onion, finely sliced
3 tbsp extra virgin olive oil
1 lemon, juiced
sea salt and freshly ground black pepper

Roast salmon, gnocchi and chestnut

by Bryn Williams

Create a luxurious supper with Bryn's homemade marjoram gnocchi, or buy ready-made gnocchi if you are pushed for time.

Preheat the oven to 200°C/400°F/Gas 6.

Bring a large saucepan of salted water to the boil. Drop the gnocchi into the water and cook for 1–2 minutes, or until they bob up to the surface and look slightly puffed. Remove from the water with a slotted spoon and place onto a plate.

Meanwhile, heat 25g of the butter in an ovenproof frying pan until foaming, then fry the salmon, skin-side down, for 2–3 minutes. Carefully turn the salmon over and roast in the oven for 5–8 minutes, or until just cooked. Remove from the pan and set aside to rest for 5 minutes.

In a separate frying pan, heat another 25g of butter until foaming, then add the chestnuts and butternut squash and cook for 3–4 minutes, or until the squash is tender. Add a little of the gnocchi cooking water to the pan, then whisk in the remaining 25g butter until the sauce thickens slightly. Season, to taste, with sea salt and freshly ground black pepper. Add the cooked gnocchi and continue to heat until the gnocchi is warmed through.

Serve the gnocchi and chestnut in large serving bowls and top with the salmon.

Serves 4

1 x marjoram gnocchi (page 220), or 400g shop bought potato gnocchi
75g butter
4 x 175g salmon fillets, skin on
150g cooked and peeled chestnuts, chopped
150g butternut squash, cut into 1.5cm chunks
sea salt and freshly ground black pepper

....

Tip: When buying fresh chestnuts, choose nuts that are heavy for their size with shiny, smooth shells. Give them a squeeze to check that the nut inside is plump and full.

Haddock 'ceviche' with crab salad
by Nick Nairn

A beautifully impressive and healthy summer lunch. Although most commonly made with raw fish, ceviche is incredible prepared with thinly sliced smoked haddock – the acidity in the lime imparts a lovely smoky flavour as it 'cooks' the fish.

To prepare the 'ceviche', cut away the thin ends of the smoked haddock fillet (you can reserve these pieces for another recipe) and slice the remaining thick fillet into 2–3mm thick slices – a very sharp knife will help here. Divide the haddock equally among 4 serving plates.

Place the lime juice, olive oil, pink peppercorns and dill into a bowl, mix thoroughly and set aside.

For the crab salad, mix the celeriac, apple, half of the mayonnaise, the crème fraîche and lemon juice together in a bowl until well combined. Add the crabmeat, the chopped parsley and the remaining mayonnaise, mixing gently until just combined.

Place a quarter of the crab salad onto each serving plate, next to the haddock slices. Garnish with the pea shoots.

Heat a griddle pan until it's really smoking hot. Drizzle the ciabatta with olive oil, season with sea salt and freshly ground black pepper and scatter over the thyme leaves, then griddle each slice for a couple of minutes on each side until the bread is nicely charred.

Meanwhile, drizzle the lime juice mixture over the haddock a few minutes before you are ready to serve. Arrange the griddled ciabatta slices next to the crab salad and ceviche and serve.

Serves 4

for the 'ceviche'
200g undyed smoked haddock fillets, skinless and boneless
25ml lime juice
25ml olive oil
½ tsp pink peppercorns, crushed
10g chopped dill

for the crab salad
75g celeriac, peeled and finely chopped
½ Granny Smith apple, skin on, core removed and finely chopped
75g mayonnaise
30g crème fraîche
1 lemon, juiced
200g cooked white crab meat
1 tsp chopped parsley
30g pea shoots or any micro greens

for the ciabatta
1 ciabatta, sliced into 3–5mm thick slices
2 tbsp olive oil
2 sprigs thyme, leaves only
sea salt and freshly ground black pepper

Malaccan black pepper crab with black beans, ginger and curry leaves

by Rick Stein

Rick adapted his Malaysian crab recipe from Charmaine Solomon's Encyclopedia of Asian Food; *now sadly out of print. It is, he says, 'one of the best dishes of Southeast Asia' and makes a scrumptious meal for two.*

If using live crabs, turn them on their backs with their eyes facing you. Drive a thick skewer or a thin-bladed knife between the eyes and into the centre of the crab. Then lift up the tail flap and drive the skewer through the underside.

For both uncooked and cooked crabs, pull off the bottom tail flaps and discard. Break off the claws, then take a large-bladed knife and cut them in half at the joint and crack the shells of each piece with a hammer or the back of a knife. Chop the body section of each crab in half, then gently tug on the legs to pull the body pieces away from the back shell. Use a knife as an added lever if you need to but the body pieces should come away quite easily with the legs still attached.

Turn each piece over and pick off the dead man's fingers (soft gills), then cut in half once more so you have 2 legs attached to each piece. Throw away the back shell or save for stock.

Mix together the ketjap manis, black beans, sugar and 3 tablespoons water in a bowl until well combined. Set aside.

Heat 75ml of the vegetable oil in a large, lidded wok over a high heat. When the oil is smoking, add the crabmeat and stir-fry for 3 minutes, until the crab is half cooked through (or until warmed through, if using cooked crabmeat). Remove from the wok and set aside to drain on kitchen paper.

Pour all but 1½ tablespoons of the oil out of the wok, then return the wok to a medium heat. Add the sliced spring onions and all of the ginger, garlic and curry leaves and stir-fry gently for 1–2 minutes, taking care not to let anything brown.

Add the black pepper and, after a few seconds, the black bean mixture. Return the crab pieces to the wok, turn over once or twice to coat in the mixture, then cover with a lid and leave to cook for 5 minutes (if the crab is raw), or 2–3 minutes (if using cooked crabmeat).

When the crab is cooked through, remove the pan from the wok, then stir in the butter and sliced red chilli, carefully turning the cooked crabmeat as you stir to coat it in the sauce. Spoon onto 1 large serving plate or 2 soup plates, scatter with the remaining spring onion and serve.

Serves 2

- 1kg raw or cooked whole crabs, such as brown crab, mud crab or blue swimmer
- 1 tbsp ketjap manis (sweet soy sauce)
- 1 tbsp Chinese fermented salted black beans, rinsed and chopped
- 1 tsp palm sugar
- vegetable oil, for frying
- 5 spring onions, thinly sliced on the diagonal, plus extra to serve
- 25g peeled fresh ginger, finely shredded
- 15g peeled garlic, finely chopped
- 20 fresh curry leaves
- 1 tbsp black peppercorns, coarsely crushed
- 15g butter
- 1 medium-hot red chilli, cut in half lengthways, sliced

Salted pollock with asparagus, wild garlic and morels

by Michael Caines

Michael Caines transforms the common pollock into a delicacy through salting the flesh the night before. The earthy flavours of asparagus, morels and wild garlic signal the arrival of spring, and are delicious in this beautifully textured dish.

Place the fish fillets onto a baking tray and sprinkle over the salt. Cover with cling film and place in the fridge for at least 8 hours. Rinse the salt off the pollock and pat dry, then wrap the fillet tightly in cling film and chill in the fridge for another hour.

Preheat the oven to 200°C/400°F/Gas 6.

Bring a pan of salted water to the boil, add the asparagus and cook until firm but not crunchy. Drain and then refresh in iced water.

Remove the pollock from the fridge, remove the cling film and cut into 4 portions. Season lightly with sea salt and freshly ground black pepper. Heat an ovenproof non-stick frying pan until hot, add 1 tablespoon of olive oil and about 20g butter. When the butter is foaming, add the fish and fry for 1–2 minutes, or until golden-brown. Turn the pollock over and roast in the oven for 4–5 minutes, or until the fish is cooked through.

Meanwhile, heat the remaining oil and butter in a frying pan and stir-fry the wild garlic for 2–3 minutes, or until wilted. Season with salt and freshly ground pepper. Stir in the asparagus.

To make the white wine sauce, heat 20g of butter in a saucepan and fry the shallots with a pinch of salt for 2–3 minutes, or until softened but not coloured. Add the mushrooms and sweat for a couple of minutes, until slippery looking. Add the fish stock, bring to a simmer and cook until the liquid has reduced by half.

In a separate pan, heat the wine and cook until reduced by a third then add to the reduced stock mixture. Add the cream, bring to the boil and continue to cook until the sauce has thickened enough to coat the back of a spoon. Meanwhile, heat a knob of butter in a frying pan and fry the morels for 4–5 minutes or until cooked through.

Strain the sauce through a sieve and whisk in the remaining 20g of butter, then season to taste with sea salt and freshly ground black pepper. Stir the cooked morels into the sauce.

To serve, squeeze a little lemon juice over the pollock and place in the middle of serving bowls. Spoon the wild garlic and asparagus around, then spoon over the white wine sauce. Drizzle with tarragon oil.

Serves 4

for the pollock
800g pollock fillet, skin removed
40g sea salt, plus extra for seasoning
12 spears asparagus, tips separated, stem sliced diagonally
2 tbsps olive oil
50g butter
175g wild garlic, cleaned and trimmed
1 lemon, juiced
1–2 tbsp tarragon oil, or extra virgin olive oil
freshly ground black pepper

for the white wine sauce
40g butter
50g shallots, sliced
175g button mushrooms sliced
250ml fish stock
250ml aromatic, dry white wine
250ml double cream
150g morel mushrooms
sea salt and freshly ground black pepper

Home smoked mackerel with beetroot and horseradish

by Lawrence Keogh

Hot smoking brings a sensational new dimension to food and is great fun too. You don't need any expensive kit, simply rig up an old biscuit tin or lidded saucepan with a wire rack, cut to sit about halfway down. Carefully pierce the lid five or six times with a screwdriver. Line the bottom with a handful or two of wood shavings (available from pet shops). Things will get a bit smoky, so open as many windows and doors as possible!

Preheat the oven to 200°C/400°F/Gas 6.

Pour the olive oil into a large baking tray and add the garlic and crushed coriander seeds, season with sea salt and freshly ground black pepper.

Remove the leaves from the baby red beetroots and plunge into boiling salted water for 20 seconds. Remove and add them to the olive oil mix. Stir in the juice and zest of 1 lemon and set aside.

Place the red beetroot, golden baby beetroot and candied baby beetroot onto a baking tray and season with sea salt and freshly ground black pepper. Sprinkle over the paprika and hot paprika and roast in the oven for 10 minutes.

Meanwhile, rub the mackerel fillets with oil and season with sea salt and freshly ground black pepper. Add the wood shavings to the smoker and place on the hob, over a medium heat. Place the mackerel fillets into the smoker, close the lid and smoke for 6–8 minutes. After a couple of minutes it will start to smoke a bit. When the fish is ready, turn the heat off and leave to sit for a few minutes before opening the tin. This will allow any residual smoke and heat to penetrate the fish.

Remove the beetroots from the oven, cut into quarters and drizzle with the honey.

To serve, remove the beetroot leaves from the oil mixture, drain and scatter onto each plate. Lay the mackerel fillets on top and arrange the beetroot around the plate. Sprinkle over the fresh horseradish and pea shoots. Squeeze over a little extra lemon juice.

Serves 4

You'll need a hot smoker and wood shavings

50ml extra virgin olive oil
4 garlic cloves, peeled
1 tbsp coriander seeds, lightly crushed
600g baby beetroot (a mix of golden, candy-stripe and red varieties, if possible)
2 lemons, 1 zested and both juiced
½ tsp smoked paprika
½ tsp smoked hot paprika
4 mackerel fillets, pin bones removed
3 tbsp clear honey
½ fresh horseradish, grated
pea shoots, to garnish
sea salt and freshly ground black pepper

Mackerel pasty with pickled cucumber salad

by Mark Sargeant

This is a really tasty summer dish and so irresistible looking: a sort of amalgam of a Cornish pasty, stargazey pie and beef Wellington, with the mackerel tail poking out.

Preheat the oven to 200°C/400°F/Gas 6. Season the mackerel with sea salt and freshly ground black pepper.

Mix the sausage meat, tarragon and parsley together in a bowl. Spread the mixture over the cut side of the mackerel, then fold the mackerel back together, along the spine. Chill in the fridge.

Meanwhile, cut the puff pastry into 4 pieces and roll each piece out to the thickness of a £1 coin.

Place a mackerel into the middle of each piece of pastry, leaving the fish tail poking out, then fold the pastry over, trim any excess and crimp the edges together to seal.

Place the pasties onto a baking tray, brush the tops with the beaten egg and bake in the oven for 25–30 minutes, or until the pastry is cooked through and golden-brown. Remove from the oven and set aside to rest for 10 minutes.

Meanwhile, mix the cucumber, sugar, vinegar and salt together in a bowl and set aside for 5 minutes, then stir in the parsley. Toss the watercress with the olive oil and squeeze of lemon juice in a second bowl. Serve both salads alongside the warm pasties.

....

Tip: If you don't feel confident preparing the mackerel yourself, ask your fishmonger to butterfly and pin bone the fish and make sure the tails are left on.

Serves 4

4 medium mackerel, butterflied, pin bones removed
4 good-quality pork sausages, filling squeezed out, skins discarded
1 bunch tarragon, chopped
½ bunch flat-leaf parsley, chopped
500g ready-roll all-butter puff pastry
2 egg yolks, beaten
sea salt and freshly ground black pepper

for the cucumber salad
½ cucumber, peeled, halved lengthways, seeds scooped out, sliced
pinch sugar
2 tbsp cider vinegar
½ tsp salt
½ bunch flat-leaf parsley, chopped

for the watercress salad
2 bunches of watercress
1 tbsp olive oil
squeeze lemon juice

Potato tart with sardines and tomatoes

by James Martin

Fresh sardines are a real treat and pan-roasted in the oven like this – rather than grilled – you won't fill your house with strong fishy smells. To make life easier, get the sardines prepared for you at the fishmongers.

Preheat the oven to 150°C/300°F/Gas 2.

Place the tomatoes, cut-side up, onto a roasting tray just big enough to accommodate them. Drizzle over the olive oil and sprinkle with the thyme, sea salt and freshly ground black pepper. Place in the oven and slowly roast for 2–3 hours until the moisture has mainly evaporated and the tomatoes have dried out. Remove the tomatoes from the oven and set aside to cool.

Turn the oven up to 200°C/400°F/Gas 6. Heat a medium-sized (about 25cm) ovenproof frying pan over a medium heat then add a drizzle of the olive oil.

Arrange the sliced potatoes in overlapping circles so they cover the bottom of the pan. Season with salt and pepper, then turn the heat down to low.

Cook for about 5 minutes until the potatoes turn golden-brown at the edges and are translucent in the middle. Place the sardines on top in a fan shape, with the tails pointing towards the middle of the pan. Drizzle with the olive oil and season with a little more salt and pepper.

Lay the oven-roasted tomatoes over the top then sprinkle with the oregano. Bake in the oven for 15–20 minutes until the potatoes are cooked and the top is golden brown. Remove the pan from the oven and let the tart cool slightly.

Serves 2

for the slow-roasted tomatoes
6 tomatoes on the vine, halved widthways
4 tbsp olive oil
4 sprigs thyme
sea salt and freshly ground black pepper

for the tart
5 tbsp olive oil
450g waxy potatoes, peeled and sliced thinly
6–8 fresh sardines, cleaned and butterflied
10 oregano leaves
sea salt and freshly ground black pepper

....

Tip: The slow-roasted tomatoes can be done the day before, or pop them into the oven a couple of hours before you start the rest of the dish.

Pollock, squid and mussel stew

by Nathan Outlaw

With two Michelin stars for his eponymous fish restaurant in Rock, Cornwall, Nathan knows how to take simple fish cooking to new heights. In this leisurely lunch dish, he takes inspiration from rustic Provençal cookery to create deep fishy flavour, redolent with garlic, saffron and tarragon. There are a few components to this dish, so take your time and make the shellfish stock well in advance.

To make the stock, preheat the oven to 200°C/400°F/Gas 6. Roast the prawns on a baking tray for 45 minutes.

Heat a large frying pan, add the remaining stock ingredients, except the orange juice, and fry gently for 2–3 minutes, or until golden-brown. Add the roasted prawns, the orange juice and enough water to just cover the pan contents. Bring to a boil, then reduce the heat and simmer for 1 hour.

Strain the stock through a sieve; reserve the liquid and discard the rest. Heat the strained liquid in a saucepan until boiling. Reduce the heat and simmer until the volume of the liquid has reduced by three-quarters. Chill in the fridge and use within 3 days, or freeze until needed.

Place the pollock onto a plate and sprinkle over the sea salt. Chill in the fridge for one hour, then rinse the pollock until all the salt is removed. Pat the fish dry with kitchen paper.

Heat the olive oil in a non-stick frying pan over a high heat. Place the pollock, skin-side up, into the pan and cook for 2–3 minutes, or until the fish is a light golden-brown, then add the potato, leek, butternut squash, thyme and garlic. Cook for a further 3–4 minutes then turn the fish over and cook for a further minute, or until the fish is cooked through. Set the fish aside and allow to rest for a couple of minutes.

For the saffron sauce, place your homemade shellfish stock along with the fish stock, tomatoes, tarragon sprig and saffron into a saucepan and bring to the boil. Simmer until the volume of the liquid is reduced by three-quarters. Place the mixture into a food processor and blend until smooth. Strain the sauce through a sieve into a large, clean lidded saucepan and return to the boil.

Serves 4

for the shellfish stock
1kg frozen prawns in their
   shells
2 tbsp olive oil
1 onion, chopped
2 carrots, peeled, chopped
4 ripe tomatoes, chopped
6 garlic cloves, halved
1 orange, zest and juice

for the pollock
4 x 200g pollock fillets, skin
   removed
2 tbsp sea salt
2 tbsp olive oil
110g cooked potato, cut into
   1cm dice
1 leek, cut into 1cm dice,
   blanched in boiling water
   for 1 minute and refreshed
   in cold water
110g cooked butternut
   squash, cut into 1cm dice
1 sprig thyme
2 garlic cloves

Add the mussels, cover with a lid and cook for 1–2 minutes, or until the mussels have opened. (Discard any mussels that have not opened.) Stir in the butter and season, to taste, with sea salt and freshly ground black pepper. Add the chopped tarragon and chervil and mix until well combined.

To serve, heat the olive oil in a non-stick frying pan over a medium heat. Fry the squid for 1–2 minutes until cooked through. Season to taste. Place some of the vegetables into the bottom of each serving bowl and top with a piece of pollock. Spoon the mussels, squid and sauce around the fish. Finish with a drizzle of extra virgin olive oil.

....

Tip: Saffron is the world's most expensive spice – hard to produce and, pound for pound, often more costly than gold. Fortunately you only need a pinch to work wonders in your kitchen. If you can afford it, buy the saffron strands as the ground variety is often mixed up with other spices to bulk it up.

for the saffron sauce
200ml shellfish stock
   (as above)
375ml fish stock
2 chopped ripe tomatoes
1 sprig tarragon, plus 3 tbsp
   finely chopped tarragon
pinch of saffron
500g fresh mussels, cleaned
   and debearded (page 78)
50g unsalted butter
3 tbsp chervil, finely chopped
sea salt and freshly ground
   black pepper

to serve
1 tbsp olive oil
2 medium squid, prepared
   and cut into rings (ask your
   fishmonger to do this)
3–4 tbsp extra virgin olive oil,
   for dressing

Wild sea trout, sorrel and peas

by Henry Harris

Accompanied by Henry's tomato, mint and crème fraîche salad (page 157) this makes a beautifully balanced summer lunch.

To trim the artichokes, cut off the top half of the artichoke and then pull away the leaves to remove the green tinged ones, leaving the delicate yellow leaves. Trim any green pieces adhering to the small base. Quarter and remove any visible hairy choke with the point of a small knife.

Melt 50g of the butter in a lidded saucepan and throw in the artichokes, vermouth, sea salt and freshly ground black pepper. Cover with a lid and cook over a medium heat for 5 minutes.

Heat a splash of olive oil in a frying pan. Season the fish fillets and place them in the pan, skin side down, for 4 minutes, or until the skin is crisp. Turn the trout over and cook for a further minute. Add a small knob of butter to the pan and a good squeeze of lemon, baste the fish and remove to 2 warm plates.

Meanwhile, add the peas to the artichokes and cook for a further 1–2 minutes. Then remove the lid from the artichoke pan and add a further 50g of butter. Bring to a brisk boil and stir in the sorrel, check the seasoning and add a few drops of lemon juice. If the sauce starts to split, add a small splash of water and stir to bring it back together.

To serve, divide the artichokes and peas between two plates, top with the sea trout and spoon the buttery juices over.

Serves 2

6 small violet baby artichokes
125g butter
110ml dry vermouth
1–2 tbsp olive oil
2 x 175g fillets wild sea trout, scaled, skin on
1 lemon, halved
110g fresh peas, podded
1 bunch sorrel, stalks removed, thinly sliced
sea salt and freshly ground black pepper

Octopus, chorizo and oregano

by Silvena Rowe

Flavours of surf and turf combine beautifully in Silvena's Spanish-style dish. Buy frozen octopus, or ask your fishmonger to prepare the octopus for you then freeze it at home before thawing, to help tenderise the meat. Since octopus can be tough if not tenderised, Silvena shares a few more tricks to ensure sweet, tender, melt-in-your mouth flesh.

Bring a large saucepan of water to a rolling boil. Beat the tentacles lightly with a meat mallet (or rolling pin) to tenderise, then peel the skin straight away.

Use tongs to dunk the octopus into the boiling water 3 times, leaving it submerged for a few seconds each time. 'Shocking' the octopus first ensures that the tentacles don't curl up during cooking and become hard and chewy. Add the vinegar and salt to help tenderise the flesh further, then return the octopus to the pan and simmer for about 1 hour, until you can easily prick it with a fork.

Leave to cool in the water and then drain and chop the tentacles into small chunks. Fry the chorizo in a hot frying pan over a medium heat for a few minutes until golden and crispy, then add the spring onions and octopus pieces, along with the oregano leaves. Cook all together for a further 2 minutes.

Serves 4, as a starter

1 octopus, about 1.75–2kg, cleaned and prepared
2 tbsp vinegar
1 tbsp sea salt
200g cooking chorizo, cubed
5 spring onions, sliced
a handful oregano, thyme or parsley

Lemon and honey spatchcock chicken
by Anthony Demetre

Marinated with exotic lemony, herby flavours, this is lovely for lunch al fresco, especially with Anthony's quinoa and broad bean salad alongside. Get your butcher to spatchcock the chicken for you, or use some strong, sharp scissors to do it yourself.

Using a pestle and mortar (or a food processor) blend the preserved lemon, garlic, rosemary, honey, olive oil, and the chopped and flaked chilli together to make a smooth paste.

If you are spatchcocking the chicken yourself, lay the bird, breast side down, on a clean work surface and cut down either side of the backbone, take out the backbone, then press down on the breast of the chicken to open it out flat.

Brush the marinade onto the chicken, cover and leave on a baking tray in the fridge for at least an hour, preferably overnight.

Preheat the oven to 220°C/425°F/Gas 7.

Cook the chicken for 20–25 minutes, or until golden-brown and cooked through. Leave to rest, then divide the chicken into 4 pieces, and pile some salad alongside.

Serves 4

150g whole preserved lemons
4 garlic cloves
1 sprig rosemary, leaves only
90g clear honey
50ml olive oil
3 green chillies, seeds removed, roughly chopped
pinch dried red chilli flakes
1.2kg chicken, spatchcocked and backbone removed
quinoa and broad bean salad (page 154), to serve

Tip: Preserved lemons add a lovely tart flavour to roast chicken, slow-cooked stews, salads and rice dishes – in fact you can throw them in just about any Middle Eastern or Mediterranean dish for a salty citrusy lift. Belazu pickled lemons are a good shop-bought option.

Chicken with chorizo, peppers and sage

by Angela Hartnett

This summery recipe makes a relaxed al fresco lunch with Angela's spiced aubergine (page 55), or some good-quality chunky bread. Ask your butcher to joint the chicken into legs, thighs and breasts for you and cut the breasts in half.

Preheat the oven to 180°C/350°F /Gas 4.

Season the pieces of chicken with sea salt and freshly ground black pepper. Heat 2 tablespoons of the olive oil in a large non-stick frying pan and brown the chicken on both sides for 4–5 minutes. When all the chicken pieces are golden, remove them from the pan and set aside.

Heat the remaining tablespoon of olive oil in a frying pan and cook the chorizo for 2–3 minutes. Add the peppers, garlic, sage and thyme to the pan and cook for another 2–3 minutes. Tip the chorizo and peppers into a roasting tin and place the chicken pieces on top.

Sprinkle the lemon zest and juice from half a lemon over the chicken. Bake in the oven for 40–45 minutes, turning the chicken pieces halfway through the cooking time.

Serves 4

1 large corn-fed chicken,
   jointed into 8 pieces
3 tbsp olive oil
110g chorizo, peeled
   and sliced
3 red peppers, cut into
   2.5cm squares
2 garlic cloves, crushed
1–2 tbsp chopped sage
2 tsp chopped thyme
1 lemon, zest and juice
sea salt and freshly ground
   black pepper

....

Tip: This can be served hot or warm and it's also great cold the next day.

Roast poussin with morels, broad beans and spätzle

by Jun Tanaka

Spätzle are a type of egg noodle, somewhere between dumplings and pasta, and can be made in all kinds of shapes – long and noodly, short and straight, or fat as little teardrops – depending on the thickness of the batter and the depth of the pot. This is the perfect dish for when you fancy a roast with a little something different. If you're cooking for more than two, use a regular chicken rather than poussin and double up the quantities of the morel mix.

Preheat the oven to 200°C/400°F/Gas 6.

For the lemon and parsley butter, blend the parsley, lemon zest and bread in a food processor. Tip the breadcrumb mixture into a bowl, add the butter and season, to taste, with sea salt and black pepper. Mix until well combined, then set aside.

Carefully slide your fingers under the skin of the poussin to create a pocket on each side of the breasts. Use a piping bag, if you have one, or your fingers to stuff the lemon and parsley butter under the skin, spreading it out evenly over the breasts. Place a garlic bulb half and a sprig of thyme into the cavity of each poussin, season with salt and pepper inside and out, and tie the legs together with butcher's string.

Heat the olive oil in an ovenproof frying pan, add the poussin and cook for 2–3 minutes on each breast, or until golden-brown. Transfer to the oven and roast for 15 minutes, or until cooked through. Remove the poussin from the frying pan and set aside to rest for 5 minutes.

Meanwhile, for the morel mix, add the lemon juice, shallot and morels to a frying pan and cook for 1 minute. Add the broad beans and peas, season with sea salt and freshly ground black pepper and cook for a further minute. Stir in the butter and then set aside.

To make the spätzle, place the flour into a large bowl and make a well in the centre. Add the eggs and gradually bring in the flour from the sides to form a runny dough. Add the crème fraîche and season with sea salt and freshly ground black pepper.

Set a metal steamer over a pan of boiling water. Spoon the dough into the steamer and push it through the holes with a spatula (if you don't have a steamer, a colander or potato ricer will do). Remove the steamer and using a slotted spoon, carefully lift out the spätzle once they bob to the surface. Stir the spätzle into the morel mix.

To serve, remove the breasts and legs from the poussin. Spoon the morel mixture onto the centre of each serving plate, place the breast on top and the legs alongside. Spoon over any reserved juices.

Serves 2

for the lemon and parsley butter
4 tbsp flat-leaf parsley
2 lemons, zest only
2 slices stale white bread
150g unsalted butter, softened
sea salt and freshly ground black pepper

for the roast poussin
2 baby chickens
1 garlic bulb, cut in half
2 sprigs thyme
2 tbsp olive oil
sea salt and freshly ground black pepper

for the morels, broad beans and spätzle
1 lemon, juiced
1 shallot, peeled, finely chopped
50g morel mushrooms
50g broad beans (shelled weight), podded and peeled
50g peas
50g butter
300g Italian '00' flour
6 eggs
2 tbsp crème fraîche
sea salt and freshly ground black pepper

Thai roast chicken with pak choi and sesame noodles

by James Tanner

A roast with a kick! James says, 'I cook this for my friends and family often and it's a great way to jazz up a whole chicken, plus any leftover chicken meat makes an excellent spiced-up sandwich or salad.'

Preheat the oven to 190°C/350°F/Gas 5.

Put the chillies and creamed coconut in a food processor with the lime zest, lime juice and coriander. Blend to a smooth paste.

Loosen the skin at the top of the crown of the chicken and push your index and middle fingers underneath to form a pocket. Score the thighs twice on both sides.

Push most of the paste into the pocket under the skin and rub the remaining paste into the thighs of the chicken.

Lay the lime slices on the bottom of a roasting pan and sit the chicken on top. Cover with foil and roast for 40 minutes. Remove from the oven, remove the foil and baste the chicken. Return to the oven, uncovered, and cook for a further 30–40 minutes, basting occasionally. Remove from the oven and rest for 5 minutes.

To cook the pak choi and noodles, simply cut the pak choi heads in half and remove the core. Heat a frying pan, add a splash of oil and fry the crushed garlic and sugar for 1 minute. Lay over the pak choi halves, add the stock and fish sauce and bring to a simmer. Cover with greaseproof paper and cook for around 3 minutes or until just tender.

Meanwhile, blanch the noodles in some salted boiling water, drain and toss in a bowl with the sesame seeds, sesame oil and sliced spring onions.

To serve, carve the chicken onto warmed serving plates, add a pile of sesame noodles and pak choi, garnish with coriander and dig in!

Serves 4

for the chicken
2 red chillies, halved
   and deseeded
150g creamed coconut
2 limes, zest and juice, plus
   2 limes, sliced
handful coriander
1.5kg chicken

for the pak choi and sesame noodles
4 small heads of pak choi
1 tbsp vegetable oil
2 garlic cloves, crushed
pinch of sugar
575ml chicken stock
2 tsp Thai fish sauce
350g fresh egg noodles
1 tbsp toasted sesame seeds
1 tbsp sesame oil
2 spring onions, sliced
4 sprigs of coriander

Hot and sour cabbage

by Paul Rankin

This is perfect winter comfort food. It's the sort of thing you baby along, instructs Paul. Taste it as you go, adding a little more salt, a little more sugar as you like.

Melt the butter in a large heavy casserole dish and add the cabbage, vinegar and a good pinch of salt.

Cover with a lid and cook over a low heat for 1 hour. Stir in the apples, raisins, ginger and sugar, and cook slowly for another 30 minutes. Finally stir in the white pepper, and check the seasoning to see if it needs more sugar or salt.

Serves 4, as a side

2 tbsp butter
1 red cabbage, core removed, finely sliced
50ml sherry wine vinegar
salt, to taste
2 apples, peeled, core removed, chopped
2 tbsp raisins
1 tbsp chopped fresh ginger
2 pinches sugar
½ tsp white pepper

Roasted root veg

by Michael Caines

Simply throw everything in the baking tray cut nice and chunky, and it will cook beautifully alongside your roast.

Preheat the oven to 190°C/375°F/Gas 5.

Place the vegetables onto a baking tray. Drizzle over with olive oil and sprinkle with oregano. Season with sea salt and freshly ground black pepper and toss well to coat. Roast in the oven for 20–25 minutes until golden and just tender.

Serves 4, as a side

2 carrots, peeled and chopped
2 large onions, peeled, and quartered
2 leeks, cut into chunky pieces
2 heads garlic, peeled, broken into cloves
2 tbsp olive oil
1 tsp dried oregano, or a handful of fresh oregano, finely chopped
sea salt and freshly ground black pepper

Mixed game pithivier

by Paul Rankin

This tasty winter warmer makes an impressive centrepiece at any gathering. You can now buy selections of ready-prepared game from your supermarket or butcher. Bought puff pastry makes the dish even quicker and easier to prepare – but everyone will think you've been slaving away for hours!

Chop the game meats and the streaky bacon then tip into a food processor along with all the pie ingredients, except the pastry and eggs. Blend until well combined and finely chopped. Tip the filling into a large mixing bowl, cover with cling film and leave to chill in the fridge.

Meanwhile, cut the pastry in 2 and roll both blocks on a floured surface into 5mm-thick squares. Chill in the fridge for at least 20 minutes, then cut into circles, one 24cm in diameter, the other 27cm. Use an overturned bowl or plate as a guide.

Place the smaller circle on a parchment-lined baking tray and brush the base completely with the beaten egg. Spread the meat filling on top, leaving a 5cm border all around, and use your hands to pat into a dome shape.

Brush the edge with egg and top with the other circle of pastry, fresh from the fridge. Use your hands to pat the pastry around the filling and seal the edge well. Try not to let any big air pockets inside, and try to not stretch the top piece of puff, or it will lose shape during cooking.

Brush the pithivier with beaten egg, making sure not to let it drip over the edges. With a small knife, cut a small cross at the top for ventilation, then use the blunt edge to make parallel semi-circles starting from near the cross and ending at the edge. Alternatively, decorate the top with pastry leaves using the leftover pastry.

Leave to chill in the fridge for 20 minutes. After about 10 minutes, preheat the oven to 180°C/350°F/Gas 4. Bake the pie for 45–50 minutes, or until the pastry is golden-brown and the filling is cooked through.

Meanwhile, for the sauce, heat the stock and cream in a saucepan until boiling and continue to cook for 2–3 minutes, or until thickened slightly. Add the alcohol and the green peppercorns, reduce the heat and simmer for 1–2 minutes. Check the seasoning.

Serve the pie whole at the table with a bowl of hot and sour cabbage (page 137) and a jug of the green peppercorn sauce alongside.

Serves 6

300g pack of game selection meat (venison, pigeon and pheasant)
150g streaky bacon
150g pork sausage meat
1 tbsp brandy
1 shallot, chopped
1 garlic clove, chopped
1 tbsp chopped parsley
1 tbsp chopped thyme leaves (or ½ tsp dried thyme)
1 tsp freshly ground black pepper
½ tsp salt
500g ready-roll all-butter puff pastry
2 eggs, beaten

for the green peppercorn sauce

150ml meat stock
150ml double cream
2 tbsp whisky or cognac
1 tbsp green peppercorns, lightly crushed

Lamb sweetbreads and liver with spring onions and samphire

by Richard Corrigan

Richard Corrigan makes a delicious spring lunch of lamb sweetbreads and liver, pan fried and served with poached samphire, spring onions and Jersey Royals. If you've never tried offal before, this is a good simple dish to cook. Offering a soft, delicate almost creamy texture matched by a subtle flavour, lamb sweetbreads are one of the great treats of the gastronomic year. Ask your butcher to order some in.

Sprinkle the flour onto a plate and coat the lambs' liver, shaking off any excess.

Add the butter, oil, lambs' liver and sweetbreads to a hot frying pan and fry for 2–3 minutes on each side, or until golden-brown and crisp.

Meanwhile, heat the vinegar and sugar in a saucepan until boiling, then add the crushed mustard seeds. Slice off the white part of the spring onions, add to the saucepan and poach gently for 2–3 minutes, or until just tender. Remove the pan from the heat. Slice the remaining green part of the onion finely and set aside.

Bring a pan of salted water to the boil, add the Jersey Royals and cook for 5–7 minutes, or until just tender, then drain. Return the Jersey Royals to the saucepan with a little butter, salt, pepper and the mint and toss to coat.

Blanch the samphire in a pan of salted boiling water for 1–2 minutes, or until hot through. Drain.

To serve, remove the poached spring onion from the saucepan and add to the samphire, then stir in a little of the poaching liquid. Arrange the samphire on serving plates with the lambs' liver and sweetbreads. Stir the dill and sliced spring onion into the remaining poaching liquid and spoon over the plates. Pile the Jersey Royals alongside.

Serves 4

75g plain flour, seasoned with salt and freshly ground black pepper
600g lambs' liver, cut into thick slices
50g butter, plus extra for the potatoes
2 tbsp olive oil
8 lamb sweetbreads
150ml white wine vinegar
200g caster sugar
3 tbsp mustard seeds, crushed
2 bunches spring onions, trimmed
250g Jersey Royal potatoes
150g samphire
2 sprigs mint, leaves picked and finely sliced
1 bunch dill, chopped
sea salt and freshly ground black pepper

Lamb cooked on hay with potato boulangère

by Tom Kitchin

Tom says, 'Cooking lamb on a bed of hay is a traditional technique revived from old cookbooks, which has become a bit of a foodie craze. It gives the lamb a delightfully earthy and smoky taste and is a beautiful way of bringing food from nature to plate.'
Buy clean eating hay from a pet shop or garden centre (rather than bedding hay).

For the boulangère potatoes, preheat the oven to 160°C/325°F/Gas 2.

Heat a heavy bottomed pan, add some oil, then add the sliced onion, leek, fennel, garlic, thyme and fennel seeds and sweat for 3–4 minutes.

Meanwhile, bring the stock to the boil in a saucepan and grease a small ovenproof dish with a little of the butter.

Slice the potatoes thinly on a mandoline or with a really sharp knife and start to layer up the dish with alternating layers of potato and the onion mix, seasoning with sea salt and freshly ground black pepper in between.

For the final layer, arrange the potatoes neatly and pour over the hot stock. Add a couple of knobs of butter, cover with foil and bake for 1 hour. Remove the foil and cook for another 30 minutes, or until cooked and crisp.

For the lamb, turn the oven up to 200°C/400°F/Gas 6. Heat a dash of olive oil in a casserole dish placed over a stove top and brown the lamb all over. Remove the lamb from the casserole dish.

Add the hay and a little more oil, just until the hay starts to smoke, then place the lamb on top and cover with the lid. Bake in the oven for 12–15 minutes, or until the lamb is pink.

To serve, remove the lamb from the hay, rest for 5–10 minutes, then carve and serve with the boulangère potatoes.

Serves 4

You'll need a cast iron casserole dish with a lid and some clean eating hay

dash olive oil
1 onion, thinly sliced
1 leek, thinly sliced
1 fennel, thinly sliced
2 garlic cloves
1 thyme sprig
1 tsp fennel seeds
500ml lamb or chicken stock
50g butter
700g potatoes
½ bag of clean pet shop hay
1 rack of lamb, French
    trimmed
sea salt and freshly ground
    black pepper

Herb-crusted roast leg of lamb

by Michael Caines

A well-cooked leg of lamb is a British classic and Michael Caines' version looks the business, while being simple to prepare. Ask your butcher to saw or chop the leg bone into 2cm pieces so that you can add it to the roasting tray, for added flavour.

To make the herb crust, blend the breadcrumbs, parsley and garlic in a food processor until the mixture resembles fine breadcrumbs. Add the olive oil and mustard and season, to taste, with salt and white pepper. Blend again, until the mixture comes together as a smooth paste (you may need to add 100ml or so of water). Place the mixture between 2 sheets of greasproof paper and roll out to an even thickness, large enough to cover the leg of lamb. Set aside.

Preheat the oven to 190°C/375°F/Gas 5.

Prepare the lamb for roasting by making several small incisions into the flesh with a sharp thin knife or a metal skewer. Press the garlic slices into the holes. Push some thyme and rosemary sprigs into the middle of the meat where the bone has been removed, then roll the lamb up into a cylinder shape. Tie with butcher's string to keep everything in place and season with salt and pepper.

Heat the olive oil in a frying pan and fry the leg of lamb, turning frequently for 4–5 minutes, or until browned all over.

Place the reserved bones on a solid-based roasting tin and top with the sealed leg of lamb. Roast in the oven for 40–45 minutes (for medium), or until cooked to your liking.

When you're happy with the doneness of your lamb, remove from the oven and set aside to rest for 30 minutes. Remove the string.

Preheat the grill to high or leave the oven on. Transfer the lamb to a clean roasting tray, brush with half of the mustard and cover with the sheet of herb crust. Grill for 8–10 minutes, or until the crust is golden-brown.

Meanwhile, place the original roasting tray back onto the heat and stir in a splash of chicken stock. You're looking to reconstitute all the cooking juices, so scrape the sides and the base of the roasting tin to release all the lovely caramelised bits. Add the remaining Dijon mustard. Bring the gravy to the boil and remove from the heat. Season, to taste, with salt and black pepper.

To serve, carve the lamb into slices, add some roasted veg and spoon over the gravy.

Serves 8

for the herb crust
275g dried breadcrumbs
110g flat-leaf parsley,
    roughly picked and washed
2 garlic cloves, peeled
4 tbsp olive oil
15g Dijon mustard
salt and white pepper

for the lamb and gravy
2kg leg of lamb, boned
    (bones reserved
    and chopped)
a few garlic cloves, peeled
    and sliced
a few sprigs thyme
a few sprigs rosemary
2 tbsp olive oil
2 tbsp Dijon mustard
150ml chicken stock
roasted root veg (page 137),
    to serve
sea salt and freshly ground
    black pepper

Pork belly with blueberry and chilli molasses glaze

by Silvena Rowe

This is one of those rare dishes that sounds quite elaborate to make, but is actually very straightforward and tastes absolutely amazing. Have your friends guess what the secret ingredient is in the glaze!

Preheat the oven to 150°C/300°F/Gas 2.

Place the pork belly in a deep roasting tray and pour over the chicken stock – it should come about halfway up the pork belly. Scatter over the spices, cover the tin with foil and cook in the oven for 2–4 hours, or until very tender.

Remove from the oven, drain off the liquid and leave to cool completely.

For the blueberry molasses, place the blueberries and water in a food processor or blender and blend to a purée. Place in a saucepan and add the sugar, lemon and chilli flakes. Bring to a boil and simmer for 40–60 minutes, or until the mixture becomes thick and syrupy. Adjust the seasoning, adding more chilli if you like a little more spice.

Preheat the oven to 240°C/475°F/Gas 8. Remove the thick layer of skin and fat from the pork belly and discard. Place the pork in a clean roasting tin and glaze the top and side of the meat with the blueberry molasses.

Place the pork in the oven for 5–6 minutes, or until the top is caramelised and slightly crisp. Cut the pork into squares and serve with Silvena's feta, yoghurt and cumin salad (page 160) as a sensational side.

Serves 4

for the pork belly
800g lean belly of pork
800ml rich chicken stock
½ tsp cumin seeds
½ tsp fennel seeds
½ tsp cardamom
   pods, crushed

for the blueberry molasses
350g fresh blueberries
   (or frozen blueberries,
   defrosted)
125ml water
2 tbsp caster sugar or honey
2 tbsp lemon juice
½ tsp mild chilli flakes
sea salt and freshly ground
   black pepper

Classic beef and ale pie

by James Martin

British stews and pies make great comfort dishes. Here is one of James's all-time favourites – the kind of thing you usually associate with a trip down the pub. The pies are really simple to make, with minimal ingredients (beef, ale, a few herbs, veg and stock), and the pastry cooked on top rather than simply plonked on at the end.

Preheat the oven to 170°C/325°F/Gas 3.

Sprinkle the flour onto a plate and season well with sea salt and freshly ground black pepper. Dredge the steak pieces in the seasoned flour.

Heat an ovenproof casserole dish over a high heat, add the steak in batches, and fry for 3–4 minutes, stirring regularly, until golden-brown on all sides. Remove the cooked steak from the dish and transfer to a warm plate and set aside. Repeat the process with the remaining steak pieces, then set aside.

Add the shallots, onions and carrots to the emptied casserole and fry for 2–3 minutes, or until just softened. Add the thyme, bay leaves and tomato purée and stir well to combine. Add the ale and stir well, scraping any sediment up from the bottom of the casserole using a wooden spoon.

Return the browned steak pieces to the casserole, add the hot stock, stir well and bring the mixture to the boil. Transfer the dish to the oven and cook for 1½ hours, or until the beef is tender and the gravy has thickened. Remove from the oven and set aside to cool slightly.

Increase the heat of the oven to 220°C/425°F/Gas 7.

Divide the beef and gravy mixture among 4 small ovenproof dishes. Cut the pastry into 4 equal pieces, each one big enough to cover the small pie dishes.

Brush a little water around the rim of each pie dish, then place on a piece of pastry over each pie and press the edges to seal the pastry to the dish. Brush with a little beaten egg, then place the pies in the oven and cook for 15–20 minutes, or until the pastry is pale golden-brown and has risen. Serve immediately.

Serves 4–6

75g plain flour
750g braising steak, cut into
   5cm cubes
2 tbsp vegetable oil
2 shallots, chopped
125g baby onions (or small
   onions), peeled
400g carrots, peeled, cut into
   large chunks
4 sprigs thyme
3 bay leaves
4 tbsp tomato purée
300ml ale (northern dark ale
   is best)
300ml hot beef stock
500g ready-roll all-butter
   puff pastry, rolled to
   5mm thickness
1 egg, beaten
sea salt and freshly ground
   black pepper

Tip: When handling pastry, run your hands under cold water to keep them cool. Make sure you dry them before touching the pastry though!

salads

Salads growing up were simple but delicious. Going out to the garden to collect eggs and pick some leaves, spring onions, a bit of beetroot. Nothing fancy, just simple clean flavours from ingredients as fresh as you can get. Home-grown, eaten within minutes of coming out of the ground, organic. It was all organic! It just wasn't fashionable to put a name to it then.

There was a time when 'salad' meant iceberg lettuce, limp cucumber and an under-ripe tomato, massacred to look like a rose. What was all that about? Thankfully times have moved on, our tastes are developing. We're travelling further afield: taking holidays abroad. Our children go on gap years. The UK is a melting pot of cultures, and these flavours and influences are now part of our everyday lives.

Take a look in your local supermarket; ingredients such as couscous, quinoa and edamame beans are no longer the preserve of health food nuts. And the choice of salad leaves! Lambs lettuce, living salads, endive. Avoid the bagged leaves that have been cut and washed for you. Even better, grow your own. You won't taste anything better.

And what about the humble potato? For God's sake, don't think that covering some potatoes in mayonnaise is a salad. Dress some boiled new potatoes with cider vinegar, spring onions, mustard and dill – great as an accompaniment to brown trout.

The term salad is far reaching and can include pretty much anything. Hot salads as a main course: why not? One of my favourite autumnal salads is a selection of roast game birds – grouse, partridge and wood pigeon – roasted root veg and bitter leaves, dressed with pan juices and crushed blackberries. At Christmas I like to serve pan-fried scallops with clementines, ham and oloroso. Sweet, tart, salty and crunchy. And that's what you want from a salad; a balance of flavours and textures, all bound together by the perfect dressing.

Salads shouldn't be complicated or fussed over. Simplicity and quality of ingredients are so important. Take inspiration from the recipes in this chapter – with a few ingredients you can prepare a quick, easy dish in minutes. You don't need a lot to get creative!

Richard Corrigan

Pea, broad bean and bacon salad

by Tana Ramsay

The combination of fresh greens with fatty salty pork is glorious. Serve alongside Tana's lamb sausages (page 208), or treat yourself to double portions for a tasty summer lunch.

Steam the peas and broad beans for 3 minutes, or until tender. Drain, then refresh in cold water.

Cook the bacon in a medium frying pan until it is golden and crispy on all sides, then drain on kitchen paper.

To make the creamy mustard dressing, whisk all of the ingredients together in a small bowl. Place the rocket, baby spinach, peas, broad beans and bacon into a large bowl. Toss the salad with enough of the dressing to coat and serve immediately.

Serves 4

150g fresh or frozen peas
150g fresh or frozen broad beans
6 rashers of smoked bacon, cut into strips
100g rocket leaves
100g baby spinach leaves

for the dressing
6 tbsp olive oil
2 tbsp white wine vinegar
1 tsp wholegrain mustard
2 tbsp crème fraîche

Fennel, radish and pepper salad

by Gennaro Contaldo

This pretty salad is full of refreshing crunch and fresh summer flavours. Serve as a starter, or alongside grilled or barbecued fish.

To make the lemon dressing, whisk the olive oil, lemon juice and mustard together in a small bowl.

Place all the salad ingredients into a large bowl. Season, to taste, with sea salt and freshly ground black pepper, then pour over as much dressing as you like and toss to coat well. Serve immediately.

....

Tip: By placing the celery stalks into iced water you will not only cause them to curl up into pretty shapes, the celery will also retain its crunch for longer.

Serves 4

200g cherry tomatoes, halved
1 red pepper and 1 yellow pepper, cut into julienne strips
1 red onion, finely chopped
2 celery sticks, cut into julienne strips and placed in cold water until they begin to curl
1 large cucumber, deseeded, thinly sliced
6 radishes, quartered
1 fennel bulb, trimmed, cut in half, core removed, thinly sliced
10 basil leaves
sea salt and freshly ground black pepper

for the lemon dressing
150ml extra virgin olive oil
4 tbsp lemon juice
1 tsp Dijon mustard

Four simple side salads

Fresh green salad by Matt Tebbutt

With Matt's classic French dressing, even the most basic salad tastes delicious.

Toss the salad leaves together in a large bowl. In a small bowl, whisk the mustard and vinegar together, add the garlic and whisk in the olive oil. Season, to taste, with sea salt and freshly ground black pepper.

Pour the dressing over the leaves and toss together well so everything gets coated. Serve immediately.

Serves 4

75g rocket leaves
1 Little Gem lettuce,
 leaves separated
75g lambs lettuce

for the dressing
1 tsp Dijon mustard
1 tbsp white wine vinegar
1 garlic clove, peeled,
 finely chopped
3 tbsp extra virgin olive oil
sea salt and freshly ground
 black pepper

Fresh herb salad by Henry Dimbleby

Don't feel restricted to the herbs listed, any fresh green herbs will do. Simply chop everything as finely as you can and enjoy the bursts of fresh flavour.

Toss the leaves and herbs together in a large bowl. In a small bowl, whisk the vinegar, mustard and olive oil together and season, to taste, with sea salt and freshly ground black pepper.

Pour the dressing over the leaves and toss together well so everything gets coated. Serve immediately.

Serves 4

150g mixed salad leaves
2 tbsp finely chopped
 mint leaves
2 tbsp finely chopped chives
2 tbsp finely chopped flat-
 leaf parsley
2 tbsp finely chopped
 oregano

for the dressing
1 tsp white wine vinegar
1 tsp English mustard
3 tbsp olive oil
sea salt and freshly ground
 black pepper

Tomato and radish salad by Galton Blackiston

Radishes make a colourful addition to any plate. This is everything you want a side salad to be – light, fresh, colourful and crunchy.

Place the tomatoes, radishes and spring onions in a bowl and mix together.

In a separate bowl, whisk the mustard, vinegar and lemon juice until well combined. Whisk in the olive oil, then add the chopped shallot. Season, to taste, with sea salt and freshly ground black pepper.

Drizzle two-thirds of the dressing mixture over the salad ingredients and stir well to coat the salad.

Serves 4

5 ripe tomatoes, roughly chopped
18 radishes, trimmed, quartered
6 spring onions, sliced thickly on the diagonal
1 tsp Dijon mustard
2 tbsp red wine vinegar
½ lemon, juiced
6 tbsp olive oil
1 shallot, finely chopped
sea salt and freshly ground black pepper

Indian-style shallot salad by Cyrus Todiwala

A perfectly zingy side salad. Great for cutting through the heat of a hot curry.

Mix all the ingredients together in a bowl until well combined. Adjust seasoning to taste then serve immediately.

Serves 4

2 banana shallots, finely sliced
1 green chilli, finely diced
2 tbsp chopped coriander
2 tbsp chopped mint
2 plum tomatoes, roughly chopped
1 lime, juiced
1 tbsp cider vinegar
sea salt and freshly ground black pepper

Quinoa and broad bean salad

by Anthony Demetre

Quinoa is a gluten-free South American grain with a nutty flavour and light couscous-like texture. It's great for soaking up the exotic Middle Eastern flavours in this salad. Serve this as a starter, as part of an al fresco spread, or to accompany Anthony's lemon and honey spatchcock chicken (page 131).

To stop the quinoa tasting bitter, place the grains in a fine-meshed strainer and rinse thoroughly with cold running water, dragging your fingers through it as you rinse to make sure the water gets to every grain.

Meanwhile, bring a pan of water to the boil. Salt it lightly then add the quinoa. Turn down to a lively simmer, and leave for about 15 minutes, until it is tender but still has a little bite to it. Drain in a sieve and then cool under running water.

Meanwhile, heat the oil in a frying pan and fry the pumpkin and sunflower seeds until golden-brown. Set aside.

Combine the quinoa, olives, preserved lemon, broad beans, parsley and mint in a bowl. Tip in the cooled seeds and season with sea salt and freshly ground black pepper.

For the dressing, whisk the honey, lemon juice and olive oil together in a small bowl and drizzle over the salad, to taste.

Tip: Vinaigrette with honey in it will remain emulsified for a long time, so this kind of dressing is great for presentations at dinner parties, for example, where you don't want the oil and vinegar separating on the plate.

Serves 4

200g quinoa
1 tbsp rapeseed oil
1 tbsp pumpkin seeds
1 tbsp sunflower seeds
2–3 tbsp Gordal or Queen green olives, stones removed and cut into segments
1 preserved lemon, finely sliced (page 131)
60g broad beans (podded weight)
a handful each of parsley and mint

for the dressing
20g clear honey
½ lemon, juiced
60ml olive oil
sea salt and freshly ground black pepper

Spicy vegetable salad with a curry-soy vinaigrette

by Ken Hom

A deliciously different salad: light and spicy and perfect alongside a quick stir-fry.

To make the curry-soy vinaigrette, combine the mustard, curry powder, soy sauce, salt, pepper and olive oil in a bowl. Mix well and set aside.

Bring a pot of salted water to the boil. Drop in the tomatoes for 5 seconds, remove with a slotted spoon, peel and seed. Cut the tomatoes into 4cm pieces and set aside.

Add the broccoli, green beans and cauliflower to the boiling water and cook for 3–4 minutes, then add the peas and cook for 1–2 minutes.

Drain the vegetables into a warm bowl, then add the water chestnuts and tomatoes, shallots and chives. Drizzle over the salad dressing and mix until well combined.

Serves 4

2 tsp Dijon mustard
2 tsp Madras curry powder
2 tbsp light soy sauce
2 tsp salt
1 tsp freshly ground
    black pepper
4 tbsp extra virgin olive oil
225g fresh tomatoes
100g broccoli florets,
    trimmed small
100g French green beans,
    trimmed
100g cauliflower, trimmed
    and broken into
    small florets
100g peas
50g fresh water chestnuts,
    peeled, sliced
3 tbsp finely chopped
    shallots, squeezed dry
    through a linen cloth
3 tbsp finely chopped chives

Couscous with pistachio and pomegranate

by Tom Kime

Tom throws yellow couscous, green coriander and ruby red pomegranate seeds together in this beautiful salad, to go with his spiced fish tagine (page 184). It's also a very good accompaniment to grilled fish or meat.

Place the couscous, olive oil and lemon juice into a bowl. Pour over the boiling water, stir once, then cover the bowl tightly with cling film. Set aside for 5 minutes, or until the couscous has absorbed all of the water, then fluff the couscous grains with a fork.

Stir the chopped pistachios, pomegranate seeds and coriander into the couscous until well combined, then season, to taste, with sea salt and freshly ground black pepper.

Serves 4–6

200g couscous
1 tbsp olive oil
½ lemon, juiced
250ml boiling water
50g pistachio nuts,
    roughly chopped
4 tbsp pomegranate seeds
2 tbsp coriander leaves,
    roughly chopped
sea salt and freshly ground
    black pepper

Tomato, mint and crème fraîche salad
by Henry Harris

Try and use as many different varieties of tomato as possible for a mix of tastes and textures. You want the tomatoes plump and ripe and at room temperature to get the best flavour.

Heat the oil in a deep heavy-based frying pan until a breadcrumb sizzles and turns golden-brown when dropped into it. Add the croutons to the hot oil and shallow fry until crisp and golden-brown. Remove from the oil using a slotted spoon and set aside to drain on kitchen paper. Season with sea salt and freshly ground black pepper.

Arrange the tomatoes in 2 small bowls. Sprinkle over the croutons and the shallot and drizzle with the olive oil.

Stir the mint into the thinned crème fraîche, then lift the mint from the cream and scatter over the tomatoes. Allow some of the cream to come along too. Finally dip a teaspoon into some hot water and lift out an oval scoop of crème fraîche from the pot and place it in the middle of each salad. Season with freshly ground black pepper.

Serves 2

olive oil, for shallow frying
1 slice sourdough, chopped
   into dice
300g mixed heirloom
   tomatoes, sliced (halve and
   quarter smaller tomatoes)
1 shallot, chopped
2–3 tbsp extra virgin olive oil
8 mint leaves, sliced thinly
1 tbsp crème fraîche thinned
   down with a splash of milk
sea salt and freshly ground
   black pepper

Creamy celery and walnut salad
by Stuart Gillies

Sweet, creamy, crunchy and lovely to look at! Stuart says, 'make sure you save the yellow leaves from the centre of the celery head – they have lots of flavour – and peel the stalks as finely as you can to get rid of the stringy bits.'

Pull the leaves from the celery stalks and set them aside. Using a mandoline or vegetable peeler, peel down the stalks to create ribbons.

Mix the celery ribbons, walnuts, Stilton, parsley and celery leaves together in a bowl.

Whisk the crème fraîche, honey, vinegar and mayonnaise together in a separate bowl until smooth.

Toss the salad with enough of the dressing to coat. Serve immediately.

Serves 4

3 sticks celery
150g walnuts, shelled
100g Stilton cheese, crumbled
50g flat-leaf parsley leaves
1 handful celery leaves
55ml crème fraîche
25g honey
½ tbsp sherry vinegar
100g mayonnaise

Tart potato salad
by Lawrence Keogh

Potato salads work best when they are dressed immediately after cooking while they are still warm, so that the dressing is absorbed into the slices. Lawrence's makes excellent picnic food, or serve with battered fish (page 202), as an alternative to chips.

Boil the potatoes in a medium pan of salted water for 10–12 minutes, or until the potatoes are tender.

Drain the potatoes and set aside to cool for a moment, then slice into thick rounds and stir together with the rest of the ingredients. Season, to taste, with sea salt and freshly ground black pepper.

Serves 4

300g waxy potatoes (such as Royal Kidney or Jersey Royals)
6 pickled onions, quartered
1 small red onion, sliced into rings
40g baby capers
40g pea shoots
2 tbsp malt vinegar
1 tbsp chopped curly parsley
sea salt and freshly ground black pepper

Minted pea and feta salad

by Donna Hay

Cool mint and salty feta get along with each other famously. For a great brunch dish, serve alongside Donna's pancetta-baked eggs (page 31) and some warm flatbread.

Pour boiling water over the frozen peas and set aside to stand for 2 minutes. Drain, then refresh in cold water.

Mix the peas, mint, lemon juice and olive oil in a bowl until well combined.

To serve, divide the spinach among the serving plates and spoon some pea and mint salad on top. Sprinkle over the crumbled feta.

Serves 4

240g frozen peas
3 tbsp chopped mint
1 lemon, juiced
2 tbsp olive oil
50g baby spinach leaves
100g feta cheese, crumbled

Whipped feta, yoghurt and cumin salad

by Silvena Rowe

Silvena's creamy cumin-spiced dressing transforms a quick lettuce salad into a side dish bursting with flavour.

Mix the feta and yoghurt together in a bowl, then add the ground cumin and season to taste.

Toast the cumin seeds in a small frying pan over a medium heat, until the seeds are aromatic and slightly darker in colour. Transfer to a dish to cool.

Place the lettuce in a large bowl, add the dressing and toss to coat well. Scatter with the toasted cumin and sesame seeds.

Serves 4

100g feta cheese, crumbled
3 tbsp plain yoghurt
½ tsp ground cumin
¼ tsp cumin seeds
4 small Little Gems, leaves
   only, washed and trimmed
¼ tsp black sesame seeds
sea salt and freshly ground
   black pepper

Mexican hearts of palm salad

by Fernando Stovell

Palm hearts are considered a delicacy in Mexico, where this is sometimes known as 'millionaire's salad'. You can't buy them fresh in the UK, but the jarred or tinned variety are available in good supermarkets and delis here (page 340). They have a unique gentle flavour that you won't find in anything else, and that perfectly complements the creamy avocado and spicy chipotle dressing. Serve as a side to Fernando Stovell's vuelve a la vida (page 23), or as a stunning starter.

For the vinaigrette, crush the garlic, onion and chipotle chilli paste in a pestle and mortar. Add half a teaspoon of orange zest. Slowly stir in the oil, then season, to taste, with salt, vinegar and sugar.

Peel the orange and cut into segments. Slice half of the radishes thinly and cut the remaining radishes into quarters.

Mix the radishes, orange segments, Little Gem lettuce and hearts of palm together in a bowl. Add a little of the salad dressing and toss until well combined.

Tip the salad onto a serving plate and top with the avocado and flaked almonds.

....

Tip: Full of vitamins and fibre, the 'right' kind of fat and more potassium than a banana, avocados make a healthy addition to any salad. If the avocado has a slight neck, rather than being rounded on top, it's a good indication that the fruit was tree-ripened, so it should be full of flavour.

Serves 4

1 orange
1 bunch radishes
1 bunch breakfast radishes
2 handfuls baby spinach leaves
1 Little Gem lettuce, leaves separated
4 pieces hearts of palm, sliced lengthways into quarters
1 small avocado, peeled, flesh thinly sliced
2 tbsp flaked almonds, toasted

for the vinaigrette

½ garlic clove
1 tbsp onion, chopped
1 tsp chipotle chilli paste
1 orange, zest only
5 tbsp sunflower oil or a very light olive oil
1 tbsp white wine vinegar
pinch of salt and sugar

Orange, herb and edible flower salad

by Silvena Rowe

Edible flowers add life to this gorgeous dish of herbs, succulent salty Kalamata olives and refreshing citrus. Serve alongside Silvena's octopus, chorizo sausage and oregano dish (page 130) for a really pretty and unusual lunch.

Combine the orange segments, herbs, olives and spring onions in a bowl.

Arrange on a plate, then scatter the flowers over. Drizzle with the olive oil and lemon juice, add the sesame seeds and season with sea salt and freshly ground black pepper.

....

Tip: Mixed selections of edible flowers can now be bought online (page 340). Alternatively, B&Q sells edible pansy and nasturtium growing kits for home cooks. Avoid eating flowers that have been sprayed with pesticides – including those bought from the florist – and never harvest anything growing by the roadside.

Serves 4

2 oranges, segments only
a handful each of mint,
    oregano and parsley leaves
16–20 Kalamata olives
5 spring onions, sliced
a handful of edible flowers,
    try nasturtiums or pansies
2 tbsp olive oil
½ lemon, juiced
1 tsp sesame seeds, toasted
sea salt and freshly ground
    black pepper

Panzanella with tuna

by James Martin

The key to a good panzanella is day old – rather than fresh – bread, which absorbs the oil, vinegar and all the ripe summer flavours in the salad without falling apart. James has added seared tuna to his classic Tuscan mix, but this is such a versatile recipe you can ring the changes with chicken, prawns or any seasonal vegetables you have to hand.

Preheat the oven to 150°C/300°F/Gas 2.

Place the tomatoes onto a baking tray, cut-side facing up. Drizzle over 1 tablespoon of the olive oil and season, to taste, with sea salt and freshly ground black pepper. Transfer the tomatoes to the oven and cook for 1 hour, or until softened and slightly dried out. Remove from the oven and set aside to cool slightly.

Meanwhile, place the tuna steaks onto a large plate. In a bowl, whisk together the lemon zest, garlic and 2 tablespoons extra virgin olive oil until well combined. Season, to taste, with sea salt and freshly ground black pepper. Pour the lemon oil over the tuna steaks and turn to completely coat them in the mixture. Set aside to marinate for 30 minutes.

Once the tomatoes are done, increase the oven temperature to 220°C/425°F/Gas 7.

Place the ciabatta pieces onto a baking sheet and drizzle over 2 tablespoons of the olive oil. Season, to taste, with sea salt and freshly ground black pepper. Transfer to the oven and cook for 5–7 minutes, or until crisp and golden-brown.

Heat the remaining tablespoon of oil in a frying pan over a medium heat. Add the shallot and fry for 2–3 minutes, or until softened.

Blend two-thirds of the roasted tomatoes, 6 tablespoons extra virgin olive oil and all of the red wine vinegar in a food processor to a fine purée. In a bowl, add half of the purée mixture to the croutons and set aside to soak for 5 minutes. Stir in the remaining roasted tomatoes, capers, piquillo peppers and basil leaves. Set aside.

When the tuna has marinated, heat a griddle pan over a medium heat until hot. Add the tuna and cook for 1 minute. Give the tuna a quarter turn and cook for a further minute. Turn by a quarter again and continue to cook for another minute, or until you can see criss-cross golden-brown griddle marks. Turn the steaks over and cook for 1–2 minutes more, or until cooked to your liking.

Remove the tuna steaks from the pan and set aside on a warm plate to rest for 1 minute. To serve, carve the tuna steaks into thick slices and place on top of the salad. Finish with a good drizzle of the tomato dressing.

Serves 4

600g baby tomatoes, cut in half horizontally
4 tbsp olive oil
4 x 200g tuna steaks
1 lemon, zest only
1 garlic clove, grated
8 tbsp extra virgin olive oil
200g day-old crusty (ciabatta) bread, torn into small chunks
1 large banana shallot, finely chopped
2 tbsp red wine vinegar
4 tbsp capers, drained and rinsed
1 x 220g jar piquillo peppers, drained, chopped
2 handfuls basil leaves, picked
sea salt and freshly ground black pepper

Tip: Look out for pole-and-line caught tuna; avoid anything purse seined (a large net that catches entire schools of fish).

Mackerel, tomato and samphire salad
by Nathan Outlaw

A sophisticated and sensational tasting dish. Once you've prepared the stock, the salad takes no time at all and makes an elegant starter or light lunch for two.

To make the tomato stock, place the tomatoes, vinegar, garlic, sugar and chilli into a bowl. Season with a bit of salt, stir until well combined, then give the mixture a good squeeze with your hands. Spoon the tomatoes into a large piece of muslin and hang it over a bowl in the fridge overnight or for at least 6 hours. Reserve the liquid collected from the tomatoes.

For the mayonnaise, mix the egg yolks, mustard and vinegar together in a bowl until well combined. Slowly whisk in the oil until the mixture thickens and then whisk in the cream. Add 150ml of the reserved tomato stock into the bowl. Season, to taste, with sea salt and freshly ground black pepper.

Pour the contents of the bowl into a saucepan over a low heat and whisk continuously until heated through. Allow to gently simmer.

Meanwhile, heat a frying pan over a medium-high heat and add a dash of oil. Once the pan is scorching hot, add the bacon and fry until crisp, then remove from the pan. Add the mackerel fillets, skin-side down, add the bacon back to the pan and cook for 1 minute. Add the cherry tomatoes, drizzle with a little oil and a sprinkling of salt and cook for a further 3–4 minutes.

Remove the bacon, mackerel and tomatoes from the pan and set aside. Add the lettuce and samphire to the same pan and cook for 1 minute.

To serve, ladle the warm mayonnaise into the middle of the plate, add the bacon, tomato and lettuce mixture on top. Finish with the mackerel and a drizzle of olive oil. Sprinkle over the basil leaves and serve.

....

Tip: Because it's an oily fish, mackerel deteriorates very fast. Keep an eye out for UK-caught mackerel in July, when they are at their peak season. Check for shiny firm fish, with clear, bright eyes. Fresh mackerel should be rigid enough not to droop if held horizontally by the head.

Serves 2

for the tomato stock
8 ripe vine tomatoes, chopped
2 tbsp white wine vinegar
2 garlic cloves, chopped
1 tbsp sugar
1 red chilli, deseeded, chopped
pinch salt

for the creamy mayonnaise
3 egg yolks
1 tsp English mustard
1 tsp white wine vinegar
300ml light olive oil
50ml double cream
sea salt and freshly ground black pepper

for the salad
1 tbsp olive oil
4 rashers of smoked streaky bacon, cut into small pieces
2 mackerel, gutted, filleted, pinbones removed
8 cherry tomatoes, halved
salt, to taste
2 Little Gem lettuces, leaves separated
110g samphire
10 basil leaves

Bulgar wheat salad

by Jun Tanaka

Jun's salad is ideal for mezze-style eating on warm summer nights. Serve with a selection of small dishes, or alongside Jun's breast of lamb with apricots and almonds (page 280).

For the dressing, crush the garlic and cumin in a pestle and mortar, stir in the lemon juice and olive oil. Season, to taste, with sea salt and freshly ground black pepper.

Heat the chicken stock, garlic and thyme in a saucepan until boiling. Add the bulgar wheat and take the pan off the heat. Set aside for 5 minutes, then drain. Remove the garlic clove and thyme.

Tip the bulgar wheat and the remaining salad ingredients into a bowl and mix until well combined. Stir in the dressing to taste.

....

Tip: For salads, look for medium grade bulgar wheat as this has already been parboiled and then dried with the tough outer husks removed.

Serves 4

400ml chicken stock
1 garlic clove
1 thyme sprig
60g bulgar wheat
10 cherry tomatoes, cut into
    quarters, seeds removed
½ red onion, finely sliced
25g golden raisins
¼ cucumber, peeled, halved,
    seeds removed, sliced
1 tbsp finely chopped
    flat-leaf parsley leaves
1 tbsp finely chopped
    mint leaves

for the dressing

1 garlic clove
15g cumin seeds, toasted
2 lemons, juiced
250ml olive oil
sea salt and freshly ground
    black pepper

Crispy chicken with braised chicory and fennel salad

by James Martin

James's mix of bitter, savoury and sweet flavours goes well with chicken or any barbecued meat or fish.

Preheat the oven to 180°C/350°F/Gas 4.

Heat a lidded, ovenproof frying pan until hot. Add the chicory, orange zest and juice, cover with a lid and place in the oven for 5 minutes, or until the chicory is just tender.

Cut the remaining 2 oranges into segments. Reserve the leftover juice and place the segments into a large bowl along with the fennel, watercress and red onion. In a small bowl, whisk the mustard, 1 tablespoon of reserved orange juice, vinegar and olive oil together until well combined. Season to taste with sea salt and freshly ground black pepper.

Heat a griddle pan, then cook the braised chicory, cut-side down, on the griddle for 1–2 minutes. Cut the chicory into thick slices and add to the fennel salad. Mix the salad and dressing together until well combined.

Now start your chicken. Slice the breasts lengthways, but not all the way through and flatten with the palm of your hand to form an oval shape. Place the flour and beaten egg into separate bowls and season each with salt and black pepper. In a third bowl, mix the breadcrumbs together with the orange zest. Dredge the chicken in the flour, then dip into the egg mixture and roll in the breadcrumbs.

Heat the butter and olive oil in a large frying pan. Add the chicken breasts, one at a time, and fry for 2–3 minutes on each side, or until golden-brown. Test the chicken breast is cooked by inserting a skewer into the thickest part of the meat. If the juices run clear, the chicken is cooked. At this point, remove the chicken from the pan and set aside to drain on kitchen paper.

Dice the chicken and add everything to a large salad bowl. Or serve the chicken breast with the salad alongside and any leftover dressing drizzled around the edge of the plate.

Serves 4

for the salad
1 tbsp olive oil
4 heads chicory, halved
   lengthways
4 oranges (2 zested
   and juiced)
2 fennel, thinly sliced
   lengthways
large handful watercress
1 red onion, finely sliced
1 tbsp wholegrain mustard
1 tbsp white wine vinegar
3 tbsp extra virgin olive oil
sea salt and freshly ground
   black pepper

for the chicken
4 chicken breasts,
   skin removed
75g plain flour
2 eggs, beaten
60g dried breadcrumbs
1 orange, zest only
50g butter
2 tbsp olive oil

Spicy chicken, cucumber and cashew nut salad

by Bill Granger

This hot chicken and cool noodle salad combines bright lime and chilli flavours to spice up a summer lunch.

Whisk the fish sauce, pepper, garlic, chillies and sugar in a bowl. Put the chicken in a separate bowl and pour over half the marinade. Cover with cling film and refrigerate for 20 minutes (keep the rest of the marinade to one side).

Heat the oil in a large frying pan over a medium-high heat. Add the chicken, in 2 batches, and cook for 3 minutes on each side, or until it is cooked through. Bill's tip here is to put another frying pan on top of the chicken and weigh it down with a couple of tins to make the chicken really crisp.

While the chicken is cooking, add the lime juice and sugar to the marinade that you set aside. Stir until the sugar has dissolved to make a dressing.

Pour boiling water over the vermicelli and leave for a minute or so until soft. Drain under cold water, place in a large bowl and add the cucumber, mint, spring onions and cashews. Add the dressing, toss well, and serve with the sliced chicken on top.

....

Tip: Once you have soaked and drained the vermicelli noodles, coating them in a little sesame or vegetable oil will ensure that they do not stick together.

Serves 4

3 tbsp fish sauce
freshly ground black pepper
3 garlic cloves, crushed
2 large red chillies,
    finely diced
2 tsp caster sugar
8 boneless skinless
    chicken thighs
2 tbsp vegetable oil
3 tbsp lime juice
3 tbsp caster sugar
200g dried vermicelli noodles
1 large cucumber, halved,
    deseeded and thinly sliced
small handful mint leaves
4 spring onions, thinly sliced
2 tbsp cashew nuts, crushed

Salad of roast suckling pig and oysters
by Richard Corrigan

This isn't a simple dish, but it looks dainty and – as you might expect from the award-winning Richard – fabulously gourmet. The succulent roast pork, topped with deep-fried sea-sweet oysters and crispy crackling is guaranteed to impress. Your butcher should be able to order the suckling pig leg and, asked nicely, will be happy to bone and skin it for you too. Failing that, boneless pork shoulder is a good substitute. Make sure you take home the skin, for that irresistible tooth-shattering crackling.

To make the crackling, cover all of the crackling ingredients with water in a large saucepan. Bring the mixture to the boil, reduce the heat and simmer for 3–3½ hours, or until the skin is soft (the cooking time is dependent on the size of the pig skin). Remove the skin from the saucepan, shaking off any excess liquid, and place onto a baking tray. Set aside to dry for 20–25 minutes.

Meanwhile, preheat the oven to 150°C/300°F/Gas 2.

Roast the pork skin in the oven for 40–45 minutes, or until golden brown and crisp. Remove the crackling from the oven and set aside.

For the suckling pig, preheat the oven to 180°C/350°F/Gas 4. Roll the pork leg up tightly into a cylinder shape and secure with kitchen string, then season with sea salt and freshly ground black pepper.

Heat 1 tablespoon of oil in an ovenproof frying pan and fry the rolled pork leg, turning occasionally, until browned all over. Transfer it to the oven to roast for 15–18 minutes, or until cooked through. Check the pork is cooked properly by inserting a skewer into the meat – the juices should run clear. Remove the pork from the oven and leave to rest.

For the dressing, heat the cider and vinegar in a saucepan until boiling. Continue to boil until the volume of the liquid has reduced right down, to 100ml. Whisk in the honey, pepper and lime juice.

Meanwhile, for the oysters, sprinkle the flour onto a plate and season with salt and freshly ground black pepper. Heat the oil and butter in a frying pan over a medium heat. Dredge the oysters in the seasoned flour, shaking off any excess and fry for 10–15 seconds on each side, or until golden-brown. Using a slotted spoon, remove the oysters from the pan and set aside to drain on kitchen paper.

To serve, carve the rolled pork leg into 8 pieces. Place 2 on each of the serving plates, top with some watercress and 2 of the oysters. Break the crackling into pieces and sprinkle on top. Drizzle the dressing around the edge of the plate.

Serves 4

for the crackling
skin from suckling pig leg
½ carrot, peeled, roughly chopped
½ onion, roughly chopped
½ leek, roughly chopped
½ celery stick, roughly chopped
4 sprigs thyme
2 garlic cloves, peeled

for the suckling pig
1 x 1kg suckling pig leg, bone removed, skin removed and reserved
1 tbsp olive oil
sea salt and freshly ground black pepper

for the dressing
250ml cider
250ml rice wine vinegar
2 tbsp honey
10g freshly ground black pepper
½ lime, juiced

for the oysters
75g plain flour
2 tbsp olive oil
25g butter
8 rock oysters (preferably Maldon), freshly shucked
1 bunch watercress, to serve
sea salt and freshly ground black pepper

Maple syrup-glazed potato salad with pancetta and calamari

by Shaun Rankin

Shaun's warm salad makes an elegant and very tasty Sunday brunch. Maple syrup and bacon is a fantastic combination, but the nutty-tasting Jersey Royals are the magic ingredient here, bringing all the beautiful flavours together.

Preheat the oven to 220°C/425°F/Gas 7.

Lay the pancetta slices onto a baking tray and place another baking tray on top. Bake for 10–12 minutes, or until the pancetta is crisp and golden-brown, then set aside to cool, still sandwiched between the trays, to keep the pancetta perfectly flat.

Heat 2 tablespoons of the olive oil in a medium frying pan, add the onion wedges and fry over a medium heat for 5 minutes, or until browned on all sides.

Place a piece of foil on a baking tray and place the onion wedges and garlic in the centre. Drizzle over 1 tablespoon of the olive oil, sprinkle over the thyme leaves and season with sea salt and freshly ground black pepper. Fold the tinfoil over to make a parcel and seal all around the edges. Bake the parcel for 15 minutes, or until the onions have softened. Remove from the oven and set aside to cool slightly.

Meanwhile, place the new potatoes in a saucepan of boiling water and cook for 12–15 minutes, or until tender. Drain in a colander, place them into cold water to stop the cooking process and set aside. Heat half the butter in a frying pan over a medium heat, then tip in the potatoes and cook until brown all over.

For the calamari, cut the squid in half lengthways. Lay the sheets of squid flat, then score a criss-cross pattern onto it using a sharp knife. Cut the sheets into strips and discard the tentacles.

Heat the remaining oil in a medium frying pan over a high heat and quickly fry the squid until opaque – this will take about 30 seconds. Remove from the heat and stir in the rest of the butter and lemon juice.

Place the potatoes in the centre of a large serving plate. Take each onion wedge and separate the layers to make petals of onion and scatter these around the potatoes. Squeeze the garlic out of the skins and dot the purée over the salad. Scatter over the crisp pancetta, squid and thyme leaves over the top of the potatoes and drizzle over the maple syrup.

Serves 4–6

6 pancetta slices
5 tbsp olive oil
2 red onions, quartered
1 garlic bulb, broken up
   into cloves
1 small bunch thyme
400g new potatoes
   (preferably Jersey Royals)
50g unsalted butter
400g whole squid, gutted,
   cleaned (ask your
   fishmonger to do this)
1 lemon, juiced
3 tbsp maple syrup
sea salt and freshly ground
   black pepper

Warm salad of mushroom, beetroot and pan-fried pigeon

by James Martin

The beginning of September marks the start of the wood pigeon season, when these plump birds become widely available at farmers' markets and larger supermarkets. The sweet nutty flavour of pigeon goes beautifully with earthy mushrooms and vibrant purple beetroot. If you can't get hold of pigeon, duck breast also works well.

Place the beetroot into a saucepan and cover with water. Bring to the boil then reduce the heat and simmer for 20–25 minutes until the beetroot is tender. Drain and cut the beetroot into quarters lengthways.

Peel the potato and slice it wafer thin with a mandoline, vegetable slicer or by hand to make game chips. Rinse the slices under cold water for 5 minutes to remove the starch.

Meanwhile, brush off any dirt from the mushrooms with a pastry brush or damp kitchen paper and trim before cooking. Heat 1 tablespoon olive oil in a frying pan, and cook the shallot gently for 2 minutes until just softened. Add the mushrooms and continue frying until the mushrooms are just tender, about 2 minutes. Tip the mixture into a large bowl then add the chestnuts, celery and salad leaves.

To make the salad dressing, whisk the mustard, vinegar and extra virgin olive oil together in a small bowl and season with sea salt and freshly ground black pepper.

To fry the chips, pour the vegetable oil into a deep-sided saucepan and heat until a small cube of bread sizzles and turns golden when dropped into it. Alternatively, heat a deep-fat fryer to 190°C/375°F. Carefully place the game chips into the hot oil and deep fry for 1–2 minutes until golden-brown. Remove from the oil with a slotted spoon, drain on kitchen paper and season with salt and freshly ground black pepper.

For the pigeon, preheat the oven to 200°C/400°F/Gas 6. Season the pigeon breast with sea salt and freshly ground black pepper. Heat an ovenproof frying pan then add 2 tablespoons olive oil and the 25g butter. Cook the pigeon breasts, skin side down, for 1 minute until golden-brown then turn and cook for another minute. Transfer the pan to the oven and roast for 3 minutes, then remove the pan from the oven and leave to rest for 5 minutes, basting occasionally with the pan juices.

To serve, toss the beetroot quarters into the salad and drizzle over the dressing. Carve the pigeon into thick slices then add to the salad. At the very last minute, add the game chips and toss lightly to combine.

Serves 4

6 raw baby beetroots, or
   4 good-sized beetroots
1 large baking potato
150g mixed wild mushrooms
   (chanterelles, girolles,
   trompettes de mort,
   shitake, oyster),
   wiped clean
3 tbsp olive oil
1 shallot, finely diced
90g cooked chestnuts
3 tbsp celery leaves
75g mixed winter
   salad leaves
1 tsp Dijon mustard
2 tbsp sherry vinegar
3 tbsp extra virgin olive oil
vegetable oil, for frying
4 pigeon breasts
25g butter
sea salt and freshly ground
   black pepper

The best way to enjoy home cooking is without a doubt with family and friends.

Most families have their own range of favourite dishes, but no matter how skilled you are in the kitchen, the trick is to create a variation in the dishes you cook at home.

I love nothing more than cooking in my time off. That may sound strange coming from a chef, but I am not alone. The kind of cooking I do at my restaurant The Kitchin in Edinburgh is very different to the dishes I enjoy at home. Despite a busy schedule in our family, we always make time for meals and sit down together with the kids to eat every day. Not only is this important for us, but it is also a chance to spend some quality time with the family while enjoying some simple but good food.

My roast pumpkin soup is one of my favourite autumnal dishes and my family love it too. It's so much fun to prepare with the kids, carving out the squash flesh and leaving a beautiful natural soup bowl for serving the soup. If that's a winner with your family, have a go at Bill Granger's chicken dumplings or James Martin's homemade pizzas next.

The key thing for all home cooks to remember is that preparing great meals from scratch doesn't have to be complicated or time consuming. The secret to success is to find the very best seasonal produce available. No matter how little time you have, there is always a wholesome family dish you can cook fairly effortlessly.

One-pot wonders, like the tagines or Bill's easy coq au vin are a great option. The food here is everything that it should be – comforting, flavoursome and affordable. Not only can these dishes be quickly assembled and cooked but you can also create a wonderful flavour from combining all of the ingredients and letting them infuse together for delicious effect.

I hope you are as inspired by these recipes as I am. It is an exciting time for British family cooking and I am proud to be a part of it!

Tom Kitchin

Roasted pumpkin soup

by Tom Kitchin

Using natural soup bowls makes the bright, silky flavour of the pumpkin stand out more. It's also a fun way to get kids excited about eating veg – there's less washing up required!

First, add all of the stock ingredients to a saucepan and bring to the boil. Reduce the heat and simmer for 1 hour. Remove the pan from the heat, set aside to rest for 20 minutes, then strain through a sieve.

Preheat the oven to 180°C/350°F/Gas 4.

Trim the base from the acorn squashes so they sit flat. Cut about 2–3cm down from the top of the squash all the way across to form a lid. Scoop out the seeds and fibres from the middle and discard. Wash thoroughly, then pat dry. Rub the squash inside and out with a little olive oil, and season the insides with sea salt and freshly ground black pepper. Drizzle the remaining olive oil over the squash lids. Place the squash and their lids onto a roasting tray and roast for 45 minutes, or until tender.

Meanwhile, divide the pumpkin wedges into 2 batches. One batch is for roasting and the other is for sweating on top of the stove. Chop the wedges for sweating into 5cm cubes and set aside. Heat the vegetable oil in a large heavy-bottomed saucepan over a medium heat. Add the onion, 1 teaspoon of the cinnamon and a pinch of salt, then fry gently until the onion is very soft. Add the cubes of pumpkin and continue to cook until tender. Add enough stock to cover and bring the mixture to the boil. Reduce the heat and simmer for 20 minutes.

Meanwhile, heat the butter in a large ovenproof frying pan until foaming. Add the pumpkin wedges and season, to taste, with salt and pepper. Fry for 2–3 minutes on each side, or until golden-brown on both sides (this is important for flavour). Sprinkle with the remaining ground cinnamon and the caraway seeds. Continue to cook, turning occasionally to ensure an even colour. After a further 5 minutes, add the honey and transfer to the oven for 6–8 minutes, until dark golden-brown and tender.

Add the roasted pumpkin to the pot of simmering pumpkin and mix together well, adding more stock if necessary. Leave to cook until the pumpkin is very soft and tender (about 10 minutes), then stir in the cream. Check the seasoning and remove the pan from the heat. Leave to rest for 10 minutes before transferring to a blender and blitzing until very smooth.

Meanwhile, for the pumpkin seeds, heat the oil in a frying pan, add the cleaned pumpkin seeds and cinnamon. Fry for 1–2 minutes until just toasted. To serve, place 1 cooked acorn squash onto each serving plate. Ladle in the soup, then top with some crispy pancetta (if using), a dollop of crème fraîche, the toasted pumpkin seeds and a sprinkling of chives. Cover with the lid and serve.

Serves 4–6

for the stock
trimmings and skin from the pumpkin (see below)
700ml chicken or vegetable stock
1 large onion, peeled
handful parsley stalks
3–4 sprigs thyme
1 cinnamon stick
½ head of garlic
3 celery sticks, roughly chopped
2 carrots, roughly chopped

for the soup
4–6 acorn squash
2 tbsp olive oil
1.5kg pumpkin (stalk, skin and seeds removed and reserved), cut into even wedges
1 tbsp vegetable oil
1 large onion, thinly sliced
2 tsp ground cinnamon
1 tbsp butter
1 tsp caraway seeds
2 tbsp clear honey
4 tbsp double cream
sea salt and freshly ground black pepper

for the pumpkin seeds
1 tbsp olive oil
seeds from the pumpkin (see above), cleaned
a pinch ground cinnamon

to serve
3 rashers pancetta, fried until crisp (optional)
50ml crème fraîche
2 tbsp finely chopped chives

Chickpea and courgette curry

by James Martin

You need not stick to courgette here. Once you have the basic ingredients for James's medium-spiced vegetable curry, use whatever is abundant and in season.

Blend half the onion, the fresh coriander stalks, ground coriander, chillies, garlic, fenugreek, asafoetida, cloves, salt and sugar in a food processor until well combined. Add half of the coconut milk and blend again to a purée.

Heat the oil in a frying pan over a medium heat. Add the cinnamon stick, crushed cardamom pods, curry leaves and mustard seeds and fry for 1–2 minutes, or until the spices are fragrant and the mustard seeds start to pop. (Take care, the seeds may pop briskly. Cover the pan with a lid to protect your eyes and face.)

Add the remaining onion and continue to stir-fry for 1–2 minutes. Add the courgettes and cook until golden-brown. Add the reserved puréed sauce and the chickpeas. Stir well and bring the mixture to a simmer. Cook for 2–3 minutes, or until the courgettes are tender and the sauce has thickened slightly.

Add the garam masala, season the mixture, to taste, with sea salt and freshly ground black pepper, then stir in the coriander leaves.

Serve with plain boiled basmati rice or the fragrant pilau rice (opposite).

....

Tip: Dried chickpeas have a nuttier flavour and a better texture than the tinned variety, and you don't have to soak them overnight. Alternatively, cover the chickpeas with cold water and bring to the boil for 10 minutes. Turn off the heat, add a pinch of bicarbonate of soda, and after 3 hours soaking time, they should be ready to cook.

Serves 4

1 onion, thinly sliced
1 bunch coriander, stalks trimmed, leaves roughly chopped
1 tsp ground coriander
3 green chillies, chopped
3 garlic cloves
½ tsp ground fenugreek
pinch asafoetida
½ tsp ground cloves
½ tsp salt
½ tsp caster sugar
400ml coconut milk
2 tbsp vegetable oil
1 cinnamon stick
4 green cardamom pods, crushed
5 curry leaves
½ tsp mustard seeds
3 courgettes, chopped
400g tin chickpeas, drained and rinsed
1 tsp garam masala
sea salt and freshly ground black pepper

Fragrant pilau rice

by James Martin

Pilau is an ancient Middle Eastern method of cooking rice so that every grain remains separate. Thirteenth century Arabic texts show the technique in its entirety and describe still current flavourings such as cardamom and cumin, which perfume James's dish.

Heat the oil in a large pan with a tight-fitting lid. Add the onion and gently cook until soft but not coloured. Stir in the garlic and spices and fry briefly, until fragrant.

Meanwhile, drain the rice and rinse until the water runs clear. In order for the grains to cook perfectly, it is important to rinse the rice thoroughly before cooking to remove all surface starch.

Add the rice to the pan and stir until well coated. Pour over the water and stir again, then bring the water to the boil, cover the pan and reduce the heat to a gentle simmer.

Cook the rice for 12–15 minutes, or until it is tender. To test if the rice is cooked, squeeze a grain of rice between your fingers; it should be firm but not hard, with each grain being separate and whole. Drain off any excess liquid, then fluff up with a fork.

Season the rice, to taste, with sea salt and freshly ground black pepper, then squeeze over the lemon juice.

....

Tip: When the rice is cooked, you can place a clean tea towel over the pan for 5–10 minutes to absorb the steam and help keep the grains dry and separate.

Serves 4

2 tbsp vegetable oil
1 onion, finely chopped
1 garlic clove, crushed to a
   paste with the side of a
   knife
3 green cardamom pods,
   crushed
½ tsp ground coriander
½ tsp ground cumin
8 curry leaves
400g basmati rice
600ml boiling water
½ lemon, juiced
sea salt and freshly ground
   black pepper

Spiced fish tagine

by Tom Kime

In Tom's Moroccan-style stew, whole fillets of plaice are cooked with aromatic spices, including ras-el-hanout, which you can either make yourself (using the recipe below) or buy ready blended.

Heat the oil in a terracotta tagine or casserole, then fry the garlic for 3–4 minutes, or until pale golden-brown. Add the onions and reduce the heat, then cook the onions slowly for 10–12 minutes, or until softened but not coloured.

When the onions have softened, push them to one side of the tagine, then increase the heat slightly and add the cumin seeds, ras-el-hanout and cayenne pepper to the empty side. Fry for a couple of minutes until fragrant, then stir everything together so that the spices coat the onion mixture.

Add the chopped tomatoes and season, to taste, with sea salt and freshly ground black pepper. Bring the mixture to a simmer and cook for 1–2 minutes, stirring well.

Add the fish stock or water, then return the mixture to a simmer. You will not have room to stir the sauce once the fish is added, so check for taste once again, and adjust the flavourings a final time, if required.

Add the plaice fillets to the tagine, then spoon over some of the sauce to cover the fish. Cover with the lid, then reduce the heat to low and continue to cook for 8 minutes, or until the plaice fillets are cooked through.

Squeeze the lemon juice over the tagine, then scatter over the coriander leaves. Take the tagine straight to the table, accompanied by a big bowl of lightly seasoned couscous or – better still – Tom's fantastic couscous salad.

Serves 4–6

You'll need a terracotta tagine or a heavy-bottomed casserole with a tight fitting lid

2–3 tbsp olive oil
2 garlic cloves, finely chopped
3 onions, finely sliced
1 tsp cumin seeds
2 tsp ras-el-hanout (see tip below)
½ tsp cayenne pepper
3 ripe tomatoes, seeds removed, roughly chopped
110ml fish stock or water
4–6 plaice fillets, skin removed
1 lemon, juiced
4 coriander sprigs, leaves only
couscous or Tom's couscous salad (page 156), to serve
sea salt and freshly ground black pepper

....

Tip: Ras-el-hanout (Arabic for 'top of the shop') is a blend of the best spices and aromatics a spice merchant has in his shop. To make your own, mix 2 tsp ground cinnamon, 1 tsp ground turmeric, 1 tsp coriander seeds, ½ tsp freshly ground black pepper, ¼ tsp freshly grated nutmeg, ¼ tsp freshly ground cardamom seeds and ¼ tsp freshly ground cloves. Store in an airtight jar.

Lemon couscous

by James Martin

A healthy, easy, bright-flavoured alternative to rice. Very fine with tagines or grilled fish.

Put the couscous in a bowl and pour over enough boiling water to cover by roughly 1½ cm. Add the olive oil, preserved lemon and lemon juice and a pinch of salt. Stir well, then cover with cling film and set aside for 3–5 minutes, or until all the liquid has been absorbed.

Gently stir the couscous with a fork to fluff it up. Season, to taste, with sea salt and freshly ground black pepper and serve immediately.

Serves 4, as a side

200g couscous
2 tbsp extra virgin olive oil
10g preserved lemons (page 131), rinsed, drained, pulp removed, flesh chopped
½ lemon, juiced
2 tbsp chopped coriander leaves, to serve
sea salt and freshly ground black pepper

Easy egg fried rice

by Ken Hom

This is a great way to use up leftover rice, but if you are cooking the rice especially, make sure it is properly cooled beforehand so it won't stick together when frying. Feel free to add any leftover vegetables to the basic recipe – chopped finely before adding to the rice. Or add a touch of chilli flakes or chilli oil for a spicy version.

Mix the eggs, sesame oil and a pinch of salt in a small bowl and set aside.

Heat a wok or large frying-pan until it is very hot. Add the oil and when it is almost at smoking point, add the cooked rice and stir-fry for about 3 minutes or until it is warmed through.

Drizzle in the egg mixture and continue to stir-fry for 2–3 minutes or until the eggs have set and the mixture is dried. Add the remaining salt and pepper and continue to stir-fry for 2 minutes then toss in the spring onions. Stir several times and turn onto a serving dish. Eat at once.

Serves 4–6, as a side

2 large eggs, beaten
2 tsp sesame oil
1 tsp salt
400g long grain rice, cooked according to the packet instructions, drained and (ideally) chilled
2 tbsp groundnut or vegetable oil
½ tsp freshly ground black pepper
2 tbsp spring onions, finely chopped

Tip: Don't be tempted to add soy sauce when cooking – it will ruin the flavour of the rice.

Sweet potato tagine

by James Martin

This vegetarian tagine is healthy and very easy to prepare. James says, 'I was never a fan of sweet potatoes, having tasted them in some disappointing desserts in the US. But the spices here work really well with the slightly sweet flavour and lovely creamy flesh of the vegetable. You can, of course, use pumpkin or butternut squash instead.'

Heat the oil in a terracotta tagine or casserole, then add the garlic and onion and fry for 2–3 minutes. Add all of the spices and fry for a further minute. Add the sweet potatoes and stir well before piling in the remaining ingredients, except the coriander. Stir well and bring the mixture to a simmer.

Chop the coriander stalks, reserving the leaves for later, and add the stalks to the pan. Reduce the heat, cover with a lid, and simmer for 15–20 minutes, or until the sweet potato is just tender. Sprinkle over the reserved coriander leaves and take the tagine straight to the table, accompanied by a big bowl of lemon couscous.

....

Tip: Sweet potatoes should be peeled deep enough to remove the hard layer beneath the skin; they will turn dark on the outside when cooked if not peeled deep enough.

Serves 4

You'll need a terracotta tagine or a heavy-bottomed casserole with a tight fitting lid

2 tbsp olive oil
2 garlic cloves, finely sliced
1 onion, thickly sliced
1 tsp ras-el-hanout (to make your own, see page 184)
½ tsp ground cinnamon
½ tsp ground ginger
½ tsp smoked sweet paprika
½ tsp ground cumin
¼ tsp freshly ground black pepper
1kg sweet potatoes, peeled and cut into large chunks
1 x 400g tin tomatoes
2 tbsp honey
½ tsp saffron
200ml water
40g preserved lemons (page 131), finely chopped
125g dried apricots, halved
110g green olives, stones removed
40g almond kernels
1 small bunch coriander
lemon couscous (page 185), to serve

Spiced chicken dumpling soup
by Bill Granger

Bill's cooking is all about maximum flavour with minimal effort. Balancing the exotic with the familiar, he makes a rich Thai-flavoured soup from ready-made chicken stock, store cupboard staples and a few fresh ingredients. A taste sensation!

To prepare the dumplings, put the chicken mince, bamboo shoots, ginger, chilli, coriander, fish sauce and cornflour into a large bowl and season, to taste. Using clean hands mix all the ingredients together until well combined. Wet your hands and roll the mixture into 24 small balls. Chill in the fridge for 30 minutes to firm up.

For the soup, put the chicken stock, coconut milk, lime leaves (or zest) and ginger slices into a large saucepan and bring to a simmer.

Reduce the heat to low, add the dumplings and simmer gently for 5 minutes or until just cooked through. Stir in the fish sauce, lime juice and sugar, to taste. Add the pak choi and rice noodles, bring back to a simmer and remove from the heat.

To serve, ladle the soup into serving bowls, dividing the dumplings evenly. Serve immediately, scattered with the chilli slices, coriander leaves and shredded kaffir lime leaves.

....

Tip: Kaffir lime leaves are essential in Thai cooking. When using older leaves for the garnish, tear either side of the central leaf vein (or midrib), and discard the stalk and central vein, which may taste bitter.

Serves 4

for the dumplings
350g minced chicken
60g tinned bamboo shoots, drained and finely chopped
2 tsp grated fresh ginger
1 long red chilli, seeds removed, finely chopped
2 tbsp chopped coriander leaves
2 tsp fish sauce
2 tbsp cornflour
sea salt and freshly ground black pepper

for the soup
800ml chicken stock
350ml coconut milk
2 kaffir lime leaves (or 2 pieces lime zest)
3cm piece fresh ginger, peeled, thinly sliced
1 tbsp fish sauce
1 tbsp lime juice
½ tsp caster sugar, or to taste
4 baby pak choi, halved lengthways.
60g dried rice noodles, soaked in water for 30 seconds and drained

to serve
2 red chillies, sliced
8 sprigs coriander leaves
2 kaffir lime leaves, finely sliced

Nasi goreng with lime and sugar barbecued chicken

by Rick Stein

Rick's journeys around the Far East inspired this delicious version of nasi goreng, a fried rice dish traditionally eaten for breakfast in Indonesia using leftovers from the night before. The basic dish is amazingly versatile, so feel free to add whatever you have in the fridge, from vegetables to cooked fish to the leftover roast. Save time by marinating the chicken the night before, and whizzing up the nasi goreng spice paste at the same time.

Mix the crushed garlic, peppercorns, sugar, fish sauce and lime juice together in a bowl. Add the chicken pieces and leave to marinate in the fridge for at least 2 hours or overnight. Thread the marinated chicken pieces onto parallel pairs of soaked bamboo skewers (this helps to stop the pieces spinning around as you turn them) and set aside in the fridge until needed.

To make the nasi goreng paste: put all the paste ingredients into a food processor and blend to a smooth paste.

Preheat your grill to high (or prepare the barbecue). Grill the chicken pieces for 6–7 minutes, turning regularly until golden-brown and caramelised on the outside and cooked through (no trace of pink should remain). Slide the meat off the skewers, cut into chunks and set aside.

For the nasi goreng, cook the rice in boiling salted water for 12–15 minutes, or according to packet instructions, until just tender. Drain, rinse well and then spread it out on a tray. Leave to cool (but do not refrigerate).

Heat 1cm of oil in a large deep-sided frying pan until a breadcrumb sizzles and turns golden-brown when dropped into it. Add the sliced shallots and shallow fry, stirring now and then, until crisp and richly golden. Remove with a slotted spoon and leave to drain on plenty of kitchen paper. Sprinkle lightly with salt and set aside until cold and crisp.

Continued overleaf

Serves 4

You'll need 8–16 bamboo skewers (18cm long), soaked in cold water for 1 hour

for the barbecued chicken
3 garlic cloves, crushed
1 tsp crushed white peppercorns
1 tbsp granulated sugar
1 tbsp Thai fish sauce
1 lime, juiced
500g skinned boneless chicken thighs, each cut into 2.5cm strips

for the nasi goreng paste
2 tbsp vegetable oil
4 fat garlic cloves, roughly chopped
50g shallots, roughly chopped
25g roasted salted peanuts
6 medium-hot red chillies, chopped
1 tsp blachan (shrimp paste)
1 tsp salt

for the nasi goreng
300g long grain rice
sunflower oil, for frying
6 large shallots, thinly sliced
2 large eggs
1 tbsp tomato purée
1 tbsp ketjap manis (sweet soy sauce)
1 tbsp light soy sauce
5cm piece cucumber, cut in quarters lengthways, sliced
8 spring onions, trimmed, thinly sliced on the diagonal
sea salt and freshly ground black pepper

Beat the eggs with some sea salt and freshly ground black pepper. Heat a couple of tablespoons of the sunflower oil in a small frying pan over a medium–high heat, pour in one third of the beaten egg and cook until it has set on top. Flip the egg over, cook for a few more seconds then turn out onto a chopping board or plate, roll it up tightly and leave to go cold. Repeat the process twice more with the remaining egg. When the egg rolls are cold, slice them into thin strips.

Heat a wok over a high heat until smoking hot. Add 2 tablespoons of the oil left over from frying the shallots, then the nasi goreng paste and stir-fry for 1–2 minutes, or until fragrant. Add the tomato purée and ketjap manis and stir-fry for a few seconds, then add the cold cooked rice and fry for a further 2–3 minutes until heated through.

Add the barbecued chicken, fried shallots and strips of omelette and stir-fry for another minute. Add the light soy sauce, cucumber and most of the spring onions and toss together well. Spoon onto a large warmed plate, scatter over the remaining spring onions and let people help themselves.

....

Tip: If you don't have any ketjap manis (sweet soy sauce), use 2 tablespoons of soy sauce with 1 tablespoon of brown sugar instead.

Malai murg tikka (chicken cream tikka)

by Cyrus Todiwala

Marinated in cream and spices, Cyrus's indulgent chicken kebabs are easy to prepare and extremely tasty. Serve as a snack, wrapped in naan bread, or as part of a bigger feast.

Squash the cardamom pods and the mace flower and roast in a frying pan over a low heat. Place all the ingredients, except the chicken, in a blender and purée to a smooth paste. Place the chicken into a large dish and pour over the paste. Cover with cling film and marinate for 6–8 hours.

To cook the kebabs, preheat the grill to high. If you are using wooden skewers, soak them in cold water for 10 minutes before using.

Thread the chicken onto skewers and cook for 4–6 minutes, or until cooked through. The chicken will colour very rapidly, so feel free to cut a piece open to check that it's done, before removing the rest from the grill.

....

Tip: Cyrus made his Malai murg tikka on *Saturday Kitchen* as part of a spectacular Indian feast. To recreate the dish presented on the show, spread some mint and mango chutney and some hot beetroot chutney over a piece of naan (page 48), top with Cyrus's simple shallot salad (page 153), pile on the Malai murg tikka and sheek kevaab (page 194), followed by the cucumber and mint raita (page 48). Roll up the naan tightly. Slice into 4–5 rounds and serve immediately.

Makes 6–8 kebabs

You'll need 6–8 thick metal skewers

3–4 cardamom pods
1 mace flower
30g cashew nuts
30g ground almonds
5cm piece fresh ginger
3–4 garlic cloves
150g Greek-style yoghurt
150ml double cream
40g Cheddar cheese, grated
1 tsp lime juice
1 tsp salt
2 tbsp vegetable oil
500g boneless, skinless chicken breast, cut into cubes

Sheek kevaab (lamb kebabs)

by Cyrus Todiwala

You can make these kebabs with any minced meat you like. It takes practice to keep the mince firm and holding well to the skewer, but it's a trick well worth mastering!

Blend the lamb, coriander, mint, ginger, garlic and chilli together in a food processor. Tip the mixture out into a bowl then stir in the powdered spices, salt and lime juice. Check for seasoning. If you prefer not to taste raw meat, either deep fry a small ball of the mince or pan fry a small patty-sized piece. Cover the mixture with cling film and chill in the fridge for 6–8 hours.

To cook the kebabs, preheat the grill to high. If you are using wooden skewers, soak them in cold water for 10 minutes before using.

Take a 5cm ball of the mince in one hand and a skewer in the other. Make the ball as smooth as possible by tossing it around in your hand. Now press the ball at roughly the middle of the skewer and press around so that the mince is now covering that part of the skewer.

Now apply a little oil or water to the palm that you use for the mince and by gently pressing the meat, carefully shape the mince around the skewer to make a sausage shape. You may find that initially the mince will fall off the skewer, but if you form a ring between your forefinger and thumb and use the rest of your fingers to guide the mince, you should be fine. The pressure has to be gently applied and the mince pushed upwards so that it thins itself out over the skewer. Ideally the size of the sausage should be around 2.5cm or a bit less in diameter.

Rest the skewer on a small tray so that the ends of the skewer rest on the edges of the tray and the kebab is suspended in the middle. Repeat with the remaining mixture and skewers. Cook the kebabs for 3–4 minutes on each side, or until just cooked through and still juicy on the inside.

These are great with Cyrus's cucumber and mint raita, and naan bread (page 48).

Makes 6–8 kebabs

You'll need 6–8 thick metal skewers

500g lamb shoulder, sinews and gristle removed, roughly chopped
20g coriander leaves and stalks, roughly chopped
20g mint leaves and stalks, roughly chopped
2.5cm piece fresh ginger, roughly chopped
6–8 garlic cloves, roughly chopped
1 large green chilli, roughly chopped
1 tsp garam masala
1 tsp ground cumin
1 tsp ground coriander
½ tsp red chilli powder
½ tsp ground turmeric
1 tsp lime juice
salt, to taste

Tip: Autumn lamb is a good match for the strong seasonings and aromatics in this dish. In addition, Cyrus says, spicy food couldn't be better for you: it helps to thin the blood during a hearty or rich meal, so that digestion takes place rather easily. Ginger helps prevents colds and flus, and turmeric will keep the body balanced and build resistance.

Crispy pork belly

by Ken Hom

According to Ken, 'This will probably be the best pork belly you have ever had!' Although it is marinated overnight, and takes almost three hours to roast, it is undeniably worth the wait. Serve with the easy egg fried rice (page 185) or some stir-fried pak choi. And save any leftover pork for lunch the following day – it makes a great sandwich.

Pierce the rind side of pork with a roasting fork or sharp knife until the skin is covered with fine holes. Insert a meat hook into the meat to secure it then put the joint rind side up over the sink.

Bring a pot of water to the boil and, using a large ladle, pour the hot water over the rind side of the pork several times. Set the pork belly aside.

Heat a wok or large frying pan until it is very hot, then add the salt, peppercorns, pepper and 5 spice and stir-fry for 3 minutes until hot and well mixed.

Remove from the heat, stir in the sugar, then allow to cool slightly. When it is warm enough to handle, rub this mixture on the flesh side of the pork. Hang the meat to dry for 8 hours or overnight in a cool place or in front of a fan. Alternatively, place the meat on a wire rack set above a roasting tin. You want the pork absolutely dry before roasting.

Preheat the oven to 200°C/400°F/Gas 6. Turn the pork rind side up on a rack and put the rack over a roasting tin with 2–3cm hot water in the bottom. Roast for 20 minutes but watch it carefully. Once the skin puffs up, turn the temperature down to 180°C/350°F/Gas 4 and continue to roast for 2 hours, checking every now and then that your tin is not dry – splash in some hot water from the kettle if it is.

Increase the heat to 230°C/450°F/Gas 8 and cook for a further 15 minutes, but again watch carefully. Remove the pork from the oven and leave it to rest (about 20 minutes). Carve it into bite-size pieces, arrange on a platter, and serve warm or at room temperature – either is delicious.

Serves 4–6

1.5kg boneless pork belly, with rind

for the marinade
4 tbsp coarse sea salt
2 tbsp ground roasted Sichuan peppercorns
2 tsp freshly ground white pepper
2 tbsp five-spice powder
1 tbsp caster sugar

....

Tip: The secret is to make sure the pork belly skin is completely dried and hard before roasting.

Saturday night pizzas

by James Martin

James's pizza dough recipe is so easy to knock up and will keep well sealed in the freezer. The 'oo' flour can be found in Italian delis and most supermarkets. If using white bread flour, make sure it's a strong one: you need the high gluten content to give the dough its lovely elasticity. The key to great homemade pizza is to turn your oven up as high as it will go and give it time to get to temperature. If you have one, put in a pizza stone to heat up too, or use a heavy baking sheet, preheated to as hot as it will get.

Basic pizza dough

Place the flour, salt and yeast into a large bowl and stir to combine.

Make a well in the centre of the flour, pour in the olive oil and gradually stir in the water until it forms a soft dough.

Tip the dough onto a floured work surface and knead for 5 minutes, until smooth and elastic. Shape into a ball and leave to rise in a lightly greased bowl, covered with cling film, until doubled in size (about 1 hour).

Remove the dough from the bowl and knead for a minute on a floured work surface – this is called knocking back the dough.

If using straight away, divide the dough up into 4 pieces. Preheat the oven and a pizza stone (or heavy baking tray) as high as it will go.

Roll out one piece of dough into a rough disc, about 5mm thick, and place on a floured baking sheet. Add your toppings (see overleaf) and slip the pizza from the tray on to the hot stone (or baking tray) that's already in the oven.

Bake until any cheese is bubbling and the crust has browned and risen (5–10 minutes). Scatter over any salad leaves or raw toppings. Repeat with the remaining dough, toppings and cheese, and serve immediately.

Continued overleaf

Makes 4 thin medium-sized pizzas

500g Italian 'oo' flour or strong white bread flour, plus extra for dusting
½ tsp salt
7g sachet dried fast-action yeast
1 tbsp olive oil
300ml warm water

A simple Margherita with rocket

Use good-quality tinned Italian plum tomatoes to make the sauce: San Marzano have dense flesh and a rich sweet flavour that works beautifully here.

Preheat the oven to its highest temperature. Place a heavy baking tray or a pizza stone into the oven.

Place the tinned tomatoes into a food processor and blitz to a purée. Spoon the tomato purée thinly over the pizza bases – just to the edges. Scatter over the grated mozzarella and pecorino then drizzle over the oils. Finish with a few basil leaves and season with sea salt and freshly ground black pepper.

Carefully transfer the pizzas into the oven, slipping the pizzas from the floured tray onto the preheated tray or pizza stone. Cook for 5–10 minutes until the base is crisp and the topping is cooked through. Scatter over the rocket and tuck in.

Serves 4

4 pizza bases (page 198)
2 x 400g tins (ideally) San Marzano tomatoes
2 large mozzarella balls, grated
50g pecorino cheese, coarsely grated
3 tbsp vegetable oil
3 tbsp peanut oil
1 large handful basil leaves
2 handfuls rocket leaves
sea salt and freshly ground black pepper

Spinach, chorizo and artichoke pizza

A sophisticated pizza with a punchy, sunny kick. Better than anything you can order in!

Heat a frying pan until hot, and then add the oil, shallots and garlic and fry for 3–4 minutes. Add the tomatoes, sugar and the chopped basil and bring to the boil. Reduce the heat and simmer for 20 minutes, until the sauce has thickened. Season, to taste, with sea salt and freshly ground black pepper and leave to cool.

Preheat the oven to its highest temperature. Place a heavy baking tray or a pizza stone into the oven.

Peel, trim and thinly slice the artichokes if you are using fresh. Spoon the cooled tomato sauce thinly over the pizza bases – just to the edges. Sprinkle over the artichokes, chorizo, mozzarella and half the spinach, then season to taste with sea salt and freshly ground black pepper.

Carefully transfer the pizzas into the oven, slipping the pizzas from the floured tray onto the preheated tray or pizza stone. Cook for 10–15 minutes, or until the base is crisp and the topping is cooked through. Remove from the oven, sprinkle over the remaining spinach leaves and serve immediately.

Serves 4

4 pizza bases (page 198)
2 tbsp olive oil
2 banana shallots, peeled, finely chopped
2 garlic cloves, finely chopped
2 x 400g tins (ideally) San Marzano tomatoes
2 tsp sugar
1 bunch basil leaves, chopped
6 baby artichokes (fresh, or good-quality jarred ones)
100g semi-cured chorizo, chopped
350g buffalo mozzarella, thickly sliced
15g baby spinach leaves
sea salt and freshly ground black pepper

Roasted vegetable pizza

The garlic and roasted tomatoes give this pizza great depth of flavour.

For the roast tomatoes, preheat the oven to 100°C/200°F/Gas ½.

Place the tomatoes, cut-side up, onto a baking tray, drizzle over the olive oil and then sprinkle with the salt and thyme and some freshly ground black pepper. Roast in the oven for 1½ hours, or until the tomatoes have dried but are still succulent. Remove the tomatoes from the oven and set aside to cool.

Preheat the oven to its highest temperature. Place a heavy baking tray or a pizza stone into the oven.

Place the whole garlic bulb onto the tray and bake for 15–20 minutes, or until soft. Remove the garlic from the oven and set aside to cool slightly, return the baking tray to the oven. Squeeze the roasted garlic flesh into a bowl.

Blend half of the roast tomatoes and 2 tablespoons of extra virgin olive oil to a fine purée. Spoon the purée thinly over the pizza bases – just to the edges. Top with the remaining tomato quarters, red onion slices, red pepper, roasted garlic, mozzarella and Cheddar. Drizzle over the remaining olive oil and a little pesto. Season with sea salt and freshly ground black pepper.

Carefully transfer the pizzas onto the preheated baking tray in the oven and cook for 5–10 minutes, or until the pizza base is cooked and the cheese is bubbling and golden-brown. Remove from the oven, scatter over the rocket leaves and serve immediately.

Serves 4

4 pizza bases (page 198)
24 baby plum tomatoes, cut lengthways into quarters
2 tbsp olive oil
2 tsp thyme leaves
1 bulb garlic
6 tbsp extra virgin olive oil
1 red onion, finely sliced
110g roasted red peppers, thickly sliced
2 large buffalo mozzarella, torn into pieces
75g mature Cheddar, coarsely grated
2–3 tbsp pesto (page 45)
1 large handful rocket leaves
sea salt and freshly ground black pepper

Deep-fried whiting in oatmeal

by Lawrence Keogh

Served with Lawrence's warm potato salad (page 159) and a homemade tomato ketchup, this is a great twist on the usual battered cod and chips.

Whisk the eggs and milk together on a shallow plate, season the flour on a separate plate with salt and freshly ground pepper, and spread the oatmeal onto a third plate.

Coat the fish in the seasoned flour then in the egg and milk mixture and finally in the oats. Chill in the fridge for 30 minutes.

Meanwhile, to make the tomato sauce, heat the olive oil in a large frying pan, then add the tomatoes and cook for 4–5 minutes, or until soft. Add the shallots and garlic and cook for a further 2 minutes. Add the sugar, tomato purée and vinegar and simmer until the volume of the sauce has reduced by half. Blend the sauce mixture in a food processor until smooth, then season, to taste, with sea salt and freshly ground black pepper.

Heat enough vegetable oil in a deep fryer or deep saucepan until very hot. Carefully lower the fish into the deep-fat fryer and cook for 4–5 minutes, or until golden-brown and crisp. Remove from the pan and set aside to drain on kitchen paper.

Season, to taste, with salt and serve with the warm potato salad, a ramekin of tomato sauce and a lemon wedge on the side.

....

Tip: For best results when deep-frying, remember that the fat must be really hot before the whiting goes in. If it's not, you'll end up with soggy, greasy fish.

Serves 4

2 eggs, beaten
100ml whole milk
150g plain flour
150g oatmeal
4 whiting fillets, skinned and pin boned
vegetable oil, for deep frying
tart potato salad (page 159), to serve
1 lemon, cut into wedges
sea salt and freshly ground black pepper

for the tomato sauce
2 tbsp olive oil
500g plum tomatoes, quartered
2 shallots, finely chopped
1 garlic clove, chopped
2 tbsp soft brown sugar
30g tomato purée
2 tbsp cider or apple vinegar
sea salt and freshly ground black pepper

Langoustine and cod puff pastry pie

by James Martin

James's fish pie is both deeply comforting and luxurious tasting. Look for cod labelled north east Arctic or eastern Baltic, where stocks are healthy, or feel free to substitute with other white flaky fish, like pollock or coley.

For the rough puff pastry, sift the flour onto a work surface and make a well in the middle. Add the butter and salt to the well and work them together with the fingertips of one hand, gradually drawing the flour into the centre with the other hand. When the cubes of butter have become small pieces and the dough is grainy, gradually add 125ml of ice-cold water and mix until well combined. Roll the pastry into a ball, wrap in cling film and chill in the fridge for 20 minutes.

Flour the work surface and roll out the pastry into a 40 x 20cm rectangle. Fold one third of the dough into the centre, then fold the other third on top. Push the edges of the pastry with the rolling pin to seal. Rotate the pastry a quarter turn. Roll the pastry out again into a 40 x 20cm rectangle and fold in the same way as before. Chill in the fridge for 30 minutes. Repeat the rolling and folding process 2 more times to give 4 rolls and folds in total. Wrap the pastry in cling film and chill for at least 30 minutes.

Meanwhile for the pie, fry half the butter in a large heavy-based frying pan and add the onion, carrot and thyme. Cook for 2–3 minutes until the mixture has softened. Add the reserved langoustine shells, cayenne pepper and tomato purée to the pan and cook for 1 minute. Pour the brandy into the pan and carefully set alight to burn off the alcohol. Add the chicken stock and bring to the boil. Reduce the heat and simmer gently for 30 minutes.

Put the mixture into a food processor and blend until smooth. Pass through a fine sieve and into a saucepan. Whisk the cream in and season with salt and pepper.

Preheat the oven to 200°C/400°F/Gas 6.

Melt the remaining butter in a frying pan, add the shallot and cook for 4–5 minutes or until softened. Add to the sauce mixture, along with the cod pieces, peas, langoustine tails and chervil. Mix until well combined. Spoon the mixture into a large pie dish and brush with the beaten egg. Roll the pastry to the thickness of a pound coin and cut out a disc big enough to cover the dish. Press the pastry on top of the filling and crimp around the edges to seal the creamy filling in.

Brush the pastry with the remaining beaten egg and pierce holes in the top to let the steam escape. Put the pie into the oven on a baking sheet for 15–20 minutes, until the pastry has risen and is crispy and golden-brown. Serve with the watercress and some mash, if you fancy it.

Serves 4

for the rough puff pastry
250 plain flour
250g butter, cut into small cubes, chilled
½ tsp salt

for the pie
50g butter
1 onion, chopped
1 carrot, roughly chopped
4 sprigs thyme
20 langoustines, cooked, shells removed and reserved
¼ tsp cayenne pepper
1 tbsp tomato purée
4 tbsp brandy
600ml chicken stock
75ml double cream
1 banana shallot, finely diced
400g cod fillet, skinned and cut into 2.5cm chunks
150g frozen peas, defrosted
3 tbsp chopped chervil
1 egg, beaten
watercress, to serve
sea salt and freshly ground black pepper

A quick coq au vin
by Bill Granger

Coq au vin is the kind of rustic French cooking anyone can perfect. Bill's version requires no marinating overnight. Instead you roast the chicken with lardons, then add white (rather than the traditional red) wine and finish things off with freshly pan-fried mushrooms. The result is crisp chicken skin, moist flesh, and delicious wine and herb infused juices.

Preheat the oven to 220°C/425°F/Gas 7.

Arrange the chicken pieces in a large roasting tin and scatter with the bacon, shallots, thyme, rosemary and chilli flakes. Season with sea salt and freshly ground black pepper, drizzle with 2 tablespoons of the olive oil and roast for 20 minutes. Add the wine to the tin and roast for another 20–25 minutes. Remove from the oven.

Heat the butter and remaining tablespoon of oil in a large frying pan over a medium heat. When the butter is foaming, add the mushrooms and garlic and fry for 3–5 minutes. Tip into the tin and season, to taste. Scatter with the parsley, and serve with some crusty bread or a creamy mash (page 214).

....

Tip: Ideally buy a lump of bacon or pancetta to cut into lardons yourself, for maximum flavour.

Serves 4–6

1.5kg chicken, jointed
150g diced bacon or lardons
10 French shallots, peeled
a few thyme sprigs
a rosemary sprig
1 tsp dried chilli flakes
3 tbsp olive oil
250ml white wine
small knob of butter
350g mixed mushrooms
  (such as oyster and
  chestnut), sliced
3 garlic cloves, crushed with
  the back of a knife
small handful of flat-leaf
  parsley, chopped
sea salt and freshly ground
  black pepper

Lamb Madras with chapatis

by James Martin

James says, 'I love Indian curries, however most are actually quite difficult to master. This is so simple and it works a treat, especially with homemade chapatis on the side.'

For the Madras curry powder, place all of the curry powder ingredients into a spice grinder and grind to a fine powder.

For the lamb Madras, season the lamb shanks all over with sea salt and freshly ground black pepper. Heat the vegetable oil in a large non-stick casserole pot and sear the lamb shanks for 1–2 minutes on all sides, until golden brown all over. Remove the lamb shanks from the pan and set aside.

Blend the chilli, garlic and ginger in a small food processor to a paste, adding a splash of water if necessary.

Place the pan used to cook the lamb back over a high heat and add the onion (add a splash of oil to the pan if it is too dry). Fry for 2–3 minutes, or until softened and starting to colour. Add 2½ tablespoons of the curry powder to the pot along with the garlic, chilli and ginger paste, curry leaves, cardamom and bay leaves. Stir well.

Return the lamb shanks to the pan and cover with the chopped tomatoes, beef stock and tamarind juice. Season, to taste, with salt and freshly ground black pepper. Cover the pan with a lid and simmer over a low heat for 2 hours, or until the lamb is very tender.

Serves 4–6

for the Madras curry powder
2 tbsp coriander seeds
2 tbsp fenugreek seeds
1 tbsp mustard seeds
1 tsp cumin seeds
½ tsp fennel seeds
1 tsp black peppercorns
1 cinnamon stick, broken into pieces
5 cloves
1 tbsp turmeric

for the lamb Madras
2 tbsp vegetable oil
4 lamb shanks
1 green bird's eye chilli
2 garlic cloves, peeled
1.5cm piece fresh ginger, peeled
1 onion, thinly sliced
12 curry leaves
3 cardamom pods
2 bay leaves
400g chopped tomatoes
200ml beef stock
2 tsp tamarind juice
sea salt and freshly ground black pepper

Meanwhile, for the chapatis, sift the flour and salt into a large bowl and gradually mix in enough of the water to form a soft dough. Cover and set aside to rest for 10 minutes.

Turn the dough out onto a floured work surface, lightly knead and then divide equally into 12 balls. Roll out each ball as thin as possible.

Heat a frying pan over a high heat and add the oil. Cook the chapatis one at a time, frying for 1–2 minutes on both sides or until golden-brown and puffed up.

For the fried shallots, dust the sliced shallots in the flour. Heat the vegetable oil in a frying pan over a high heat and fry the shallots for 2–3 minutes, or until golden-brown and crisp. Remove from the oil and drain on kitchen paper.

To serve, remove the lamb shanks from the pan and place one on each serving plate. Place the pan back over a high heat and simmer until the liquid has reduced to a thick sauce, enough to coat the back of a spoon. Pour the sauce over the lamb shanks and garnish with the crisp shallots.

for the chapatis
325g chapati flour, plus extra for dusting
1½ tsp salt
170–230ml water
1 tbsp vegetable oil

for the fried shallots
2 shallots, finely sliced
2 tbsp plain flour
2–3 tbsp vegetable oil

....

Tip: After baking, keep the chapatis in a closed container: the steam inside will help to keep them soft for a long time – at least 1–2 hours.

Homemade lamb sausages in prosciutto

by Tana Ramsay

No fancy equipment or ingredients are needed here. Tana wraps minced lamb in slices of delicious prosciutto for these easy, spicy bangers, which she serves with a yoghurt and cucumber dip, and sweet spring greens.

Preheat the oven to 190°C/375°F/Gas 5. Lightly grease a baking tray.

Place the lamb mince in a large bowl and break it up using a fork. Add the coriander, cumin, onion, parsley, chilli and breadcrumbs and stir. Add the egg, season, to taste, with sea salt and freshly ground black pepper, and mix until well combined.

Divide the mix in 12 portions, shape each portion into a sausage using your hands, then wrap in a slice of prosciutto, leaving both ends open.

Place the sausages onto the prepared baking tray and bake for 20–25 minutes, or until golden brown and cooked though.

Meanwhile, for the minty cucumber dip, mix all of the ingredients together in a bowl and season, to taste, with salt and freshly ground pepper.

To serve, place the sausages onto each of 4 serving plates and spoon some salad alongside. Serve the yoghurt and cucumber dip in small bowls at the table.

....

Tip: Look for mince that has more red meat than white fat or ask your butcher to mince a piece for you. Scrag, neck and belly all make good, flavoursome mince, as does shoulder.

Serves 4

vegetable oil, for greasing
500g lamb mince
1 tbsp ground coriander
2 tbsp ground cumin
½ red onion, finely chopped
3 tbsp finely chopped
    flat-leaf parsley
1 red chilli, seeds removed,
    finely chopped
4 tbsp fresh breadcrumbs
1 egg, beaten
12 slices of prosciutto
pea, broad bean and bacon
    salad (page 150), to serve
sea salt and freshly ground
    black pepper

for the yoghurt and
cucumber dip

200g natural yoghurt
¼ cucumber, peeled and
    diced
2 tbsp mint, finely chopped
sea salt and freshly ground
    black pepper

Steak, fat chips and béarnaise sauce

by James Martin

To make this extra special, treat yourself to the best-quality steak you can afford, bought from a decent butcher. Look for a good-sized steak, at least 4cm thick, and take the meat out of the fridge 20 minutes before cooking to get it up to room temperature.

Heat the vegetable oil in a deep fat fryer to 160°C/320°F.

For the béarnaise sauce, place the vinegar and diced shallot into a small saucepan and bring to the boil. Turn down the heat and simmer until the liquid has reduced by half.

Strain the liquid into a heatproof bowl and add the egg yolks. Place the bowl over a pan of very gently simmering water. The bowl should sit snugly in the top of the pan.

Whisk the eggs and vinegar together until light in colour, then gradually add the melted butter, whisking constantly until the sauce is thick and velvety. Season with sea salt and freshly ground black pepper and add the chopped tarragon leaves.

Turn off the heat and leave the bowl over the warm pan while you grill your steak and fry your chips.

Slice the potatoes into 1.5cm thick long chips. Place into the deep-fat fryer, a few at a time, and cook for 5–6 minutes until just tender, but without colour.

Using a slotted spoon, remove the chips from the fryer and drain on a plate lined with kitchen paper. Turn up the deep-fat fryer to 190°C/375°F.

Season the steaks with sea salt and freshly ground black pepper. Get a frying pan really hot then add the butter and olive oil. When the butter is foaming, add the steaks in batches and cook to your liking. For medium, they'll probably need 2–3 minutes on each side. Remove the pan from the heat and leave the steaks to rest.

Meanwhile, place the semi-cooked chips back into the deep-fat fryer in batches and cook for another 2–3 minutes until golden-brown and crispy. Season with salt to taste. Keep warm on a tray in the oven if necessary.

To serve, carve the steak into thick slices, place onto plates and spoon the béarnaise sauce over. Pile some chips alongside.

Serves 4

for the béarnaise sauce
3 tbsp tarragon or white wine vinegar
1 large banana shallot, finely diced
3 egg yolks
225g butter, melted
2–3 tbsp chopped tarragon leaves
sea salt and freshly ground black pepper

for the steak and chips
vegetable oil, for frying
3 large floury potatoes, peeled
4 x 250g rump or rib eye steaks
50g butter
2 tbsp olive oil
sea salt and freshly ground black pepper

Sausage, pumpkin and sage casserole
by Matt Tebbutt

This comforting casserole is just the thing to warm up a sparkling Bonfire night.

Preheat the oven to 180°C/350°F/Gas 4.

Heat half the butter in a large casserole pot over a medium heat and fry the sausages for 4–5 minutes, or until golden-brown all over.

Add the remaining butter, onion and shallots and fry for 3 minutes, or until softened. Add the garlic and sage leaves and cook for a further 3 minutes, stirring well.

Add the pumpkin, stir to combine and turn up the heat to high. Add the white wine vinegar and continue to cook until most of the liquid has evaporated. Add the sugar, then pour in the tomatoes, beans and stock into the pot, season with salt and pepper and bring to the boil. Transfer the casserole to the oven for 1 hour, or until the sausages are cooked through and the pumpkin is tender.

Ladle into bowls and sprinkle with the flat-leaf parsley.

....

Tip: When choosing a pumpkin, the smaller ones have more flavour. Some of the larger pumpkins can be quite watery, with a mushy, stringy texture.

Serves 4

50g butter
6 best-quality sausages, pricked several times with a fork
1 onion, thinly sliced
3 banana shallots, peeled, chopped finely
2 garlic cloves, finely chopped
1 tbsp chopped sage
1 small pumpkin, peeled, seeds removed, cut into equal-sized pieces
1 tbsp white wine vinegar
1 tsp caster sugar
200g tinned chopped tomatoes
1 x 400g tin cannellini beans, drained and rinsed
500ml chicken stock
2 tbsp chopped flat-leaf parsley
sea salt and freshly ground black pepper

Tagliatelle with Bolognese ragu

by James Martin

The best Bolognese is cooked long and slow to deliver complexity of flavour and lovely tender meat. Be sure to mix the sauce with the tagliatelle before serving. As James says, 'Most people think of ragu as a pile of dried pasta with a dollop of sauce but classically, and always in Italy, the meat is combined with the pasta.'

To make the ragu, heat a large flameproof casserole, add the pancetta and fry for 3–4 minutes, until the pancetta softens and the fat starts to melt. Add the mince in small batches and fry over a high heat until browned. Remove each batch of mince from the pan with a slotted spoon, set aside and keep warm while you fry the remaining batches.

Add the olive oil and butter to the pan in which you cooked the mince, then add the onion and sweat for 1–2 minutes, or until softened. Add the carrots and celery to the pan and cook for another minute.

Stir in the browned mince, then add the milk and bring to the boil. Reduce the heat and simmer for 5 minutes.

Add the tomato purée and cook for a further minute. Add the red wine and simmer until the volume of liquid has reduced by a quarter.

Add the beef stock and return the ragu to the boil. Season to taste with salt and pepper. Reduce the heat and simmer for 1½–2 hours, or until the ragu has thickened and the meat is tender.

Cook the tagliatelle in boiling salted water according to the packet instructions, then drain and mix with the sauce. Serve with plenty of Parmesan.

Serves 4–6

200g pancetta, chopped
1kg minced beef
3 tbsp olive oil
25g butter
1 onion, roughly chopped
2 carrots, peeled, finely chopped
2 celery sticks, finely chopped
150ml whole milk
4 tbsp tomato purée
175ml red wine
750ml beef stock
500g tagliatelle
150g grated Parmesan, to serve
sea salt and freshly ground black pepper

Spicy stuffed meatballs

by Henry Dimbleby

These Indian-style meatballs are adapted from a recipe by Henry's mother, the cookery writer Josceline Dimbleby. Easy to make and lightly spiced, they make a great family dish with rice or noodles, or simply accompanied by Henry's herb salad (page 152).

For the meatballs, take the seeds out of the cardamom, place into a coffee grinder or pestle and mortar with the coriander and blitz to a fine powder. Chop the garlic with the salt until it forms a paste (or add it to the pestle and mortar).

Place the beef and pork into a bowl and mix together vigorously to soften the texture – this will help stop the cheese escaping. Add the garlic and ground spices, turmeric and chilli powder then mix really well with your hands and add the beaten egg.

Wet your hands and shape the mixture into ping-pong sized balls. You should have about 12 meatballs.

Lightly oil a clean work surface with the groundnut oil and gently press the balls into flattened circles.

Put a teaspoon of cream cheese in the centre of each meat circle and carefully bring the meat up round it to enclose the cheese completely, making rather larger meatballs. Roll gently and make sure there are no holes.

Heat a large frying pan, add the remaining oil and fry the meatballs for 10 minutes over a medium–high heat, turning regularly until nicely caramelised all over. Place the balls into a serving dish and keep warm.

Turn the heat right up then add the tomatoes to the pan, flash-fry then remove the pan from the heat and stir in the yoghurt.

To serve, pour the tomatoes over the meatballs and garnish with the chopped coriander, almonds and fried shallots.

Serves 4

8 cardamom pods
2 tsp coriander seed
4 large garlic cloves
large pinch salt
300g lean minced beef
200g minced pork
½ tsp turmeric
red chilli powder, to taste
1 egg, beaten
1–2 tbsp groundnut oil
115g cream cheese
200g baby plum tomatoes,
   cut in half lengthways
1 tbsp plain yoghurt

to serve
2–3 tbsp chopped coriander
   leaves
2 tbsp flaked almonds,
   toasted
4 shallots, finely sliced and
   deep-fried

Tip: You can stuff meatballs with ingredients other than cheese: mango chutney works particularly well, or whiz up some parsley, garlic and butter in the blender for an indulgent meatball kiev.

Marvellous mash

However you like to make it, mash is the ultimate comfort food. For the best results with mashed potato, the Potato Council recommends using floury spuds like Maris Piper, Golden Wonder or King Edward – the older (as in the longer out of the ground), the better. However, some chefs, including Vivek Singh, favour a waxy variety: the mash may not be as fluffy but the flesh is a lovely buttery yellow colour and the flavour is arguably superior. Bryn's creamy wet polenta makes a great change, and Vivek's spicy masala mash is fantastic with your favourite curry, or to liven up any plate.

Classic mash by Adam Byatt

Light and fluffy, and great with some good-quality bangers. If you prefer a creamier mash, double the butter or fold in 100ml crème fraîche or single cream at the end.

Place the chunks of potato in a saucepan of cold salted water, cover and bring to the boil, then boil gently for 15–20 minutes until tender.

Bring the milk and butter just to the boil in a separate saucepan.

Drain the potatoes in a colander, then stand the colander over the saucepan for a few minutes so the potatoes steam in their own heat.

Return the potatoes to the pan and mash until smooth using a potato masher or ricer, then fold in the hot milk and butter and beat well. Season to taste with sea salt and freshly ground black pepper.

Serves 4

750g floury potatoes, peeled, cut into even-sized chunks
pinch salt
100ml whole milk
50g butter
sea salt and freshly ground black pepper

Olive oil mash by José Pizarro

A smooth, silky mash that's rich in flavour, and relatively healthy too.

Place the potatoes in a large saucepan and just cover with cold water. Add a pinch of salt, the garlic, bay leaves and 2 tablespoons of the olive oil, then bring the water to the boil. Reduce the heat until the liquid is simmering, then continue to simmer for 10–15 minutes, or until the potatoes are tender. Drain well.

Drain the potatoes in a colander, then stand the colander over the saucepan for a few minutes so the potatoes steam in their own heat.

Return the potatoes to the pan and mash until smooth using a potato masher or ricer. Slowly add in the olive oil, stirring until well combined. Season to taste with sea salt and freshly ground black pepper.

Serves 4

1kg floury potatoes, peeled, cut into even-sized chunks
pinch salt
2 garlic cloves, peeled
2 bay leaves
75–110ml extra virgin olive oil
sea salt and freshly ground black pepper

Creamy wet polenta by Bryn Williams

A delicious alternative to mashed potato. Try it with stews, ragus, mushrooms or any hearty meat, chicken or fish dishes you like.

Bring the chicken stock, milk and cream to the boil in a lidded saucepan. Add the garlic, thyme, peppercorns and bay. Remove the mixture from the heat, cover with a lid and set aside to infuse for 1 hour.

Pass the infused stock through a sieve and into a large saucepan. Return to the boil and gradually pour in the polenta in a slow, steady stream, whisking all the time to ensure there are no lumps. Continue cooking for 15–20 minutes, stirring or whisking the polenta often to give you a thick, smooth mash. If you are using instant polenta, which is part-cooked, stir for about 5 minutes. Add the Parmesan, stir, taste and season with sea salt and freshly ground black pepper.

Serves 4

400ml chicken stock
110ml whole milk
110ml double cream
1 garlic clove
1 thyme sprig
5 peppercorns
1 bay leaf
150g coarse or instant
  polenta
30g Parmesan, freshly grated
sea salt and freshly ground
  black pepper

Masala mash by Vivek Singh

Mashed potato is common in India – just not alongside a plate of sausages! The Punjabis stuff parathas with it and the Bengalis eat it spiked with chillies, onion and mustard oil.

Place the potatoes into a large pan and just cover with cold water. Add a pinch of salt and bring to the boil. Reduce the heat until the liquid is simmering, then continue to simmer for 15–18 minutes, or until the potatoes are tender. Drain well.

Return the drained potatoes to the pan to drive off any excess moisture. Mash the potatoes until smooth using a potato masher or ricer.

In a large saucepan heat the ghee or butter, add the cumin seeds and when they start crackling, add the onion and cook until light brown. Now add the turmeric, ginger and green chilli and sauté for 30 seconds. Add the salt and the potato and mix well on a slow heat until the potato is heated through and covered evenly by the colour of the turmeric. Throw in the coriander and the tomato and mix well for a couple more minutes. If you like, add some butter to give extra shine and richness.

Serves 4

2 Desiree potatoes, peeled,
  cut into even-sized chunks
2 tbsp ghee or butter
½ tsp cumin seeds
1 red onion, chopped
¼ tsp ground turmeric
2 green chillies, chopped
1cm piece of fresh ginger,
  chopped
1 tsp salt
pinch of chopped coriander
1 tomato, deseeded
  and diced

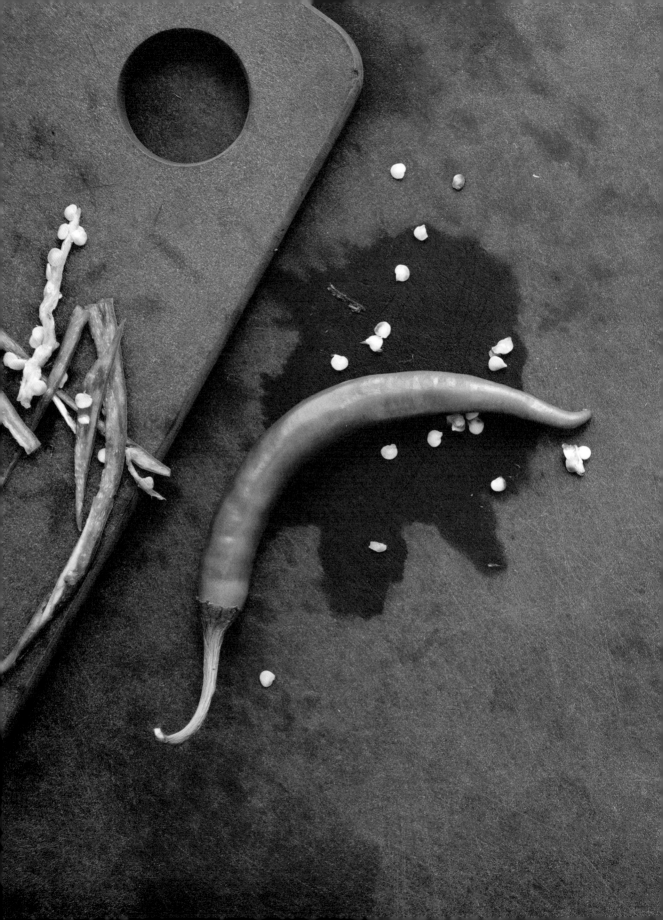

I know that some people find cooking for lots of people quite daunting and will say 'Oh, it's OK for you, you're a chef!' But the trick is really simple: it's all about planning and preparation before the event. If you came into my restaurant kitchen during the day, you would see me and my chefs beavering away on preparation. That's the key to a calm, relaxed service in the evening and it's no different for you cooking at home.

Another tip I would give is to never cook more than one hot course for a meal. If you do, you are going to be in the kitchen all night. Where's the fun in that? Make a terrine or try my smorgasbord of smoked fish as a starter or to put out for buffet style eating; they're what my nan would call 'cut and come again' dishes.

I do like the Chinese tradition, mentioned by Ken Hom, of getting guests to have a go at making the dumplings with you. I'm not sure about the adults – it might get very messy – but I know my kids would love this idea, as they would having a go at making pasta and gnocchi. They'd definitely be happy eating them!

I can hear some people saying 'Ah, but what about flavour?' Well, I will vouch that every one of the recipes here packs loads of flavour and, in fact, in some cases such as the terrines, the hotpot and the pandhi curry, the method of preparation beforehand actually enhances the flavour of the finished dish. Then of course, there is Thomas Keller's unusual roast chicken dish – mad but brilliant, and so tasty.

I'd call this 'the boy scout chapter' – it's all about being prepared. And the brilliant thing is that the recipes here are versatile because they can be used simply for an everyday family meal or dressed up into a grand occasion. Another great thing is that each one of them will allow you to maximise the time you can enjoy with friends and family and minimise the time in the kitchen on the day.

So, armed with this chapter of the book, you should never have to lose out on the fun again. Instead you will be able to wow your guests with delicious dishes and be there to accept the compliments. And, of course, these stress-free recipes are sure to make everyone want to come back for more!

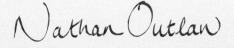

Marjoram gnocchi

by Bryn Williams

Gnocchi may look impressive but they are not complicated to make. Bryn's are flavoured with marjoram but you could substitute any fresh green herb, or even some chopped olives. Serve simply with a little butter and Parmesan, or make into a feast with roast salmon and a creamy butternut squash sauce (page 115).

Preheat the oven to 180°C/350°F/Gas 4.

Bake the potatoes for 1 hour, or until completely cooked through. Use tongs to transfer the potatoes to a cutting board. Cut the potatoes in half lengthways and scoop out the flesh, transferring it to a bowl.

Mash with a flexible spatula until smooth, then add the egg yolks, flour, Parmesan, salt and the chopped marjoram. Mix well to form a silky, pliable dough.

Divide the mixture into 4 equal pieces. Dust the work surface and your hands with flour, then roll each piece into a long sausage shape, 1cm in diameter. Use a sharp knife to cut each sausage crosswise into 2.5cm lengths and place them on a floured board or tray. They should look like rows of little pillows! Don't worry if they're not all uniform – that's part of the charm.

Bring a large pan of salted water to a rolling boil. Drop half the gnocchi into the water; cook until they bob up to the surface and look slightly puffed. Remove from the water with a slotted spoon. Repeat to cook all of the gnocchi and serve hot.

Serves 4

3 large Desiree or other floury potatoes
4 egg yolks
170g Italian 'oo' flour, plus extra for rolling
30g freshly grated Parmesan
1 tsp salt
handful of fresh marjoram, finely chopped

Beetroot gnocchi with butter, sage and orange sauce

by Gennaro Contaldo

Gennaro's gnocchi are a spectacular crimson colour – great for showcasing your new pasta-making skills to friends! Wear gloves to prepare the beetroot or you'll end up with bright red hands.

To make the gnocchi, place the potatoes into a pan of salted water and bring to the boil. Simmer for 15–18 minutes, or until tender.

Drain the potatoes and return them to the heat to drive off any excess moisture. Allow them to cool for a minute and then mash well using a potato masher or ricer.

Blend the beetroot in a food processor to a purée, then pass through a fine sieve.

Tip the flour onto a clean work surface and make a well in the centre. Add the beaten egg, mashed potato, beetroot purée and salt to the well, then use your hands to mix well to obtain a smooth dough-like consistency.

Split the dough into 4–6 equal pieces and roll each piece out into a long sausage shape. Use a sharp knife to cut each sausage crosswise into approximately 2cm pieces of gnocchi, and set aside.

Bring a large pan of salted water to a rolling boil. Drop half the gnocchi into the water; cook until they bob up to the surface and look slightly puffed. Remove from the water with a slotted spoon.

As soon as you drop the first batch of gnocchi into the boiling water, start making the sauce – you need to work quickly because the gnocchi doesn't take long.

Melt the butter in a large frying pan and add the sage leaves. Allow the sage to infuse for about 30 seconds and then add the orange juice and salt, to taste.

Scoop out the cooked gnocchi with a slotted spoon, allowing them to drain a little, then add them to the sauce, mixing well. Repeat to cook all of the gnocchi. Cook for a minute or so until the sauce begins to thicken slightly.

Remove the pan from the heat, stir in the Parmesan and serve immediately, sprinkled with some orange zest.

Serves 4

for the gnocchi
1kg floury potatoes, peeled and roughly chopped
400g cooked beetroot, peeled and roughly chopped
300g plain flour
1 egg, lightly beaten
pinch of salt

for the sauce
110g butter
6 sage leaves
1 orange, juiced, plus zest of 2 oranges, to serve
salt, to taste
4 tbsp freshly grated Parmesan

Basic pasta dough

by Gennaro Contaldo

A pasta machine will make life easier here. They are relatively inexpensive and the small one is compact enough to store easily when not in use. If you don't have a machine and are relying on your rolling pin, the main challenge will be getting the pasta thin enough to work with. In this case, try rolling lots of small pieces of pasta rather than a few big ones, and don't worry about making perfect strips.

Mix the flour and semolina together on a clean work surface or in a large bowl. Make a well in the centre and break in the eggs. With a fork or with your hands, gradually mix the flour with the eggs, then knead with your hands for about 5 minutes, until you get a smooth dough; it should be pliable but not sticky. Shape the dough into a ball, wrap in cling film and leave for about 30 minutes or until you are ready to use.

Divide the pasta into 4 portions and put each one through your pasta machine, starting at the highest setting. As the pasta gets thinner, turn down the settings until you get to number 1 and the dough is almost wafer thin. Lightly dust the pasta with a little flour every time you run it through the machine.

Place the sheet of pasta on a lightly floured work surface and shape or cut it straight away, according to your recipe. Pasta dries very quickly, so don't leave it more than a minute or two before cutting or shaping it. You may cover with a slightly damp cloth to stop it from drying.

Serves 4–6

300g Italian 'oo' flour
100g fine semolina (durum wheat) flour
4 eggs, at room temperature

....

Tip: Wrapping the dough in cling film and leaving it to sit at room temperature will allow the gluten to relax. This will make it easier to stretch later.

Fresh pasta, southern Italian-style

by Francesco Mazzei

Eggless pasta dough

Francesco's eggless pasta is part of the traditional culture of southern Italy and Sardinia, and invaluable for vegans or anyone with an egg allergy. It has a firmer texture than its northern sister and absorbs flavours well, making it ideal for heavier sauces and ragus.

Put the flour in a mixing bowl. Dissolve the salt in the tepid water.

Add about two-thirds of the water to the dough and start kneading by hand or in a food processor fitted with a dough hook attachment. Add almost all the remaining water and continue kneading to obtain a stiff, perfectly smooth dough. Only add the last of the water if necessary.

Cover the dough with a slightly damp cloth and set aside to rest for approximately 2 hours. To test whether it is ready to use, press your thumb hard into the dough – the imprint should not start to spring back.

Place the sheet of pasta on a cool, lightly floured work surface and shape or cut it straight away, according to your recipe. You may cover with a slightly damp cloth to stop it from drying. Alternatively, cover with cling film and freeze for up to a month.

Serves 4

500g fine semolina (durum wheat) flour, or Italian '00' flour, plus extra for dusting
pinch salt
210ml warm water

....

Tip: Use plenty of boiling salted water to cook and don't expect to cook fresh pasta to precise times. The sooner you cook the pasta after making it, the shorter the time will be. Francesco recommends three-quarter cooking the pasta in boiling water, then finishing it in your chosen sauce.

Lagane in a borlotti bean and guanciale soup

Lagane (origin of the modern word 'lasagne') is one of the earliest recorded pasta shapes. If you're in the mood for a delicious and authentic southern Italian recipe, packed with hearty flavour, Francesco's dish is a great one to take your time over.

Roll out the pasta dough using a pasta machine or rolling pin. Transfer the dough to a work surface dusted with flour. Using your hands, stretch the dough until it almost doubles in length. Divide the dough in 2 and place the pieces side by side. Dust with flour, and then roll each piece up like a Swiss roll. Slice finely, so each piece is about 4mm in diameter.

Place the crushed garlic, chilli, basil and olive oil into a bowl and leave to marinate. Meanwhile place the remaining ingredients into a large saucepan along with 200–225ml warm water. Add a pinch of salt and simmer for 45–50 minutes, or until the beans are cooked.

Remove the vegetables and guanciale from the stew. Set the meat aside, but blend the vegetables with a ladleful of the broth in a food processor until smooth. Return this purée to the soup and bring back to a simmer. Add sea salt and freshly ground black pepper to taste.

Bring a large pan of salted water to the boil, add the pasta and simmer for 3–4 minutes, then drain.

Heat a griddle pan until hot. Add the guanciale and sear on each side until charred. Remove from the pan and cut into chunks. Add the par-boiled lagane to the soup and simmer for a minute, then add the guanciale back at the last minute. Serve with the reserved garlic, chilli and basil oil drizzled on top.

Serves 4

120–150g eggless pasta dough (page 225)
fine semolina (durum wheat) flour, for dusting
4 garlic cloves, 1 crushed and 3 roughly chopped
1 red chilli, finely chopped
2 leaves basil
1 tbsp olive oil
250g fresh borlotti beans, shelled (or 200g dried beans soaked in cold water overnight and drained)
1 large plum tomato
1 carrot
1 celery stick
½ onion
2 tsp extra virgin olive oil
2 sprigs fresh rosemary
200g guanciale (fatty bacon, prepared from pig's cheeks) or pancetta
sea salt and freshly ground black pepper

Cavatelli with broccoli and colatura

Cavatelli – from the Italian for 'little caves' – is an easy pasta shape to try as a beginner. It's a little like gnocchi, with little dents or ridges that are great for holding chunky sauces. You can make the shells by hand or use a pasta machine with a cavatelli or gnocchi attachment. Alternatively, fresh orrechiette or your favourite dried pasta shells will work beautifully with Francesco's sauce.

Roll out the pasta dough using a pasta machine or rolling pin. Transfer the dough to a work surface dusted with flour. Treat the piece of dough as if it were a rolling pin or play dough that gets longer and longer as you roll it back and forth. Keep rolling until you have a long rope about 2cm in diameter.

Put the 2 ends of the rope together and cut the dough in half in the middle. Cut the 2 pieces into small nuggets about 1cm long.

To shape the cavatelli: flatten each nugget with your thumb, allowing the edges to curl up on either side to make a slightly open, narrow tube shape. Place on a rack or tray dusted with flour then cover with a slightly damp cloth until ready to cook.

Heat a frying pan over a high heat and add the olive oil. Fry the garlic and chilli for 2–3 minutes, or until golden-brown. Add the chopped anchovies and cook, stirring frequently, until they break down in the pan.

Meanwhile, drop the cavatelli and broccoli into a large pan of salted boiling water, and blanch for 1–2 minutes. Drain, reserving some of the pasta cooking liquid.

Add the cavatelli and broccoli to the frying pan, add the colatura and mix well, then add a splash of the pasta cooking liquid. Stir well to coat the pasta in the sauce.

To serve, spoon the pasta onto serving plates and sprinkle over the grated bottarga.

Serves 4

1 x quantity eggless pasta dough (page 225)
fine semolina (durum wheat) flour, for dusting
2–3 tbsp olive oil
1 garlic clove, finely chopped
1 red chilli, finely chopped
2 anchovies, chopped
200g broccoli, cut into small pieces
1 tbsp colatura (anchovy sauce)
2g grated bottarga (the salted, pressed and dried roe of tuna or grey mullet)

A classic lasagne

by Theo Randall

Theo says, 'the great thing about lasagne is that you can make it the day before, pop it in the fridge, then whack it in the oven the next day when guests arrive without warning. It's brilliant no-stress family food.' If you don't have so many mouths to feed first time round, freeze in slices for a quick midweek supper.

To make the béchamel, pour the milk into a saucepan and bring to a simmer then turn off the heat. In a heavy saucepan, melt the butter then whisk in the flour and hot milk. Whisk constantly until smooth. Add the bay leaf, cover with a circle of greaseproof paper and cook slowly for 5–6 minutes. Remove the paper and bay leaf and season with sea salt and freshly ground black pepper. Stir in the Parmesan and egg yolks and set aside to cool.

Meanwhile, for the ragu, melt the butter in a large casserole dish until foaming. Add the celery, carrots, onion, pancetta and rosemary and fry for 5 minutes. Stir in the veal and prosciutto and cook for a further 5 minutes.

Add the tomatoes, white wine and milk and bring to the boil. Reduce the heat and cook slowly for 1½ hours – the meat should be broken down into small pieces and the sauce should have a rich, thick consistency.

Preheat the oven to 170°C/325°F/Gas 3.

Blanch the fresh pasta sheets in boiling salted water for 1 minute (or cook according to packet instructions), then refresh in cold water.

Rub olive oil into the sides of a baking dish. Place a layer of pasta onto the base of the dish and then add an even layer of beef ragu, followed by a layer of béchamel sauce. Repeat this process until you have used all the pasta and finish with a thick layer of béchamel on top. Sprinkle the top with a generous layer of Parmesan.

Bake in the oven for about 45 minutes, or until bubbling and pale golden-brown on top.

Tip: Lasagne is always better with fresh pasta sheets; because they're made with egg yolk, they have a much richer taste. You can buy fresh sheets of pasta in all good supermarkets, or try making your own with the basic pasta dough on page 224.

Serves 8

for the béchamel
1 litre whole milk
75g butter
125g Italian 'oo' flour
1 bay leaf
125g grated Parmesan, plus extra for topping
2 egg yolks
sea salt and freshly ground black pepper

for the ragu
110g butter
2 tbsp chopped celery
2 tbsp chopped carrots
2 tbsp chopped red onion
110g smoked pancetta, chopped
1 sprig rosemary, leaves picked, chopped
1kg trimmed veal or beef flank, finely chopped
50g prosciutto, roughly chopped
1 x 400g tin tomatoes
125ml white wine
110ml whole milk

1 x 250g pack fresh lasagne sheets

A smorgasbord of smoked fish

by Nathan Outlaw

If you have friends popping by, but don't want to be stuck in the kitchen cooking, Nathan's gravalax, smoked mackerel pâté, beetroot salad and deep-fried oysters is the perfect spread to put together in advance. Preparation is key here. Allow two days for the beetroot-cured salmon, which will keep for a good week or two in the fridge, or a couple of months in the freezer. Deep-fry the oysters and prepare the pâté and beetroot salad nearer the time.

Beetroot-cured salmon

This homemade gravalax is marinated with a mix of sweet and sour: raw beetroot, fennel seeds, tarragon (with its sensational anise flavour) and lots of salt.

Place the beetroot, fennel seeds, tarragon, salt and sugar in a food processor and blend together to make a purée for the cure.

Lay the salmon skin side down on a large tray and spread the cure over it, ensuring the salmon is evenly covered. Cover with cling film and then place in the fridge for about 10 hours.

Turn the salmon over, cover with cling film again and continue to cure for another 20 hours.

Scrape and then wash off the cure, then pat the salmon dry with kitchen paper. Wrap in cling film and keep in the fridge, or carve the salmon into thick slices, season with freshly ground black pepper and serve with slices of granary bread.

Continued overleaf

Serves 10

500g raw beetroot, peeled
 and cut into 3cm cubes
1 tsp fennel seeds
1 small bunch tarragon
500g sea salt
250g caster sugar
1 side of organically
 farmed salmon (or wild if
 available), pinboned and
 trimmed
freshly ground black pepper
granary bread, to serve

Beetroot salad

Wash the beetroot and place in a pan. Add enough water to cover the beetroot then add a pinch of sea salt and a dash of the vinegar.

Bring the water to the simmer and cook until the beetroot is soft but not breaking up – the cooking time will vary depending on the size of the beetroot but it could take up to an hour. Allow the beetroot to cool in the water and then peel and dice.

Place the beetroot into a bowl and then add the shallot, garlic, a pinch of salt, freshly ground black pepper and the remaining vinegar. Cover with the olive oil and set aside until ready to serve.

Serves 10

500g raw beetroot
50ml white wine vinegar
1 banana shallot, finely
   chopped
1 garlic clove, finely chopped
110ml olive oil
sea salt and freshly ground
   black pepper

Smoked mackerel pâté

Place all the ingredients in a food processor and pulse until smooth. Chill until ready to serve.

5 fillets smoked mackerel
2 tbsp plain yoghurt
4 tbsp cream cheese
½ lemon, juiced
1 tsp creamed horseradish
sea salt, to taste

Deep-fried oysters

If you know someone who isn't mad about oysters, this is a brilliant way to get them keen. Coated in flour, egg and breadcrumbs and deep-fried, Nathan's come up with a sophisticated twist on everyone's favourite, the fish nugget!

Place the flour, egg and breadcrumbs into 3 separate bowls. Season the flour with sea salt and freshly ground black pepper.

Dip each oyster into the flour, then the egg and finally the breadcrumbs. Lay the coated oysters out on a tray and set aside until ready to cook.

Heat the oil in a deep-fat fryer or large saucepan to 180°C/350°F. Cook the coated oysters in batches for 1–2 minutes or until golden-brown. Drain on kitchen paper and keep warm.

115g plain flour
1 egg, beaten
75g breadcrumbs
14 oysters, shucked
oil, for deep frying
sea salt and freshly ground
   black pepper

Rabbit and rosemary terrine with chutney

by Stéphane Reynaud

Terrines are such a versatile dish, packed full of flavour and appropriate for every occasion – from a lazy summer picnic to dinner with family and friends. This makes a lovely lunch, or a highly impressive first course, which you can prepare in advance.

Preheat the oven to 180°C/350°F/Gas 4.

Place the rabbit, chicken livers and pork into a bowl. Add the port, white wine, shallots, 1 sprig of the rosemary and the spices and toss well to coat the meat. Leave to marinate for at least 5–10 minutes, then discard the marinade.

Meanwhile, place the bread into a large bowl, pour over the cream and allow to soak for 5 minutes, or until the bread has softened. Gently squeeze out the bread, discarding the cream.

Add the meat to the bowl with the bread, then add the beaten eggs and mix until well combined. Season with sea salt and freshly ground black pepper. Spoon the mixture into a large ovenproof terrine mould, pat down well to pack tightly together, then place the remaining sprig of rosemary on top. Place the mould into a roasting tray, fill with enough hot water to come halfway up the sides of the mould, then bake in the oven for 1 hour, or until the terrine is cooked through. Cool completely, then cover with cling film and leave to chill for 48 hours before serving.

For the chutney, place all the chutney ingredients into a saucepan and bring to a simmer over a low heat. Cook for about 1 hour, stirring occasionally, or until the chutney has thickened to a slightly syrupy consistency. Remove the pan from the heat and allow the chutney to cool completely. If not using immediately, spoon into a sterilised airtight jar and store in the fridge until needed.

To serve, thickly slice the terrine and serve with a spoonful of chutney on the side.

Tip: Use non-reactive pots when making chutneys. The acid in the mixture will react to iron, copper and brass, causing discolouration and imparting a metallic taste to the chutney.

Serves 6–8

You'll need 1 large terrine dish (1 litre capacity)

for the terrine
600g rabbit, bones removed and chopped into 2.5cm pieces
200g chicken livers, cleaned, trimmed and chopped
200g pork loin, trimmed and chopped
50ml white port
175ml white wine
2 shallots, finely chopped
2 sprigs rosemary
1 tsp grated fresh ginger
1 tsp quatre épices (French four spice)
1 slice soft white bread
200ml single cream
2 eggs, beaten
1 tsp salt
1 tsp freshly ground black pepper

for the chutney
500g tomatoes, skin and seeds removed, chopped
3 apples, peeled, cored and chopped
3 onions, chopped
50g fresh ginger, finely chopped
1 tsp ground cumin
3 tbsp tomato ketchup
100g golden raisins
200g soft brown sugar
300ml cider vinegar

Chicken terrine with herbs

by Michel Roux

This is a cinch to make and delicious to have in the fridge for an impromptu snack. Michel says, 'the idea is that everyone can keep going back again and again to make a sandwich, accompanied by a pear or fig chutney or a dollop of Cumberland sauce. If you don't have a mincer, ask your butcher to prepare the meat for you.'

Mince the chicken, ham, pork and veal twice in a mincer using a medium-sized mincer blade disc. Alternatively, chop the meat into tiny pieces with a sharp knife.

Put the minced meat into a well-chilled bowl, set on a larger bowl of ice, and stir with a wooden spoon until thoroughly mixed. Stir in the cream, egg, alcohol (if using), thyme and white wine until well combined. Add the salt and some freshly ground black pepper. This is called the farce.

Heat 40g of the butter in a small saucepan and sweat the shallots for 2–3 minutes, then set aside to cool. Stir in the herbs.

Melt the remaining butter in a small saucepan and remove from the heat. Dip the chicken breast strips in the melted butter, then dip in the shallot and herb mixture until well coated. Set aside on a plate. Line the terrines with strips of pork fat.

Spread half of the farce in the bottom of the terrines, then add a layer of chicken breast strips, top with the remaining farce, then more slices of pork fat. Cover with the lid and chill in the fridge for 2 hours.

Preheat the oven to 180ºC/350ºF/Gas 4.

Place the terrines in a large baking tray and half-fill the baking tray with boiling water. Cook the terrines for 30 minutes uncovered, then cover with the lids and cook for a further 15 minutes. Remove the terrines from the oven, remove the lids and place a weighted board (maximum weight 250g) onto the terrines to compress them gently until they have completely cooled. Cover with cling film and leave to chill in the fridge for a day or two before serving.

Serves 14–16

You'll need 8 mini terrine dishes (250ml capacity) or 2 large terrine dishes (1 litre capacity)

1 x 1.4kg chicken, flesh removed and chopped, skin and bones discarded
110g unsmoked ham, chopped
300g pork shoulder or neck, chopped
300g veal rump, chopped
300ml double cream, very cold
1 egg
75ml Armagnac or Cognac (optional)
2 tbsp fresh thyme leaves
200ml dry white wine
3 tsp salt
freshly ground black pepper
100g butter
2 shallots, finely chopped
4 tbsp chopped fresh parsley
4 tbsp chopped fresh chives
2 tbsp chopped fresh tarragon
1 chicken breast, sliced into 1cm strips
250g pork back fat (available from your butcher), finely sliced

Amazing brined roast chicken

by Thomas Keller

How good can a simple roast chicken be? Superchef Thomas Keller ensures golden crisp skin and the tenderest meat with six hours of aromatic brining, plus air-drying and tempering time. Simply seasoned with sea salt and thyme, this chicken is fantastic with roast potatoes and a classic chasseur sauce (overleaf). Or for an extravagant, savoury sweet brunch, Keller serves his roast chicken with the chasseur sauce, waffles (page 28), vanilla butter and maple syrup. Genius at work!

Place all the brine ingredients in a large saucepan. Cover with a lid and bring to the boil for 1 minute, stirring to dissolve the salt. Remove from the heat and set aside to cool completely before using.

Rinse the chickens under cold running water, then submerge them in the brine – use a plate if necessary. Chill in the fridge for 6 hours.

Preheat the oven to 240°C/475°F/Gas 8.

Remove the chickens from the brine, rinse under cold, running water, then dry it very well with kitchen paper, inside and out. (The less the meat steams in the oven, the drier the heat, the better.)

Season the cavities with a light sprinkling of salt and pepper, then truss the birds. To do this, place each chicken on a tray with the legs toward you. Tuck the wing tips under the bird. Cut a 90cm piece of kitchen twine and place it on top of the neck end of the breast.

Lift the neck end of the bird and pull the twine down around the wings and under the chicken, then bring the ends up over the breast, toward you, and tie the twine into a knot, pulling it tight to plump the breast. Bring the ends of the twine around the ends of the drumsticks and straight up. Tie as before to pull the drumsticks together and form a compact bird; tie again to secure the knot.

Set the trussed birds aside for 30 minutes. (The trussed chickens can be refrigerated for a few hours, but take them out of the fridge at least 30 minutes before cooking.) Having the chicken at room temperature before cooking will ensure it cooks evenly in the oven. Salt the birds – aim for a uniform coating that will result in a salty, flavourful skin (about 1 tablespoon). Place 2 heavy-based ovenproof frying pans over a high heat, add half the oil to each and heat until hot.

Continued overleaf

Serves 6

for the brine
5 litres water
175g sea salt flakes
100g honey
12 bay leaves
6 garlic cloves, skin left on, smashed
2 tbsps black peppercorns
10g fresh rosemary leaves
10g thyme leaves
50g flat-leaf parsley
2 large lemons, zest and juice

for the chicken
2 x 1.2kg free range, organic chickens
2 tbsp rapeseed oil
2 tsp chopped thyme leaves
sea salt and freshly ground black pepper

Put the chickens breast-side up into the pans, and then into the oven with the legs facing the back of the oven. Roast for 40 minutes, checking the birds every 15 minutes and rotating the frying pans if the chickens are browning unevenly.

After 40 minutes, check the temperature of the birds by inserting an instant-read thermometer between the leg and the thigh. The temperature should read approximately 68°C/155°F. (The chicken will continue to cook as it sits, reaching a temperature of about 73°C/165°F.)

When the birds are done, remove from the oven, add the thyme leaves to the pans, and baste the birds several times with the juices and thyme leaves. Let them rest in a warm place for about 10 minutes.

To carve the chicken, cut the twine between the legs and pull on one end; the entire piece will pull away easily. Cut each bird into 4 pieces. Remove the legs by cutting through the joint where the thigh joins the body. Cut the breast down the middle and serve it on the bone, with one wing joint still attached to each. If you like, cut off and discard the wing tips.

Chasseur sauce

Thomas's French 'hunter's sauce' will complement any simple chicken dish you fancy.

Serves 6

Heat the rapeseed oil over a medium heat, then add the shallots, carrot, garlic cloves and button mushrooms and fry until very lightly coloured.

Add the tomato and stir until well combined. Pour in the wine and reduce the sauce slowly until the liquid has almost evaporated.

Add the herbs and chicken stock, bring to a simmer and and cook for 30 minutes, skimming the scum at regular intervals. Strain the sauce through a fine sieve.

The jus should have the consistency of a thin sauce. Reduce further if needed, but don't overdo it!

2 tbsp rapeseed oil
3 shallots, cut into
    medium dice
1 carrot, cut into
    medium dice
3 garlic cloves, chopped
25g button mushrooms,
    cut into medium dice
1 tomato, cut into
    medium dice
40ml white wine
1 sprig fresh parsley
1 sprig fresh thyme
1 bay leaf
10 black peppercorns
125ml dark chicken stock

Duck confit with lentils

by Daniel Galmiche

A traditional French method for preserving duck by first salting, then slow cooking the meat in its own fat, before crisping up briefly in the oven or pan to serve. It's a simple process, resulting in meltingly tender, savoury meat. Serve with Daniel's earthy puy lentils, or you can pack the confit in a well-sealed container in the fridge for weeks, for an impromptu winter feast.

To make the duck confit, put the duck legs in a small shallow tray, skin-side down, and season with the salt, pepper, garlic and thyme. Cover with cling film, press down and leave to marinate in the fridge for a good 3 or 4 hours, or even overnight. The longer you leave it the more intense the flavour will be.

Preheat the oven to 130°C/250°F/Gas 1.

Take the duck out of the tray, discarding the marinade. Rinse under cold running water and pat dry with kitchen paper.

Put the duck in a large heavy-based casserole or cast iron pan and pour the melted goose (or duck) fat on top. Cover with a lid or greaseproof paper sealed with foil, place in the oven and bake for 3–4 hours, or you can gently simmer the duck on the stove, covered with a lid, for 3–4 hours.

Remove from the oven, or take off the heat if you're cooking on the stove, skim off any fat then cover with foil and set aside. If you want to refrigerate the duck for another time, put the duck legs in a clean sealable plastic container and add the strained fat. Cool and store in the fridge – it will keep for several weeks if the duck legs are properly covered by at least 2.5cm of fat and there are no air pockets.

Continued overleaf

Serves 4

for the confit
4 duck legs, each about 175g, including fat
40g sea salt
4 garlic cloves, unpeeled and crushed with the flat edge of a knife or your hand
4 thyme sprigs, leaves only
1kg goose or duck fat, melted
2 tbsp honey

for the lentils
200g puy lentils, picked over and rinsed
1 shallot, finely chopped
1 small carrot, peeled and diced
1 bouquet garni made with 1 thyme sprig and 1 parsley sprig, tied together with kitchen string
1 garlic clove, unpeeled
2–3 tablespoons vinaigrette
1 handful chervil, leaves only, chopped

Meanwhile, cook the lentils. Place them in a small saucepan and cover with cold water. Bring to the boil and skim the white foam from the surface. Add the shallot, carrot, bouqet garni and garlic, reduce the heat and simmer for a further 10 minutes or until al dente.

Strain the lentils, reserving 2 tablespoons of the cooking liquid. Discard the shallot, bouquet garni and garlic. Add the vinaigrette, the reserved cooking liquid and the chervil. Season, to taste, with salt and pepper.

Brush the duck legs with the honey and pan-roast them, skin-side down, in a non-stick pan over a medium heat for 5 minutes or until crisp and golden-brown. The honey will caramelise very quickly so be careful not to let it burn.

To serve, apoon the lentils onto serving plates and top with the duck legs. Alternatively, arrange the duck legs on top of the lentils in a large pot and serve at the table. The texture and delicate flavours of this dish are second to none.

....

Tip: Don't chuck the leftover fat away – it's fine to use again.

Duck confit with flageolet ragout and celeriac mash

by James Martin

James's hearty French cassoulet is anything but healthy – and all the more tasty for it.

Place the duck legs into a roasting tray and sprinkle with the salt. Sprinkle over the thyme, then cover the tray with cling film and chill in the fridge overnight.

Heat a heavy frying pan over a low to medium heat, then add the duck legs to the pan and cover them completely in the duck fat.

Bring the duck fat to a gentle simmer and cook the duck legs gently for 2–2½ hours, or until the meat is very tender. Remove the duck legs from the fat, reserving the fat, and place onto a clean roasting tray, draining off any excessive fat.

Shred the meat from 2 of the confit duck legs. Set the other 2 aside. Heat a little of the reserved duck fat in a frying pan over a medium heat. Add the shallot and garlic and fry for 1–2 minutes, or until softened. Add the tinned tomatoes, bring the mixture to a simmer and cook for a further 2–3 minutes.

Add the shredded duck meat, flageolet beans, stock and rosemary and return the mixture to the boil. Boil for another 2–3 minutes, then season, to taste, and whisk in the butter.

Heat a little more of the reserved duck fat in a frying pan over a high heat. Add the reserved duck legs, skin-side down, and fry for 2–3 minutes, or until the skin is crisp and the duck meat is warmed through.

Meanwhile, for the celeriac mash, place the potatoes and celeriac into a pan of salted water and bring to the boil. Reduce the heat and simmer for 15 minutes, or until just tender. Drain well and return to the pan to steam over the heat for 1 minute.

Pass the cooked potatoes and celeriac through a ricer (or mash with a potato masher) until smooth, then return to the pan. Add the butter and cream and mix well, then season, to taste, with salt and freshly ground black pepper.

To serve, pile some of the celeriac mash onto each of 2 serving plates, then spoon the ragout alongside. Top each portion with a crispy confit duck leg.

Serves 2

for the confit
4 x 175g duck legs
30g table salt
2–3 thyme sprigs, leaves only
300g duck fat, melted
1 banana shallot, finely sliced
1 garlic clove, finely diced
200g tinned tomatoes
1 x 400g tin flageolet beans, drained and rinsed
200ml chicken stock
1 sprig rosemary, leaves finely chopped
50g unsalted butter
sea salt and freshly ground black pepper

for the celeriac mash
500g floury potatoes, peeled, cut into chunks
500g celeriac, peeled, cut into chunks
75g butter
110ml double cream
sea salt and freshly ground black pepper

Veal blanquette

by Michel Roux Jr

This is French comfort food at its finest – rich and creamy, and full of robust flavour. Slow-cooked over a couple of hours, it will fill your home with the most wonderful smells.

Place the veal into a large saucepan, cover generously with cold water and bring to the boil. Reduce the heat until the water is simmering gently, then simmer for 30 minutes, skimming off any froth that collects on the surface at intervals.

Add the vegetables, bouquet garni and a large pinch of salt. Continue to simmer for a further 1 hour 20 minutes, adding more water as necessary to cover the veal and vegetables. (The pan contents should be covered by the water at all times.)

While the meat is simmering, carefully decant about 500ml of the cooking liquid and pour over the small cocktail onions in a separate pan. Bring the cooking liquid to the boil, then reduce the heat until the liquid is simmering. Continue to simmer the onions for 10–15 minutes, or until tender. Add the mushrooms, cover the pan with a lid and continue to simmer for a further 10 minutes, or until the vegetables are tender.

Drain the onions and mushrooms, collecting the cooking liquid in the pan with the veal in it. Keep the drained onions and mushrooms warm. When the veal pieces are tender, remove from the pan and add to the onions and mushrooms. Keep warm.

For the sauce, strain the cooking liquid into a clean saucepan, discarding the bouquet garni and the vegetables. Bring the cooking liquid to a rapid boil for 12–15 minutes, or until reduced by half. Stir in the double cream, then return the mixture to the boil for a further 4–5 minutes.

Meanwhile, in a bowl, mix together the egg yolks and crème fraîche until well combined. Remove the pan from the heat, then stir in the egg–crème fraîche mixture. Stir continuously until the mixture is completely incorporated and the sauce has thickened slightly. Season, to taste, with sea salt and freshly ground black pepper, then strain the mixture through a fine sieve onto the veal, onion and mushrooms. Warm through for 3–4 minutes.

Serve in a big bowl with some boiled potatoes, pilau rice or bread for dunking.

Serves 6–8

1kg breast of British or rose veal, cut into 4cm chunks
1 large onion, left whole, studded with 2 cloves
2 carrots, peeled
1 leek, white part only
1 bouquet garni (bundle of flat-leaf parsley, thyme and bay)
24 small cocktail onions, peeled
250g small button mushrooms, trimmed
300ml double cream
2 egg yolks
2 tbsp crème fraîche
sea salt and freshly ground black pepper

A hearty roast pheasant lunch

by Michael Caines

Served with braised chicory, quince purée and wild mushrooms, this hearty roast pheasant recipe will make you yearn for cold, autumn days. There are quite a few steps to Michael's dish, so it really helps to plan the meal. The quince purée and the braising of the chicory can be done the day before. The walnuts can be caramelised in the morning.

For the quince purée, heat the sugar, 500ml water, butter and lemon juice in a non-reactive saucepan until the sugar has dissolved and the mixture is well combined. Add the quince and bring the mixture to the boil. Reduce the heat and simmer the mixture until the quince has softened. Strain off the liquid, reserving a little of it.

Transfer the drained quince to a food processor and blend to a smooth purée. Pass this through a fine sieve, loosening the strained mixture with a little of the reserved cooking liquid if necessary. Then pour into a clean saucepan, season, to taste, with sea salt and freshly ground black pepper, and cover with cling film until required.

For the braised chicory, preheat the oven to 180°C/350°F/Gas 4. Place the onion, salt and 50g of the butter into an ovenproof saucepan. Fry the onion, stirring well, until softened. Add 1 litre of water, the bouillon, sugar, bouquet garni and chicory and bring to the boil. Cover the pan with foil and transfer to the oven for 25–30 minutes, or until tender and cooked through. Remove from the oven and set aside to cool.

Once cool, drain the braised chicory, squeeze out any excess water, and then slice across into thin strips. This whole process can be done the day before.

For the caramelised walnuts, preheat a deep-fat fryer to 190°C/375°F. Heat the sugar and 100ml water in a saucepan until dissolved. Add the walnuts and bring the mixture to the boil. Continue to cook until the temperature of the sugar syrup reaches 110°C/225°F (use a sugar thermometer to check this). Remove the walnuts from the syrup using a slotted spoon and carefully lower them into the deep-fat fryer. (Take care: the liquid coating the walnuts may spit upon contact with the oil.) Fry the walnuts until golden-brown, then remove from the oil using a slotted spoon and set aside to drain on kitchen paper. Sprinkle with sea salt.

Serves 4

for the quince purée
110g sugar
40g butter
½ lemon, juiced
500g quince, peeled, core removed, chopped
sea salt and freshly ground black pepper

for the braised chicory
1 large onion, chopped
15g salt
70g butter
pinch of chicken bouillon (or pinch chicken stock cube)
20g sugar
1 bouquet garni
4 large chicory, any discoloured outer leaves removed
110g smoked bacon lardons, finely sliced
50g garlic pureé (made by pounding 50g garlic to a paste in a pestle and mortar)

To finish off the chicory, heat the remaining 20g butter in a separate frying pan over a medium heat. Add the lardons and fry until lightly brown, then add the cooked chicory and continue to cook until the water has evaporated. Add the garlic purée, stir well, then season to taste. Keep warm by putting a lid on top of the pan.

For the pheasant, increase the oven temperature to 200°C/400°F/Gas 6. Season the pheasant breasts with plenty of salt and pepper. Heat the oil and a knob of butter in an ovenproof frying pan over a high heat. Add the pheasant breasts, skin-side down, and fry until golden-brown. Turn the breasts over and transfer the pan to the oven. Roast the pheasant for 5–6 minutes, or until cooked the way you like it. Remove from the pan, leaving behind the pan juices, and set aside to rest.

Add the mushrooms to the same pan the pheasant was cooked in and fry in the resting juices until softened, adding a splash of water (or chicken stock, if you have it) to deglaze the pan if necessary. Stir in the chopped parsley, then stir in the remaining butter until melted, and season with salt and pepper.

To serve, place some of the braised chicory on the centre of each serving plate. Spread a line of quince purée alongside using the back of a spoon. Place one pheasant breast on top of each portion. Spoon over the mushrooms in their sauce and garnish with the caramelised walnuts.

for the caramelised walnuts
vegetable oil, for deep-frying
100g caster sugar
handful of walnuts, shells
    removed
sea salt flakes, to taste

for the pheasant
4 x 175g pheasant breasts
1–2 tbsp oil
110g unsalted butter
200g wild mushrooms,
    wiped clean
2 tbsp chopped flat-leaf
    parsley
sea salt and freshly ground
    black pepper

....

Tip: Pheasant breasts have very little fat, so it's important to keep them well basted when roasting and rest once cooked, to keep them juicy. Smear with plenty of butter, or try wrapping in a coat of bacon.

Chinese pork potsticker dumplings

by Ken Hom

These delicious northern Chinese dumplings are first fried and then finished off steamed in the same pan. Fill them with your favourite meats, veg or fish for a Sunday treat. You can make them a day ahead and refrigerate or freeze them (take them directly from the fridge or freezer to the pan). Or follow Chinese tradition and invite friends to come stuff, shape, and cook the dumplings along with you, making the preparation and cooking part of the fun.

To make the dough, put the flour into a large bowl and gradually stir in the hot water, mixing all the time with a fork or with chopsticks until most of the water is incorporated. Add a splash more water if the mixture seems dry. Remove the mixture from the bowl and knead it with your hands, dusting the dough with a little flour if it's sticky. Continue kneading until it is smooth – this should take about 8 minutes. Put the dough back in the bowl, cover with a clean damp towel and let it rest for about 20 minutes.

While the dough is resting, combine the stuffing ingredients in a large bowl and mix them together thoroughly.

After the resting period, take the dough out of the bowl and knead it again for about 5 minutes, dusting with a little flour if it is sticky. Once the dough is smooth, shape it into a roll about 23cm long and about 2.5cm in diameter.

With a sharp knife, slice the roll into 18 equal segments. Using your hands, roll each of the dough segments into a small ball and then, with a rolling pin, roll each ball into a small, round, flat 'pancake' about 6cm in diameter. Arrange the round skins on a lightly floured tray and cover them with a slightly damp cloth to prevent them from drying out until you are ready to use them.

Put about 2 teaspoons of filling in the centre of each 'pancake' and moisten the edges with water. Fold the dough in half and pinch together with your fingers. Pleat around the edge, pinching to seal well. The dumpling should look like a small Cornish pasty with a flat base and rounded top. Transfer each finished dumpling to the floured tray and keep it covered until you have stuffed all the dumplings in this way.

Makes about 18 dumplings

for the dough
140g plain flour, plus extra for dusting
125ml very hot water

for the stuffing
110g minced pork (fatty, not extra lean)
75g Chinese leaves or spinach, finely chopped
1 tsp diced fresh ginger
½ tbsp Shaoxing rice wine or dry sherry
½ tbsp dark soy sauce
½ tsp light soy sauce
½ tsp salt
¼ tsp freshly ground black pepper
1½ tbsp finely chopped spring onions
1 tsp sesame oil
½ tsp sugar
1 tbsp cold chicken stock or water

to cook
about 1 tbsp groundnut or peanut oil
75ml water

for the dipping sauce
3 tbsp soy sauce
1 tbsp white rice vinegar
2 tsp chilli oil

To cook, heat a large non-stick frying pan until it is very hot. Add the groundnut oil and place the dumplings flat-side down into the pan. Turn down the heat and cook for about 2 minutes until they are lightly browned. Add the water, cover the pan tightly and simmer gently for 12 minutes or until most of the liquid is absorbed. Check the water halfway through and add more if necessary. Uncover the pan and continue to cook for a further 2 minutes. The potstickers should be crisp and browned on the bottom, sticking lightly to the pan but easy to remove with a spatula. The trick to making these dumplings is not to overcook them, or they will live up to their name by sticking firmly to the pot!

Combine the dipping sauce ingredients in a small bowl. To serve, remove the dumplings from the pan with a large slotted spoon and serve with the dipping sauce.

Tip: If you're pushed for time, gyoza (Japanese) wrappers can be found in the freezer section of most larger supermarkets or Asian stores, and can be used as a good substitute for homemade potsticker dough.

Pandhi curry (Coorg pork stir-fry)

by Vivek Singh

Vivek's summer curry, from the Coorg region of Karnataka, requires double cooking; the pork is first braised slowly to cook until tender and then stir-fried to finish the dish, with the high heat caramelising the onions and meat, adding a depth of flavour. Keep the seasoning slightly less than what you'd like to end up with: the prolonged cooking makes the flavours very intense.

Place the cubes of pork into a large dish. Add the remaining pork ingredients, cover, then marinate overnight in the fridge.

Once the pork has marinated, transfer the cubes to a large heavy-based pan. Add just enough water to cover the pork and cook, covered, over a very low heat for 1–1½ hours or until the pork is falling apart. (It helps to use as little water as possible to cook the pork this time around. The liquid will have stronger flavours and you can add it back to the stir-fry later.) Drain the pork and reserve the cooking liquid.

For the stir-fry, heat the oil in a wok over a high heat. When the oil is smoking, add the dried red chillies and stir-fry until they have darkened and are fragrant. Add the curry leaves and fry for 30 seconds, or until crisp and fragrant. Add the split green chillies and red onion slices and stir-fry for 2–3 minutes until softened.

Add the cooked pork cubes and fry, stirring continuously, for 3–4 minutes, or until golden-brown. (If the meat looks dry, add 1–2 tablespoons of the reserved cooking liquid and continue to cook until it has evaporated – this will glaze the pork.) Season, to taste, with sea salt and freshly ground black pepper, finish with a squeeze of lime, and spinkle over the coriander cress (if using), or the chopped coriander.

....

Tip: Try this curry with Vivek's apple and fennel raita (page 49) to refresh the palate – the sharp acidity from the apple is perfect for cutting through rich pork.

Serves 4

for the pork
750g pork shoulder or pork belly, diced into 2.5cm cubes
2 tbsp ginger and garlic paste (garlic, ginger and vegetable oil, blended to a paste)
1 tsp ground turmeric
2 tsp salt
8–10 whole black peppercorns
3 bay leaves
2 star anise
4 tbsp clear honey
3 tbsp dark soy sauce
10 kokum (cocum) berries, soaked in 100ml hot water to soften (available from some Asian grocers)

for the stir-fry
2 tbsp vegetable oil
4 dried red chillies
10 curry leaves
2 green chillies, split
3 red onions, sliced
½ lime, juiced
1 small bunch coriander cress, or finely chopped coriander, to serve
sea salt and freshly ground black pepper

Country captain shepherd's pie

by Cyrus Todiwala

This Indian-style version of a British classic uses lamb shoulder or leg (rather than mince) slow-cooked with spices and topped with cumin-flavoured mash. It is based on one of the earliest examples of fusion cooking, wherein spices were gently introduced to the British in India over 200 years ago. Cyrus chose this dish to cook for the Queen and the Duke of Edinburgh at the royal couple's first Diamond Jubilee celebration of 2012.

Preheat the oven to 140°C/275°F/Gas 1.

Place the cumin and coriander seeds into a dry frying pan on a low heat and toast them until they change colour slightly, then remove from the pan.

Grind the spices, ginger and garlic together in a spice grinder, adding as much water as you need to make it into a fine paste.

Heat a large ovenproof casserole dish until medium hot, add the oil and continue to heat until a haze forms. Add the lamb and brown well on all sides until the meat is well sealed.

Remove the lamb from the pan and set aside, then add the cinnamon, cardamom, cloves, peppercorns and the shredded chillies to the pan. Fry the spices for 1–2 minutes until the cloves swell a little.

Add a little water to the pan to deglaze it, scraping up any meat residue and dissolving it in the water. Add the chopped onions and cook until the liquid evaporates, then gently fry the onions until soft (about 4–5 minutes). Add the spice paste and cook for 5–6 minutes, mixing well, then return the lamb to the pan. Coat the lamb with the mixture then season lightly with sea salt and freshly ground black pepper, and cover the pan.

Place the pan into the oven and cook for 2–2½ hours, stirring the casserole occasionally and making sure the onions do not catch on the bottom of the pan.

Continued overleaf

Serves 4

1 tsp cumin seeds
1 tbsp coriander seeds
50g fresh ginger, peeled
50g garlic
2–3 tbsp sunflower oil
1.25kg cleaned lamb shoulder or leg (kept whole)
2 x 2.5cm pieces cinnamon (or cassia bark)
3–4 green cardamom
2–3 cloves
3–4 black peppercorns
2–3 large dried red chillies, shredded
3 medium onions, chopped
250g fresh or tinned tomatoes, chopped
1 heaped tbsp chopped coriander
sea salt and freshly ground black pepper

for the mash topping

3–4 large baking potatoes, peeled and roughly chopped
1 tbsp butter
½ tsp cumin seeds
2–3 garlic cloves, finely chopped
1 dried red chilli, shredded
250g fresh spinach leaves, coarsely shredded
2 eggs
75ml double cream
sea salt and freshly ground black pepper

Add the chopped tomatoes and mix well (add a little more water if it looks dry) then cover and return to the oven for another 15 minutes.

Check that the lamb is cooked – the meat will have retracted from the bone and will feel soft to the touch. Lift the lamb out of the casserole and place onto a tray to cool slightly. Carefully remove all the whole spices from the gravy and discard.

When the lamb is cool enough to handle, shred the meat off the bone and place back into the casserole with the gravy. Place back onto a medium low heat and cook until the gravy has thickened nicely. Add the freshly chopped coriander, check the seasoning, and spoon into an ovenproof dish, big enough that the filling reaches 2cm from the top of the dish.

For the topping, place the potatoes into a saucepan and cover with water, bring to the boil and simmer until tender. Drain, return the potatoes to the pan and back on the heat to drive off any extra moisture. Pass the cooked potatoes through a ricer (or mash them to a smooth purée) and set aside.

Place the butter onto the board with the cumin seeds, then finely chop the two together. Heat a frying pan and add the cumin butter and gently fry until the cumin colours gently, but don't heat it too much or the butter will burn.

As soon as the cumin changes colour, lift out the seeds and add to the potatoes, transferring as little butter as is possible. Add the chopped garlic and chilli to the butter in the frying pan and gently fry for 1 minute. When the garlic is light golden-brown, add the spinach leaves, toss for a minute or so until soft, season lightly then remove from the pan and place the wilted leaves straight onto the dish of shredded lamb, spreading evenly over the top.

Add the eggs and cream to the potato and mix well until smooth then check the seasoning. Spread the potato over the spinach evenly, ruffle the surface a little; it doesn't have to be smooth, just evenly spread.

Place back in the oven for 10 minutes then increase the oven temperature to 180°C/350°F/Gas 4 and cook for another 15 minutes until golden brown. Serve with crusty bread or as you like.

Mum's hotpot with vinegar onions
by Marcus Wareing

This is a quick and simple dish to prepare with long slow cooking being the key to its success. Braising is an ideal way to cook tougher cuts of meat, such as chuck and blade steak (also known as shoulder). If you prefer large pieces of meat rather than cubes, thick flank is suitable too.

Preheat the oven to 160ºC/320ºF/Gas 3.

Heat 2 tablespoons of the oil in a 2 litre flameproof casserole. Add the onions and garlic with a little fine salt and fry until light golden-brown. Remove with a slotted spoon, place in a bowl and reserve.

Add another 2 tablespoons of oil to the pan and fry the mushrooms until cooked through. Tip the cooked mushrooms into the bowl containing the onions.

Chop the beef into large cubes and coat in the flour, which should be seasoned with salt and freshly ground black pepper.

Heat the remaining oil in the casserole and fry the beef, in 2 batches, until well browned all over. Remove from the pan and set aside.

Pour in the wine and scrape the pan with a wooden spoon to loosen the browned bits. Simmer until it has a syrupy consistency, then add the stock, sauces, and herbs. Stir well and bring to a simmer.

Return the onions, mushrooms and beef to the pan, and add sea salt and freshly ground black pepper. Cover and place in the oven to braise for 2 hours, adding the potatoes after an hour.

Meanwhile, to make the pastry, sift the flour and salt into a bowl. Rub in the butter, then slowly mix in 3–4 tablespoons of cold water to make a stiff dough, bringing the dough together to make a ball with your hands. Wrap the dough in cling film and refrigerate for at least 1 hour – remove the dough 15 minutes before using.

Serves 4

for the hotpot
6 tbsp vegetable oil
2 onions, finely chopped
2 garlic cloves, crushed
pinch table salt
200g button mushrooms, quartered
500–600g braising steak
2–3 tbsp plain flour
200ml red wine
600ml hot beef stock
4 tbsp brown (HP) sauce
dash Worcestershire sauce
1 small bunch fresh thyme
2 bay leaves
500g small new potatoes, peeled and cut into chunks
sea salt and freshly ground black pepper

To prepare the vinegar onions, gently warm the vinegar in a pan, tip it into a large bowl and stir in the onions. Cover and set aside.

Remove the casserole from the oven and rest for about 30 minutes. Increase the oven temperature to 200°C/400°F/Gas 6. Roll out the pastry and, with a sharp knife, cut out a lid about 2.5cm larger in diameter than the casserole dish. Discard the herbs from the casserole, taste and adjust the seasoning if necessary. Brush water around the rim of the casserole dish. Place the pastry lid on top, sealing well to the edge, and brush all over with water. Pierce a hole in the centre.

Return to the oven to cook for 20–30 minutes until the pastry is a deep golden-brown colour. Leave to rest in a warm place for 10 minutes – the capacity of the meat tissue to hold water increases as it cools, so the idea is for it to reabsorb some of the liquid lost during cooking.

Serve with the vinegar onions, and a crisp green salad, if you like.

for the vinegar onions
400ml malt vinegar
1 large Spanish onion,
    finely sliced into rings

for the pastry
200g plain white flour
pinch salt
100g cold unsalted butter,
    cubed

In this chapter you will find dishes to tantalise and tease the taste buds of friends and family. Whether you are looking to showcase your cooking skills with a really complicated dish or decide to take a more relaxed approach, the *Saturday Kitchen* chefs have produced some amazing recipes to suit varying degrees of competence.

We all lead busy lives, so before deciding on your dinner menu I suggest that you give some thought to how much time and effort you are able to give to cooking (and shopping). Even if you are an uber-confident cook it is better to choose just one complicated dish. Consider a soup or a really simple first course. Many fish dishes only require a short cooking time and make a great first course or main.

Puddings – hot or cold – should be chosen carefully. You could opt for something quick and easy. But don't dismiss the idea of a hot soufflé or a fondant pot: these puds have the wow factor and can be prepared well before your guests arrive and then popped into the oven when you start to clear away the main course.

The secret is to plan ahead. You will find that many of the components to these dishes can be gotten ready beforehand – I am thinking here of my own rustic ratatouille which I like to serve with cod (though it is just as good served with meat), which can be prepared a day in advance, then carefully reheated.

When deciding on your menu try and choose seasonal food. Fresh asparagus can be a meal in itself. Ripe melon with Parma ham makes a beautiful starter. A delicious dinner does not have to be challenging and stressful. Think carefully about the balance of your meal and, above all, have fun cooking for your guests. That's what dinner parties are all about!'

Galton Blackiston

Chilled soup of carrot, pink grapefruit and hazelnuts

by Anthony Demetre

Anthony's recipes are always exciting and innovative – this soup is wonderfully simple and elegant too.

Slice the carrots as thin as possible, ideally using a mandoline.

Heat a large pan until hot, then add the butter, carrots and garlic, and sweat lightly for a couple of minutes. Add the water, thyme and rosemary, and season with sea salt and freshly ground black pepper. Bring to a simmer, then cover with a lid and cook for 5–6 minutes, or until the carrots are tender.

Remove the pan from the heat and stir in the milk. Allow to cool slightly, then pour into a liquidiser and blitz until smooth. Chill in the fridge for at least 30 minutes.

To serve, divide the soup among 4 serving bowls. Arrange the grapefruit segments, olives, nuts and coriander cress on top of the soup, then drizzle over the hazelnut oil.

....

Tip: When choosing carrots look for ones that are dark orange in colour, indicating a high level of beta-carotene. Avoid grapefruits with any bruising or coarse, puffy skin as they tend to be dry inside.

Serves 4

500g carrots, peeled
50g butter
1 garlic clove, peeled and crushed
750ml water
1 sprig thyme
1 sprig rosemary
150ml whole milk
2 pink grapefruit, peeled and segmented, segments halved
a handful of large green olives (Gordal work well), stones removed, halved and sliced
a handful of hazelnuts, crushed and toasted
1 punnet micro coriander cress, or 1 tbsp finely chopped coriander
4 tbsp hazelnut oil
sea salt and freshly ground black pepper

Scallops with leek and chestnut
by Stéphane Reynaud

Earthy chestnuts and sweet scallops make a deeply satisfying winter dish.

If you are buying scallops in the shell, rinse them clean under cool running water, pat dry with kitchen paper and trim off any tough, sinewy flesh. Remove the orange coral (the roe) and set it to one side.

Heat half the olive oil in a saucepan, add the garlic, leek, spring onion and ginger, lower the heat and fry for 10 minutes.

Add the wine and chestnuts and cook for another 5 minutes. Then add the cream (and the reserved roe, if you have it) and cook for 5 more minutes. Season with salt and freshly ground black pepper.

Heat the remaining oil in a frying pan and sear the scallops over a high heat for 2 minutes each side. Pile the chestnut fondue onto the plate and serve topped with 3 scallops each.

Serves 6

18 scallops
3 tbsp olive oil
3 garlic cloves, crushed
2 leeks, white part only, rinsed and sliced
2 spring onions, sliced
25g fresh ginger, peeled and chopped finely
200ml white wine
400g pre-cooked and peeled chestnuts
200ml whipping cream
sea salt and freshly ground black pepper

Tip: Scallops that are bright white in colour have often been soaked in brine to makes them swell and appear larger. Avoid these, as the scallops tend to have a soap-like flavour, and steam when cooked. Look for diver-caught, unsoaked scallops that are creamy or slightly off-white.

Scallop mousse with asparagus

by Alain Roux

The combination of asparagus and scallops is irresistible here. Alain's French classic makes an impressive starter for any dinner party.

Preheat the oven to 160°C/325°F/Gas 3.

For the mousse, brush the ramekin dishes generously with the butter and sprinkle inside with the herbs.

Blend the scallops and eggs in a food processor for 1 minute or until smooth. Add the cream, salt and cayenne pepper, and whizz for a further minute. Divide the mousse mixture evenly between the ramekins and cover each ramekin with foil.

Line a roasting tray or a deep ovenproof dish with kitchen paper and place the ramekins on top. Add enough boiling water to come half way up the sides of the ramekins. Cook in the oven for about 20–25 minutes. To check the mousse is cooked, push a fine skewer or the blade of a small knife into the centre for about 10 seconds. It should come out completely clean and feel hot. Set aside and keep warm.

For the garnish and sauce, heat the butter in a frying pan and fry the asparagus for 2–4 minutes, or until just tender. Remove half of the asparagus from the pan.

Add the shallot and wine to the pan, and bring to the boil. Pour in the cream and boil for a further 2 minutes. Pass the sauce through a fine sieve into a clean saucepan, using the back of a spoon to rub the sauce through. Add the lemon juice, sea salt and freshly ground black pepper and keep warm.

Slice the 2 large scallops in half horizontally and drizzle with the oil. Season with salt and cook on a hot grill for 30 seconds on each side. Season with salt and freshly ground black pepper and keep warm.

Remove the foil from the ramekins, loosen the timbales with a small knife and turn each one out onto a warm plate. Place a slice of grilled scallop on top of each timbale and arrange the asparagus alongside. Drizzle a little sauce on each plate and serve.

Serves 4

You'll need 4 ramekin dishes (approximately 8cm x 4cm)

for the mousse
15g soft butter
3 tbsp mixed fresh herbs (tarragon and flat-leaf parsley, dill or chives), leaves picked
5–7 king scallops (about 150g scallops, white part only)
2 eggs
200ml double cream
pinch each of salt and cayenne pepper

for the garnish and sauce
25g butter
150g wild or fine asparagus tips
1 small shallot, finely chopped
75ml dry white wine
100ml double cream
¼ lemon, juiced
2 large scallops, white part only
1 tsp vegetable oil
sea salt and freshly ground black pepper

Wild mushroom and sweetcorn biryani parcels

by Atul Kochhar

Served with a glorious blackberry raita and a wild mushroom and toasted almond side, Atul's dinner looks spectacular as well as being lots of fun to prepare.

For the parboiled rice, add the rice, bay leaf, cardamom and cloves to a pan of boiling salted water. Cook the rice until it is almost tender, then drain well and set aside.

Preheat the oven to 200°C/400°F/Gas 6.

For the biryani, heat the oil and butter in a frying pan. When the butter is foaming, add the cumin, cardamom and bay leaf and fry for 1–2 minutes, or until the spices are fragrant and beginning to pop.

Add the chopped garlic and fry until lightly brown, then add the chopped onion and fry for another couple of minutes, or until golden-brown. Add all of the mushrooms and the sweetcorn kernels and continue to fry, stirring well, for a further 3–4 minutes, or until softened.

Add the spice powders and stir well to coat the vegetables. Continue to fry for 1–2 minutes, or until fragrant, then add the white truffle paste (if using), tomato purée and cream and stir well to combine.

Add the parboiled rice and chopped coriander and season, to taste, with sea salt and freshly ground black pepper.

Brush 1 side of each sheet of filo pastry all over with some of the melted butter. Place 1 sheet of filo pastry on top of another to create 2 layers of pastry, then spoon a quarter of the biryani mixture into the centre of the pastry. Fold the sides over the rice filling, then scrunch up the pastry into a parcel. Brush all over with more melted butter. Repeat the process with the remaining filo pastry and biryani mixture.

Place the biryani parcels and a few sprigs of coriander onto a baking tray and bake in the oven for 12–15 minutes, or until the pastry is golden brown and crispy and the coriander has dried.

Continued overleaf

Serves 4

for the parboiled rice
150g basmati rice
1 bay leaf
2 green cardamom pods
2 cloves

for the biryani
1 tbsp vegetable oil
1 tbsp butter, plus 110g butter, melted
1 tsp cumin seeds
2 green cardamom pods, lightly crushed
1 bay leaf
2 garlic cloves, peeled, chopped
200g onions, finely chopped
2 large portobello mushrooms, wiped clean, chopped
110g mixed wild mushrooms, wiped clean, chopped
75g sweetcorn kernels
1 tsp ground coriander
½ tsp ground cumin
½ tsp red chilli powder
½ tsp garam masala
1 tbsp white truffle paste (optional)
½ tbsp tomato purée
2 tbsp single cream
2 tbsp chopped coriander
8 large sheets ready-made filo pastry
a few sprigs of coriander
black truffle shavings (optional)
sea salt and freshly ground black pepper

Meanwhile, for the mushrooms, heat the oil and butter in a pan over a medium heat. When the butter is foaming, add the crushed garlic, coriander seeds and chilli flakes and fry for 1–2 minutes, or until the garlic has softened. Throw in the toasted almonds, followed by the mushrooms, and stir well. Continue to fry for 1–2 minutes, or until the mushrooms have softened, then drizzle over the lemon juice. Season, to taste, with sea salt and freshly ground black pepper.

To make the raita, whizz the blackberries in a food processor until smooth, then push the fruit through a sieve over a bowl to make a perfectly smooth purée. Mix and blend all the raita ingredients together, cover and put in the fridge to cool. Serve chilled.

To serve, spoon the mushroom and almond mixture into the centre of each plate. Cut the biryani parcels in half and place 2 halves on top of each serving. Sprinkle over the dried coriander sprigs and truffle shavings, if using. Serve the raita alongside.

Tip: You have to work quickly with filo pastry, otherwise it dries out. It is a good idea to keep it in the plastic wrapping or cover with a damp cloth while you're working with it.

for the mushrooms
½ tbsp vegetable oil
½ tbsp butter
1 garlic clove, crushed to a paste with the edge of a knife
½ tsp crushed coriander seeds
¼ tsp dried chilli flakes
50g almonds, lightly toasted, and halved
110g mixed wild mushrooms, wiped clean, sliced
1 tbsp lemon juice
sea salt and freshly ground black pepper

for the raita
110g fresh blackberries
300g Greek-style yoghurt
1 tsp toasted cumin seeds, ground to a powder

Gruyère and bacon soufflé suissesse
by Galton Blackiston

If you thought soufflé was decadent, this recipe rises to another level. Crispy bacon, reduced cream and nutty Gruyère cheese make for a lavish starter or an indulgent meal in its own right.

Preheat the oven to 200°C/400°F/Gas 6 and generously grease the ramekin dishes.

Pour the milk into a saucepan, add the thyme, bay leaf and nutmeg, and bring to a simmer. Turn off the heat and leave to infuse for a few minutes.

Fry the bacon in a hot pan until crisp on both sides, then drain on kitchen paper. Melt the butter in a saucepan and add the flour and mustard. Cook for a couple of minutes until a nutty aroma is released.

Strain the infused milk, pour it slowly into the saucepan containing the flour and mustard and whisk continuously until thick, then beat in the egg yolks and season with sea salt and freshly ground black pepper. Allow to cool slightly.

Whisk the egg whites in a clean bowl until firm, adding a pinch of salt. Then add a third of the egg white into the soufflé base mix, and beat in. Stir in the chives and then carefully fold in the remaining egg whites. Spoon the mixture into the buttered ramekins and bake for 5–7 minutes, or until the tops begin to brown. Remove from the oven and set aside.

Preheat the grill to high. Meanwhile, gently warm the double cream in a saucepan and season with sea salt and freshly ground black pepper. Increase the temperature and cook until the volume of liquid has reduced by one third. Add the crispy bacon and mix well. If needed, add some more salt and pepper.

Pour the cream into 6 serving bowls and turn the Gruyère and bacon soufflés out onto the cream. Cover the soufflés with the grated Gruyère cheese and place under the grill. Once golden-brown and bubbling, remove from the grill and serve immediately.

Serves 6

You'll need 6 ramekin dishes (approximately 7cm x 4cm)

500ml whole milk
2 sprigs thyme
1 bay leaf
pinch ground nutmeg
150g heavily cured bacon, finely chopped
65g butter, plus extra for greasing
55g plain flour
a pinch English mustard powder
5 eggs, separated
2 tbsp chopped chives
300ml double cream
110g Gruyère cheese, very finely grated
sea salt and freshly ground black pepper

Roast cod with winter ratatouille
by Galton Blackiston

A classic dish with well-loved flavours that are perfectly balanced.

For the ratatouille, preheat the oven to 200°C/400°F/Gas 6. Place all your cubed veg, onion and garlic into a deep-sided roasting tin and toss together. Drizzle over some of the olive oil and season, to taste, with sea salt and freshly ground black pepper.

Place the roasting tin over a medium heat and give the vegetables a good stir and a shake to coat everything in the oil. Once the vegetables start to sizzle, transfer the roasting tin to the oven and cook for 35–40 minutes, stirring through occasionally.

Add more of the oil, as necessary, until the vegetables are tender, but still have a bit of 'bite'. Check for seasoning.

Meanwhile, for the lemon beurre blanc sauce, bring the shallots, white wine vinegar, lemon juice, lemon zest and white wine to the boil in a saucepan. Continue to boil until the volume of liquid has reduced to 2 tablespoons.

Add 1 tablespoon of cold water and return the mixture to the boil. Reduce the sauce again until only 1 tablespoon of liquid remains in the pan.

Reduce the heat to low, then whisk in the butter, a cube at a time, waiting until each cube has melted before adding the next. Continue to whisk until the sauce is pale and thick, then remove the pan from the heat and season, to taste, with salt, freshly ground black pepper and a little more lemon juice, if necessary.

Strain the sauce through a sieve into a clean saucepan and set aside until needed (don't refrigerate or the sauce will separate). Gently reheat the sauce just before serving, stirring continuously.

Meanwhile, for the roast cod, reduce the oven temperature to 180°C/350°F/Gas 4.

Heat the oil and butter in a frying pan over a medium heat. When the butter has stopped foaming, place the cod fillets into the pan, skin-sides down, and fry until the skin is crisp and golden-brown. Season, to taste, with salt and pepper. Carefully turn the fillets over and continue to fry until golden-brown on both sides.

Either continue to fry in the pan until the fish is just cooked (being careful not to overcook it), or transfer the fillets to a roasting tray and cook in the oven for 4–5 minutes, or until just cooked through. You'll know the cod is done when the flesh is opaque.

To serve, divide the winter ratatouille equally among 6 serving plates. Place one roasted cod fillet on top of each serving and spoon over the lovely lemon sauce.

Serves 6

for the ratatouille
175g swede, peeled, cut into 1cm dice
175g parsnip, peeled, cut into 1cm dice
175g carrot, peeled, cut into 1cm dice
175g beetroot, peeled, cut into 1cm dice
175g butternut squash, peeled, cut into 1cm dice
1 onion, sliced
2 garlic cloves, finely chopped or grated
5–6 tbsp olive oil
sea salt and freshly ground black pepper

for the lemon beurre blanc
2 shallots, peeled, finely sliced
1 tbsp white wine vinegar
4–5 tbsp lemon juice, and zest of 1 lemon
4 tbsp white wine
225g salted butter, cut into cubes
sea salt and freshly ground black pepper

for the roast cod
vegetable oil and butter, for frying
6 x 110g line-caught cod fillets, skin on (fillets taken from the middle of the fish if possible)
sea salt and freshly ground black pepper

Sea bream with fennel and orange

by Jason Atherton

Sea bream is good value and Jason makes this a high-end dish with show-stopping flavour combinations and gourmet presentation, including his technique for making orange 'pearls' to decorate the plate.

For the orange dressing, heat the orange juice in a small saucepan and cook for 3–4 minutes or until it has reduced by two thirds. Stir in the zest, set aside to cool and then leave to chill in the fridge.

Put the orange segments into a sous vide bag or airtight, plastic freezer bag. Place the bag in a small saucepan of boiling water for 10 seconds. Remove the bag from the water and gently press apart the segments with your fingers to make orange 'pearls'.

Add the orange pearls to the chilled reduced orange juice. Stir in the white wine vinegar, olive oil and half of the fennel fronds. Set aside.

For the fennel and onion salad, place the sliced fennel and red onion into a bowl of iced water and leave to stand for 10 minutes. Drain, pat dry using kitchen paper and place into a large bowl.

Add two thirds of the olives, the olive oil, wine vinegar and remaining fennel fronds to the bowl and season, to taste, with salt. Stir until well combined and set aside.

For the sea bream, score the fish 4–5 times on the skin side and season, to taste, with sea salt and freshly ground black pepper. Heat the oil in a large frying pan and fry the fish, skin-side down, for 1–2 minutes on each side. Remove the fish from the pan and set aside to rest for 2 minutes.

To serve, drizzle some dressing around the edge of each serving plate and place a bream fillet, skin-side up, in the centre. Drizzle a little sauce over the fish. Pile the fennel salad on top and scatter the reserved olive pieces around the plate.

Tip: If you can't find sea bream, feel free to use red snapper or sea bass instead.

Serves 4

for the orange dressing
3 oranges (blood oranges when in season), 1 peeled and segmented, 2 zested and juiced
2 tbsp white wine vinegar
100ml olive oil
fennel fronds (see below)

for the fennel and onion salad
2 fennel bulbs, thinly sliced, fronds reserved
1 red onion, sliced
75g marinated black (Kalamata) olives, stones removed, quartered lengthways
25ml olive oil
1 tbsp white wine vinegar

for the sea bream
2 whole sea bream, filletted
3 tbsp vegetable oil
sea salt and freshly ground black pepper

Sole-in-a-bag with courgettes and black olives

by Bryn Williams

Served with the wet polenta on page 215, this makes a lovely feast for the family or an easy dish at dinner parties, as all the preparation is done beforehand. The black olives and basil add a salty, herby tang here, but the overall effect is surprisingly delicate.

Preheat the oven to 180°C/350°F/Gas 4.

Place the spring onion, courgette, black olives and basil in a bowl. Season with salt and pepper, pour over the olive oil and mix together well.

Cut 4 pieces of greaseproof paper or foil, each one measuring about 30 x 30cm. Divide the vegetables into 4 equal piles on the pieces of paper or foil. Place 3 sole fillets on each of the vegetable mounds, and fold each fillet in half to save them from overcooking. Season the sole with salt and pepper.

Divide the butter evenly between each pile. Then fold the paper or foil over to create 4 parcels and, before you close them, pour a quarter of the white wine into each one. Seal the parcels tightly by folding over the edges and crimping them together. Leave a little space inside the parcels for the steam.

Place a large, heavy-based frying pan or roasting tin over a high heat and pop the parcels into it. When the parcels start to expand, remove them from the heat and place in the oven for 7 minutes. Remove and serve at once.

Serves 4

1 spring onion, trimmed and thinly sliced
1 yellow courgette, trimmed and thinly sliced
1 green courgette, trimmed and thinly sliced
50g black olives, stones removed and cut in half
1 bunch basil, chopped
1 tbsp olive oil
3 lemon sole, skinned and filleted to make 12 fillets
50g butter
50ml white wine
sea salt and freshly ground black pepper

Tip: Serve the parcels just as they are, so people can open them up at the table. With the steam billowing out, and the room filling with delicious smells, the effect is really theatrical and great fun.

Mini stargazey pies

by Tristan Welch

So called because the heads of the fish look out from the pastry crust to gaze upward at the stars. Tristan's imaginative twist on a Cornish classic is sure to wow your guests.

Serves 4

You'll need a small (4cm) pastry cutter

for the mustard sauce
250ml chicken stock
125g crème fraîche
25g English mustard
pinch salt
½ tsp mustard powder
squeeze of lemon juice

for the pies
16 baby onions, peeled
250g ready-roll all-butter
    puff pastry
1 egg yolk, beaten
4–8 sardines, filleted,
    carcasses and heads
    reserved
1–2 tbsp rapeseed oil
25g butter
150g diced streaky bacon
    or lardons
1 tbsp white wine vinegar
16 quail eggs
sea salt and freshly ground
    black pepper

For the mustard sauce, bring the stock to the boil in a non-reactive saucepan. Whisk in the other ingredients until well combined. Bring back to the simmer. Taste to check for the right amount of mustard and seasoning, then pass the sauce through a fine sieve into a jug and set aside.

For the pie, bring a pan of water to the boil and cook the baby onions for 6–7 minutes, or until tender. Drain and refresh in cold water, then slice each onion in half. Set aside.

Preheat the oven to 200°C/400°F/Gas 6.

Roll out the puff pastry until 3–4mm thick, then cut into 4 equal-sized squares. Using a small circular pastry cutter the size of a golf ball, cut out 2 holes in each pastry square. Place each square onto a baking tray and brush with the beaten egg yolk. Chill in the fridge for 15 minutes.

Bake the pastry squares in the oven for 18–20 minutes, or until deep golden brown and crisp. Remove from the oven and set aside.

Turn the grill on to high.

Place the sardine fillets, heads and tails on a solid grill tray, brush with the rapeseed oil and season with sea salt and freshly ground black pepper. Grill for 2–3 minutes, or until golden-brown and just cooked through (the fish should be opaque all the way through and flake easily).

Heat a frying pan until medium hot, add the butter and bacon lardons and fry gently for 3–4 minutes, or until golden-brown. Add the onions and stir in enough sauce to coat all the ingredients in the pan. Reserve the remaining sauce and keep warm.

Bring a small pan of water to the boil, add the vinegar and a pinch of salt. Reduce the heat to a simmer.

Crack the quail eggs into a small bowl of iced water, then pour off any excess (there should only be enough water to just cover the eggs). Swirl the simmering water with a wooden spoon to create a whirlpool effect, then gently pour the quail eggs into the centre of the whirlpool. Poach for about 1–2 minutes, or until the egg whites have set and the yolk is still runny. Remove with a slotted spoon and drain on kitchen paper.

To assemble the pies on each serving plate, place the onions and bacon on the bottom, arrange the sardine fillets on next and place 4 eggs around each fillet. Hand blend the sauce and spoon over the froth (to keep the dish light). Top with the puff pastry, poke the heads and tails out of the holes and serve.

Spoots with diced veg, chorizo and sautéed squid

by Tom Kitchin

Tom says, 'A great shellfish to try is razor clams, or spoots as we call them in Scotland because of the way they "spoot" the water out. I would always recommend buying them live to ensure that they are absolutely fresh. And use the cooking liquid to make the accompanying sauce. The result is a well-balanced, tasty and fresh dish with really subtle flavours.'

Heat a large pan with a tight fitting lid over a high heat. When the pan is hot, add the razor clams, shallots and white wine and immediately cover the pan with the lid so that the clams steam. After 30 seconds, all the razor clams should spring open. Strain the cooking liquid from the steamed razor clams into a clean pan. Set aside.

When the razor clams are cool enough to handle, remove the clam flesh from the shells using your hands (reserving the shells for serving), and discard any that have not opened fully during cooking.

Slice the razor clam meat thinly at an angle around the brown intestine then set aside.

Heat 1 teaspoon of the vegetable oil in a frying pan over a medium heat. Add the chopped carrot, courgette and fennel and gently sauté for 3–4 minutes, or until softened. Set aside.

Return the reserved cooking liquid to the heat and bring to a simmer. Continue to simmer until the volume of liquid has reduced by half. Add the chopped chorizo, cream, the finely chopped veg, broad beans, fresh chives or parsley and anchovy fillets to the cooking liquid. Stir well.

Once the cream thickens slightly, add the sliced razor clams, lemon zest and juice, and finish with a knob of butter. Stir well until the butter has melted. The key to enjoying the tastiest razor clams is to not overcook them. As soon as the shells open, remove from the heat as they will become very tough if overcooked.

Heat the remaining teaspoon of vegetable oil in a frying pan over a high heat. Season the squid meat, to taste, with sea salt and freshly ground black pepper. When the oil is smoking, add the seasoned squid to the pan and fry for 1–2 minutes, or until the flesh has turned opaque. (Be careful not to overcook or the squid meat will be tough.)

To serve, place 2 razor shells into each of 2 serving bowls and pile in the razor clams, vegetables and creamy juices. Put the squid on top and garnish with the fresh herbs and edible flowers, if using.

Serves 2

8 razor clams, washed well under running water to remove any grit
2 shallots, peeled, finely chopped
110ml white wine
2 tsp vegetable oil
1 carrot, peeled and finely diced
1 courgette, peeled and finely diced
1 fennel, finely diced
110g chorizo, finely diced
110ml whipping cream
110g broad beans (podded weight), pods removed, inner membranes removed
50g chives or parsley, finely chopped
3 anchovy fillets, finely chopped
1 lemon, zest and juice
25g butter
110g squid, cleaned, flesh cut into triangles (ask your fishmonger to do this)
sea salt and freshly ground black pepper

for the garnish (optional)
3 sprigs dill, chopped
1 bunch chives, chopped
1 bunch amaranth leaves
2 sprigs chervil, leaves only
10g wild edible flowers

Murg Adraki (ginger chicken)

by Atul Kochhar

The warmth and fragrance of ginger is at the heart of this classic north Indian dish. Atul's sophisticated twist, with chicken roulades sliced into rounds, looks sensational but is straightforward enough to master at home.

For the chutney, heat 2 tablespoons of the oil in a frying pan, fry the cumin seeds for 1–2 minutes then add the sesame seeds, ginger and green chilli and season with a little salt. Stir for 2–3 minutes and then cover the mixture with a circle of greaseproof paper and let it cook slowly for 40–45 minutes until the ginger is almost cooked.

Let the mixture cool then transfer to a food processor and blend to a fine paste with the tamarind paste and palm sugar.

Heat the remaining oil in a separate pan, add the asafoetida, red chilli and mustard seeds. As the mustard seeds pop, add the curry leaves, stir for 30 seconds then pour into the ginger chutney mixture and mix well. Set aside.

Meanwhile, prepare the chicken. Place each breast of chicken on a large piece of cling film and flatten them with a meat mallet. Mix the minced chicken breast with the spring onion, ginger, garam masala and a little salt and divide into 4 portions.

Place 1 portion of mince on a flattened chicken breast and roll into a roulade with the cling film. Tighten the ends of cling film by twisting and tying a knot on each end.

Bring the chicken stock to a simmer in a saucepan and poach the roulades for 25–30 minutes or until the chicken is completely cooked through. Remove the roulades from the stock and let cool. Heat a little oil in a frying pan. Remove the cling film from the chicken roulades and sear them on all sides until lightly coloured and crisp.

While the chicken is poaching, make the sauce. Heat the oil in a pan, gently fry the cumin seeds and ginger then add the green chilli and chopped onions. Fry until the onions are caramelised to a golden-brown then add the chilli powder, coriander and turmeric. Cook for 2–3 minutes then season with salt and add the chopped tomatoes.

When the tomatoes have softened, place the mixture in a food processor and blend to a fine paste, moistened with a little stock if necessary. Set the sauce aside and keep warm.

To serve, trim the sides of the chicken to form even cylinders and then cut into 3 equal pieces. Spoon the sauce and chutney on the plate and place 3 pieces of roulade on top of the sauce. Garnish with the fried ginger and cress leaves.

Serves 4

for the chutney
2½ tbsp rapeseed oil
1 tsp cumin seeds
2 tsp sesame seeds
200g fresh ginger, thinly sliced
1 fresh green chilli, slit open
100g tamarind paste
100g palm sugar
pinch asafoetida
1 dried red chilli
½ tsp mustard seeds
5–6 curry leaves
salt, to taste

for the chicken
4 chicken breasts, skin on
300g chicken breast, minced
1 spring onion, chopped
2 tbsp ginger, finely chopped
pinch garam masala
salt, to taste
1 litre chicken stock
oil, for frying

for the sauce
2 tbsp rapeseed oil
1 tsp cumin seeds
50g fresh ginger, chopped
1 green chilli, slit open
2 onions, finely chopped
1 tsp red chilli powder
2 tsp ground coriander
1 tsp turmeric
salt, to taste
2 tomatoes, chopped

for the garnish
fresh ginger, julienned and crisp fried
celery cress

Spatchcocked poussin with a chimichurri sauce

by Stuart Gillies

A poussin is fantastic here, but if you have more mouths to feed, use chicken, partridge or even grouse and simply increase the cooking time. Spatchcocked poussin take no time to cook and the result is wonderfully juicy, tender meat.

You can ask your butcher to spatchcock the poussin for you, but if you are doing it yourself, use some strong, sharp scissors to cut down either side of the spine, take out the backbone, then press down on the breast of the poussin to open it out flat.

To make the chimichurri sauce, mix the shallots, parsley, chillies, oregano and chives together in a bowl. Stir in the vinegar, olive oil, Tabasco sauce and lemon juice.

Preheat the grill to medium-high.

Heat an ovenproof griddle pan until hot. Place the poussins and lemon halves onto the griddle pan and fry for 2–3 minutes on each side, or until golden-brown on both sides.

Transfer to the grill and cook for about 8–10 minutes, or until cooked through. Squeeze the roasted lemon halves over the poussins (take care as the lemon halves will be hot).

To serve, spoon the dressing straight onto the chicken and spread it over the top, and if you like, pile some celery, blue cheese and walnut salad alongside.

Serves 4

4 poussin, spatchcocked and
    backbone removed

for the chimichurri sauce
3 tbsp shallots, finely
    chopped
1 bunch flat-leaf parsley,
    finely chopped
2 jalapeño chillies, roughly
    chopped
2 tbsp chopped oregano
½ bunch chives, finely
    chopped
2 tbsp sherry vinegar
2 tbsp olive oil
splash Tabasco sauce
½ lemon, juiced
2 lemons, halved
creamy celery and walnut
    salad (page 159), to serve

Rabbit with Moroccan-style couscous and calamari

by Shaun Rankin

If you've never eaten rabbit before, this recipe is a good place to start. Ask your butcher to remove the loins from the rabbit saddle together with any sinew, so that you are left with two clean fillets.

Lay the loin fillets side by side, top to tail, so they form an even shape together.

Carefully wrap the pancetta or Parma ham around both the fillets, making sure you overlap the slices so the fillets are covered as a single piece. Lay some cling film on a flat surface, place the covered loin about 5cm from one edge and then roll it up into a tight sausage. Tie the cling film in knots at both ends, forcing any air out.

Warm the chicken stock in a saucepan. Place the couscous grains in a bowl and pour over the hot chicken stock. Cover the bowl with cling film and leave in a warm place for 5 minutes. To finish the couscous, run a fork through to fluff up the grains then add 1 tablespoon of the olive oil together with the mixed herbs, black olives, sun-blushed tomatoes and toasted pine nuts. Finish with a squeeze of lemon juice and season with salt and freshly ground pepper. Keep warm.

Steam the rolled loin for 4 minutes. Remove the rabbit from the steamer and, once cool enough to touch, carefully remove the cling film.

Heat 1 tablespoon of the olive oil in a frying pan, add the rabbit fillet roll and cook for 2–3 minutes, or until the pancetta is golden-brown. Add the remaining tablespoon of olive oil in a separate frying pan, add the squid strips and fry for 20 seconds. Remove the pan from the heat.

Cut the rabbit into 1cm slices. Melt the butter in a saucepan and add a good squeeze of lemon juice. Keep warm.

To serve, spoon the warm couscous onto serving plates and arrange the rabbit on top.

Add the calamari to the dish and drizzle with the lemon butter. Season with sea salt and freshly ground black pepper.

Serves 2

1 rabbit saddle, cleaned and boned
6 slices of pancetta or Parma ham
200ml chicken stock
150g couscous
3 tbsp olive oil
2 tbsp chopped mixed herbs such as dill, tarragon and coriander
20g pitted black olives, sliced
20g sun-blushed tomatoes, halved
20g pine nuts, toasted in a dry frying pan
½ lemon, juiced
50g squid strips, cleaned
20g butter
sea salt and freshly ground black pepper

Veal cutlet with a burnt chilli courgette pickle

by Nic Watt

Nic's deliciously different veal recipe is great for a dinner party. The marinade takes a few minutes to mix together. Leave it for 24 hours and you will have a dish packed full of Japanese flavour that can be cooked in a flash.

Combine the miso, ginger, yuzu or lemon zest, shallot, garlic, shichimi pepper (or chilli powder), soy, sake, mirin and oil in a shallow dish. Whisk together until well combined, then add the veal cutlets to the dish and rub the marinade all over them. Marinade for 24 hours. In hot weather, store the marinating veal in the fridge, but let it come to room temperature for half an hour or so before cooking and pat dry with kitchen paper.

For the burnt chilli courgette pickle, blacken the chilli using a mini blowtorch, or by holding the chilli with metal tongs over a gas flame. Roughly chop the chilli, including the blackened skin and seeds.

Cut the courgette on the diagonal, then make 3 cuts, following the diagonal, 2–3mm apart, but not going all the way through. Make a final cut all the way through – you will have a little fan of courgette. Repeat with the remaining courgettes.

Season the sliced courgette with sea salt and allow to stand for a few minutes, just enough to soften. Pour over the sushi vinegar. Combine the red chilli, courgette, ruby grapefruit segments and coriander in a small bowl.

Preheat the oven to 180°C/350°F/Gas 4 and preheat a griddle to hot.

Griddle the veal cutlets on each side until browned. Transfer to a roasting tray and roast for about 6 minutes, turning once in the oven. Allow the veal cutlets to rest for a couple of minutes.

Squeeze a little ginger juice over the resting cutlet and serve with the burnt chilli courgette pickle.

....

Tip: A splash of fresh ginger juice adds zest and flavour to this dish. To make your own, grate fresh ginger, wrap up the shredded root in cheesecloth and press hard to squeeze out the juice.

Serves 4

for the veal cutlets
3 tbsp barley miso
3 tbsp finely chopped fresh ginger
3 tbsp yuzu (or lemon) zest, finely diced
2 tbsp finely chopped shallot
1 tsp crushed garlic
pinch shichimi pepper or red chilli powder
2 tsp soy sauce
2 tsp sake
2 tsp mirin
4 tbsp rice bran oil (available online)
4 x 250g veal cutlets, bone in

for the burnt chilli courgette pickle
1 red chilli
1 yellow courgette, halved lengthways
1 green courgette, halved lengthways
pinch sea salt
3 tbsp sushi vinegar
½ ruby grapefruit, cut into segments
5–6 sprigs coriander
fresh ginger juice, to taste

Breast of lamb with apricots and almonds

by Jun Tanaka

Jun uses an economical cut of lamb to produce a sensational dish. Serve alongside his bulgar wheat salad (page 168) for a delicious balance of flavours.

For the almond paste, put the almonds, garlic, vinegar and bread into a food processor and blend until smooth. With the motor running, slowly add the olive oil followed by the water. Season, to taste, with sea salt and freshly ground black pepper. Cover and set aside.

For the lamb, season the breast with sea salt and freshly ground black pepper and sprinkle the chopped herbs on the inside. Roll the lamb breast up and secure with string.

Place the lamb breast into a pan, pour over the duck fat and simmer gently for 1½ hours.

Remove the lamb breast from the pan, remove the string, wrap in cling film and chill briefly in the fridge.

Meanwhile, melt the butter in a frying pan, add the apricots and almonds, fry for 1–2 minutes, then stir in the honey. Season, to taste, with sea salt and freshly ground black pepper.

To serve, preheat the oven to 180°C/350°F/Gas 4.

Slice the lamb into ½cm slices, place on a baking tray and warm in the oven for 1 minute.

Spoon a thin layer of almond paste onto serving plates and top with the lamb. Scatter the almonds and apricots on the lamb.

Serves 4

1kg breast of lamb, bones removed
1 tsp finely chopped rosemary
1 tsp finely chopped thyme
1 litre duck fat
25g butter
3 fresh apricots, stone removed, sliced into wedges
110g whole almonds
1 tbsp honey
sea salt and freshly ground black pepper

for the almond paste
100g flaked almonds, toasted
1 small garlic clove
25ml sherry vinegar
½ slice white bread, soaked in water
20ml olive oil
75ml water
sea salt and freshly ground black pepper

Tip: Lamb breast is full of flavour, but it needs long, slow cooking to tenderise the otherwise tough, scraggy meat. Any fat that floats to the top can be skimmed off during the cooking process.

Pork schnitzel with fried egg and apple
by Tom Kerridge

Tom reminds us of the winning combination of pork and apple with his simple autumn dish, which combines generosity of flavour with an elegant presentation. This is a real dinner party pleaser, especially if you get your hands on some luxurious duck eggs.

Put the peppercorns, star anise and cloves into a small, sealed muslin bag. Place the bag into a saucepan along with the vinegar and 100g of the sugar and bring to the boil. Then remove from the heat and leave to cool.

With a small melon baller (or a tablespoon), shape the apples into balls and add them to the vinegar mixture. Set aside for at least 10 minutes for the apples to absorb the vinegar.

Bring 100ml of water, the remaining caster sugar and the lemon juice to the boil in a saucepan. Add the diced Bramley apple and cook until soft. Remove from the heat, cool slightly, then blend with a hand-blender and pass through a sieve into a clean saucepan.

Cut the pork tenderloins in half and place beween 2 sheets of cling film. Using a meat mallet, or a rolling pin, bash to about 1cm thick. Remove the cling film. Tip the flour, eggs and breadcrumbs into separate shallow dishes. Place the pork slices in the flour, then the egg and then the breadcrumbs, tossing to coat thoroughly.

Heat a non-stick frying pan until hot, add a little oil and butter and fry the pork on each side until golden-brown and just cooked through. In a separate frying pan, heat a little oil and butter and fry the duck eggs, season with sea salt and freshly ground black pepper and place on top of the pork.

Bring the butter and 200ml of water up to the boil in a small saucepan, season and add the sliced celery. Cook until the celery just loses its bite. Drain well.

To serve, reheat the apple purée, if necessary, and serve the pork with the apple purée, pickled apple and celery around, garnished with celery leaves.

Serves 4

5 peppercorns
2 star anise
4 cloves
110ml white wine vinegar
125g caster sugar
2 classic English apples
1 lemon, juiced
1 Bramley apple, peeled
    and diced
2 x 400g pork tenderloins,
    trimmed of excess fat
75g plain flour
3 eggs, lightly beaten
125g breadcrumbs
vegetable oil and butter,
    for frying
4 duck (or hen's) eggs
50g butter
4 celery sticks, peeled
    and sliced
celery leaves, for garnish
sea salt and freshly ground
    black pepper

Wagyu beef with beetroot, kale and sautéed potatoes

by Galton Blackiston

The wonderful earthy flavours of curly kale, shallot rings and potatoes make the most of Galton's top-quality beef. Wagyu (which means 'Japanese cattle') refers to several breeds of cattle genetically predisposed to intense marbling and a high percentage of fat, producing a meat that is extraordinarily tender and flavourful. You can order the wagyu ahead from your butcher, or subsitute with the best-quality beef available.

To make the beetroot purée, place the beetroot and salt in a saucepan over a medium heat and completely submerge in the apple juice. Cover with a lid and cook until the beetroot is tender. Remove from the heat, pour out a little of the juice and blitz the rest in a food processor, using the reserved juice if necessary to thin the purée a little. You want it thick and velvety. Season with sea salt and freshly ground black pepper, to taste.

For the kale, bring a pan of salted water to the boil, and half fill a large bowl with iced-water. Add the kale to the boiling water and cook for 2 minutes, until tender, drain, dunk into the bowl of iced-water, then drain and squeeze out any excess water.

For the shallot rings, heat a deep-fat fryer to 190°C/375°F, or alternatively heat vegetable oil in a deep-sided, heavy-bottomed pan until a breadcrumb sizzles and turns golden-brown when dropped into it.

Set up 3 bowls, one with the flour, another with the beaten egg and a third with the breadcrumbs. Dredge the shallot rings first in the flour, then the egg, then the breadcrumbs. Gently lower them into the hot oil and deep fry until golden-brown. Remove with a slotted spoon and then drain onto kitchen paper.

For the potatoes, cook the potatoes in boiling salted water with a sprig of mint. Once tender, drain, and cut in half. Heat the butter and rapeseed oil in a large frying pan over a medium–hot heat, add the potatoes and gently fry until golden-brown. Season with sea salt and freshly ground black pepper, and add the chopped mint.

Heat the rapeseed oil in a frying pan till hot. Season the beef all over with sea salt and freshly ground black pepper. Add a knob of butter to the hot pan and pan fry on both sides till coloured. Because of the finely marbled fat, take care not to overcook the meat as the fat melts quickly and burns easily – you'll need 2–3 minutes each side. Remove the beef from the pan and set aside to rest for a couple of minutes.

Serves 4

for the beetroot purée
250g raw beetroot, peeled and diced
300–400ml apple juice
sea salt and freshly ground black pepper

for the kale
250g kale, leaves picked
knob butter
freshly ground black pepper

for the shallot rings
vegetable oil, for deep-fat frying
50g plain flour
2 eggs, lightly beaten
75g breadcrumbs
1 banana shallot, peeled, sliced thinly

for the sautéed potatoes
400g new potatoes
3 sprigs mint, leaves finely chopped
1 tbsp rapeseed oil
50g butter
sea salt and freshly ground black pepper

for the wagyu beef
1 tbsp rapeseed oil
knob butter
4 x 150g 1cm thick steaks from the wagyu feather blade (or rump)
150ml beef jus, or reduced beef stock
sea salt and freshly ground black pepper

Heat the beef jus through in a small pan, ready to serve. If you don't have beef jus, add good-quality beef stock to the pan used to cook the beef, and cook over a medium heat until the volume has reduced and it has thickened and become flavoursome.

To serve, melt a knob of butter in a pan over a medium heat, add the kale, heat through and finish with a twist of freshly ground pepper. Spoon the beetroot purée onto each plate and top with the beef. Place the curly kale and potatoes alongside, spoon over the delicious beef jus and top with shallot rings.

The ultimate cottage pie

by Adam Byatt

Adam's beef short rib and onion cottage pie is heartwarming and fabulously swanky, with sparkling sprigs of rosemary adding drama to the traditional humble pie. 'It's difficult to impress with a dish everyone's mum cooked,' says Adam, 'so you've got to go all out to make it special.' The meat and veg mix can be made the day before serving and kept in the fridge. Or you can freeze it in individual portions for up to three months.

With a large knife, cut through the meat that lies between each of the rib bones so that you have 8 pieces in total (or ask your butcher to do this for you).

Cook the sliced onions with a drizzle of vegetable oil in a saucepan over a medium heat. Don't add any seasoning as you want the onions to caramelise completely – this will take up to 20 minutes.

Put the sliced carrots into a saucepan over a high heat with a splash of vegetable oil. Season with salt (to prevent the carrots from colouring too quickly) and add the star anise to the pan. Cook for 2 minutes, then turn the heat down to medium and continue cooking for about 10 minutes, stirring regularly, until the carrots just start to soften.

Prepare the mash and transfer to a piping bag if you have one (or a small plastic bag with the tip snipped off), then set aside until ready to use. Preheat the oven to 150°C/300°C fan/Gas 2.

Lightly season the ribs with salt and pepper. Splash some vegetable oil into a very large flameproof casserole dish and place over a medium heat until very hot, then add the seasoned short ribs. Fry until lightly browned on all sides. Remove the ribs from the pan and place onto a wire rack suspended over a tray.

Place the empty pan back on the heat and add the roughly chopped vegetables, the garlic halves, peppercorns and thyme. Cook for 5 minutes or until golden.

Pour the wine and port into the pan, bring to a boil and then reduce the heat to a simmer. Cook until syrup-like in consistency and reduced in volume by three-quarters.

Return the ribs to the pan with any juices that have gathered in the resting tray, cover with the stock and bring to a simmer. Skim off any impurities, then cover the surface of the liquid with a 'lid' of parchment paper and place the pan in the oven. Cook for just under 3 hours until the meat is tender and falling off the bones.

Continued overleaf

Serves 4

You'll need 4 individual cast iron or earthenware dishes

4kg beef short ribs (also known as Jacob's ladder)
6 onions, peeled, 3 thinly sliced, 3 chopped
50ml vegetable oil
6 carrots, 4 thinly sliced, 2 roughly chopped
4 star anise
1 quantity classic mash (page 214)
1 leek, roughly chopped
1 head garlic, cut in half crossways
2 tsp black peppercorns
6 sprigs thyme, leaves only
300ml red wine
110ml port
4 litres beef stock
4 pieces centre-cut bone marrow (10cm long, cleaned of any sinew)
1 bunch fresh rosemary, to serve
sea salt and freshly ground black pepper

Remove the pan from the oven and leave to cool, then take the meat out and set aside. Pass the cooking liquid through a fine sieve into a clean pan and reduce by half, skimming off any impurities during the process. Remove the meat from the bones, discarding any sinew, and shred the meat into long strips with your fingers. Combine the reduced cooking liquid with the shredded meat, caramelised onions and carrots (without the star anise).

Preheat the oven to 200°C/400°F/Gas 6.

Divide the mixture equally between 4 ovenproof dishes and place a piece of bone marrow in the middle. Pipe the mash around the bones (or use a spoon if you don't have a piping bag) and fill the bones with sprigs of rosemary.

Place the dishes in the oven and cook for 15–20 minutes, or until golden and bubbling. Serve hot, with the rosemary set alight.

....

Tip: Adam sets light to the rosemary just before bringing his pies to the table. It's a great way to create drama and provides a wonderful aroma too.

Spicy sticky ribs with sweet shallots and peanuts

by Paul Rankin

These spicy, sticky ribs are tender and wickedly moreish; excellent for a laid-back evening with friends when nobody minds getting their fingers dirty. The ribs take a couple of hours to cook, which gives you plenty of time to get on with other things.

Preheat the oven to 180°C/350°F/Gas 4.

Cut the ribs into 2 or 3 pieces and place in a large, flameproof roasting tray. Mix the rest of the ingredients until well combined and pour over the ribs. Toss lightly.

Set the roasting tray over a medium flame and bring to the boil. Cover tightly with foil and place in the oven for 2 hours, turning the ribs in their cooking liquor every 20 minutes.

Increase the oven temperature to 220°C/425°F/Gas 7. Remove the foil and continue basting the ribs every 5 minutes or so, until the sauce has reduced to a shining glaze.

Meanwhile, for the sweet shallots and peanuts, heat the oil in a large heavy frying pan, add the shallots, garlic and a good pinch of salt. Cook for 4–5 minutes, or until golden-brown. Add the chillies and the sugar and continue cooking until lightly caramelised. Toss in the spring onions followed by the crushed peanuts.

Allow the ribs to cool slightly then serve with Thai sticky rice or plain Jasmine rice, and the sweet shallots and peanuts.

....

Tip: Adding water to the roasting tray will create steam to keep the meat moist, while keeping the bottom of the pan and foil from scorching.

Serves 4

for the ribs
1.5kg pork ribs
250ml water
125ml Chinese rice wine
   (Shaoxing)
1 tsp salt
4 tbsp dark soy sauce
3 star anise
1 cinnamon stick
4 garlic cloves, crushed
5 large slices of fresh ginger
2 spring onions, roughly
   chopped
pinch chilli flakes
2 pieces dried tangerine peel
110g demerara sugar

for the sweet shallots
and peanuts
4 tbsp vegetable oil
2 banana shallots,
   finely sliced
3 garlic cloves, finely sliced
good pinch salt
2 large red chillies,
   finely sliced
1 tbsp caster sugar
2 spring onions, finely sliced
3 tbsp crushed peanuts

A modern steak and chips

by Anna Hansen

The Modern Pantry's Anna Hansen is full of fresh ideas about fusion food. Here she brings an Asian twist to a classic British dish with her tamarind and miso-marinated steak with besan chips. Onglet steak, otherwise known as skirt or hanger steak, is an inexpensive cut of meat and full of flavour. It should be served rare or medium rare.

For the den miso, place all the ingredients into a saucepan and whisk over a medium heat until the sugar and miso have completely dissolved. Remove the pan from the heat and set aside to cool. Store in an airtight container in the fridge.

For the steak, mix the tamarind paste, den miso, garlic and thyme in a bowl until well combined. Coat the steaks in the marinade and set aside to marinate for at least 3 hours, preferably overnight.

Meanwhile, for the besan chips, heat the oil in a heavy-based saucepan. Add the spices, ginger, chilli and coriander and cook for a few minutes until aromatic.

Sift the chickpea flour into a large bowl, then whisk in the water until smooth. Pour the paste into the saucepan, add the salt and pepper and stir over a moderate heat with a wooden spoon or spatula for 10–12 minutes, or until the mixture thickens and comes away from the sides of the pan (the process is similar to making firm polenta, but the besan takes a little longer to thicken).

Grease a small oven tray and sprinkle with the black onion seeds and a little polenta. Pour over the besan mixture, cover with cling film and quickly flatten out the mixture. Chill in the fridge until the mixture has hardened.

Heat a griddle or a heavy-based frying pan over a high heat until hot but not smoking (if the pan is too hot, the outside of the meat will burn before it has cooked enough). Brush the steaks with the oil and season with sea salt and freshly ground black pepper. Cook for a couple of minutes on each side, or until cooked to your liking. Transfer the steaks from the pan to a rack, cover with foil and set aside to rest on a plate for about 10 minutes. This helps the meat to 'relax' and maximises taste and tenderness.

Continued overleaf

Serves 6

for the den miso
25ml sake
25ml mirin
150g white miso
75g caster sugar

for the steak
125g tamarind paste
75ml den miso (see recipe above)
2 garlic cloves, finely sliced
1 tsp chopped thyme
6 x 150–175g onglet steaks, trimmed
50ml olive oil
sea salt and freshly ground black pepper

for the besan chips
1 tbsp vegetable oil, plus extra for greasing and deep-frying
1 tsp cumin seeds
15 fresh curry leaves, chopped
1 tsp ground turmeric
1 tbsp minced fresh ginger
½ green chilli, finely chopped
½ bunch coriander, finely chopped
200g chickpea or gram flour
600ml water
½ tsp salt
¼ tsp freshly ground black pepper
1 tsp black onion (nigella) seeds
2–3 tbsp polenta

for the watercress
1 tbsp pomegranate molasses (see tip, overleaf)
2 tbsp cider vinegar
5 tbsp extra virgin olive oil
2 bunches watercress

Preheat a deep-fat fryer to 180°C/350°F. Carefully turn the hardened besan out onto a chopping board and cut into chips, then dust with polenta. Deep-fry for 2–3 minutes, or until golden-brown. Remove the chips from the pan with a slotted spoon and set aside to drain on kitchen paper.

To make the watercress salad, whisk the pomegranate molasses, vinegar and olive oil together in a small bowl, and season with salt and pepper. Place the watercress in a large salad bowl, pour over the dressing and toss well so that everything gets coated.

....

Tip: Pomegranate molasses is a thick tangy syrup that can be used to boost flavour in a whole range of dips, dresses and glazes. You can find it in most larger supermarkets and Middle Eastern stores, but you can easily make your own. Simply pour a 710ml bottle of pomegranate juice into a saucepan, along with 60g sugar and the juice of a large juicy lemon. Bring to the boil, whisk to melt the sugar and combine the ingredients. Simmer for 1 hour, until the juice reduces down to about a quarter. Remove from the heat and let it cool for 30 minutes in the pan. The molasses has a syrupy consistency that will thicken as it cools. While still warm but not boiling, pour into a sterilised jar where it will keep for up to 6 months in the fridge.

Beef stroganoff

by Lawrence Keogh

Lawrence's luxurious take on the great Russian classic makes an easy supper for family and friends. A deeply savoury casserole, with a comforting creamy sauce, it tastes even better the next day.

For the rice, preheat the oven to 200°C/400°F/Gas 6.

Heat an ovenproof sauté pan until hot, add half the butter and the onion and sweat for a few minutes until softened but not coloured. Add the rice and stir well then fry for another minute, again without colouring, and add the hot stock, bay leaf, sea salt and freshly ground black pepper.

Bring to the boil, stirring with a wooden spoon, then cover with buttered greaseproof paper and a lid and place in the oven. Cook for 15 minutes until the rice is cooked but firm. Remove the bay leaf, add the last of the butter and separate the grains of rice with a fork. Season with salt and pepper, then transfer to a clean warmed serving dish and keep covered with a clean piece of greaseproof paper until ready to serve.

Meanwhile, make the stroganoff. Sprinkle the beef strips with the paprika and season with salt and pepper. Heat a large frying pan with the vegetable oil. Quickly flash-fry the beef strips, making sure you keep them as rare as possible, then tip the meat into a colander, rseerving any juices that drain off.

Using the same pan add the butter, shallots and sliced mushrooms and cook these for 1 minute. Add the tomato purée and cook a few more minutes, stirring the ingredients together. Add the white wine vinegar and cook until completely evaporated. Add the white wine and cook until reduced by half, then pour in the double cream, bring to a boil, and season with salt and pepper.

Add the seared beef and the reserved juice and gently warm through, taking care not to boil or you will overcook the beef.

To serve, pour the stroganoff into a large warmed serving dish and sprinkle with dill pickle. Zig zag the soured cream over the top then sprinkle with chopped parsley and a dust of paprika. Serve with the rice alongside, and a simple green salad would be lovely too.

Serves 4

for the pilau rice
50g butter
50g onion, chopped
250g basmati rice
500ml hot chicken stock
1 bay leaf
sea salt and freshly ground
   black pepper

for the stroganoff
450g tail end beef fillet, cut
   into long strips
1 tsp hot paprika
2 tsp sweet paprika
2 tbsp vegetable oil
30g butter
2 shallots, finely chopped
115g button mushrooms,
   sliced
1 tsp tomato purée
50ml white wine vinegar
75ml white wine
200ml double cream
115g dill pickle, julienned
125ml soured cream
1 tbsp finely chopped
   flat-leaf parsley
pinch sweet paprika
sea salt and freshly ground
   black pepper

puddings

As a fortunate and frequent guest chef on *Saturday Kitchen*, I particularly enjoy making a pudding, even more than a savoury dish, because I have such a sweet tooth. Desserts are a lifelong passion that has led me to achieve one of the greatest recognitions in my career, *Meilleur Ouvrier de France en pâtisserie* (one of the Best Craftsmen of France in pastry).

I am so happy that some of my favourite desserts are featured in this mouth-watering collection amongst those of my colleagues and friends. I cannot resist congratulating James Martin on his delicate peach and raspberry pavlovas, and a delightfully simple jam roly poly. He is certainly an inspiring, multi-faceted chef.

The recipes in this chapter offer the perfect solution for any occasion, from the fragrant indulgence of my spiced roasted pineapple to the extraordinary and inventive red wine soufflé by Will Holland.

Our cooking experience on the live show no doubt seems very familiar to the busy food lover at home with little time to produce a stunning finale to a meal with friends or a sweet family treat. We have six to eight minutes maximum on the live show to make our desserts, so there is no room for hesitation or the smallest mistake. But with a little planning, and some coordination, you can rest assured that everything in this book can be assembled in a few minutes, look stunning and taste great.

As busy as I am in my life, I never turn down the opportunity to appear on *Saturday Kitchen* because it is the most pleasurable albeit gruelling challenge. When I am at home in Switzerland, I love catching up on the show, for entertainment and also to check out the new dishes. I hope you have as much fun making these puddings at home as we all had preparing them in the studio.

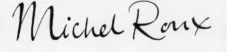

Crêpes with orange butter sauce
by Michel Roux

Fragrant with orange blossom water, these thin citrus pancakes make a beautiful dessert. For the best results, use a clean, smooth-surfaced frying pan, ideally non-stick. And be prepared to sacrifice the first couple of crêpes, while you get the temperature of the pan and the spoonfuls right – the more you make, the better they'll be.

In a food processor or large bowl, add the flour, sugar, salt, eggs and a third of the milk and mix to a smooth batter. Gradually stir in the rest of the milk and all of the cream, checking for lumps. Leave the batter to rest in a warm place for about 1 hour. Just before cooking, stir in the orange flower water.

Brush a small (18cm–20cm) frying pan with a little of the clarified butter and place over a medium heat. When it's nice and hot, ladle in the batter and gently rotate the pan evenly to cover the base in a thin layer of batter.

Return the pan to the heat and cook for 1 minute on each side, or until the edges start to brown and the surface dries. Don't be tempted to toss them, because they're a little delicate. Instead, use a spatula to ease around the edges, loosen, flip and cook the other side.

Stack the crêpes between sheets of greaseproof paper, until all of the batter has been used up. Keep warm in the oven until ready to serve.

For the sauce, strain the orange juice through a sieve into a saucepan and add the icing sugar. Gradually bring the mixture to the boil and cook until the volume of liquid has reduced by half. Turn off the heat and whisk in the butter, a little at a time.

To serve, scatter the orange segments over each crêpe and roll up. Spoon over the orange sauce and garnish with a sprig of mint.

Serves 4

125g plain flour
15g caster sugar
pinch salt
2 eggs
325ml whole milk
50ml double cream
few drops orange
    flower water
20g clarified butter
    (see tip below)

for the orange butter sauce

10 oranges, 6 juiced,
    4 segmented
100g icing sugar
125g butter, diced, softened
4 sprigs mint

Tip: To make your own clarified butter (butter without the milk solids or water) cut 250g unsalted butter into smallish chunks and melt in a heavy saucepan over a gentle heat until the butter breaks down into separate layers. Skim off the white froth from the top, then remove the saucepan from the heat. Let the water and milky residue settle to the bottom of the pan, then carefully pour the clear fat into a storage jar. Leave to cool then cover and keep in the fridge, where it will last a long time.

A classic cherry clafoutis

by Matt Tebbutt

Served with a delicious cherry cream, Matt's summer pudding is super simple – just a layer of sweet batter poured over cherries and baked in the oven – yet so impressive looking. Traditional clafoutis recipes call for leaving the cherry stones in, which adds a subtle almond flavour, but removing them makes the clafoutis quicker to devour.

For the cherry cream, heat the sugar, star anise and 200ml water until simmering. Add the cherries and poach for 2–3 minutes, or until just tender. Remove the cherries and set aside then return the syrup to the heat and continue to cook until thickened. Return the cherries to the syrup and set aside to cool completely. Fold in the whipped cream.

For the clafoutis, preheat the oven to 180°C/350°F/Gas 4. Grease the baking dish.

Place the milk, cream, vanilla pod and seeds into a saucepan over a medium heat, bring to the boil and cook for 1 minute. Discard the vanilla pod (see tip below) and set the mixture to one side.

Whisk the eggs and sugar together in a bowl until light and frothy, then stir in the flour and baking powder. Gradually pour the milk mixture onto the eggs, whisking all the time until the batter is smooth and creamy. Be careful not to overbeat the mix.

Arrange three-quarters of the cherries in the bottom of the ovenproof dish and pour the batter over the fruit. Scatter the remaining cherries over the top. Bake in the oven for 1 hour, or until the pudding is set yet still has a slight wobble in the middle.

Serve the clafoutis warm, topped with a spoonful of the cherry cream.

Tip: Use the vanilla pod to make your own vanilla sugar to use in cakes, bakes or ice creams. Simply put the pod in a jar filled with caster sugar, seal and leave to infuse for a couple of weeks. Alternatively grind the pod in a coffee grinder, add to caster sugar and shake well, for an instant flavouring for your pot of tea, hot chocolate or coffee.

Serves 6–8

You'll need a 20cm ovenproof baking dish

for the cherry cream
200g caster sugar
3 star anise
350g ripe cherries, stones removed
250g double cream, lightly whipped

for the clafoutis
small knob butter, for greasing
125ml whole milk
125ml double cream
1 vanilla pod, split, seeds scraped out (and reserved)
3 large eggs
175g caster sugar
60g plain flour
1 tsp baking powder
600g ripe cherries, stones removed

Orange and almond cake with basil cream

by James Martin

James's deliciously moist almond cake is made with whole oranges: the fruit is simmered until very tender, then roughly chopped. If you want to save time on the day of making, the oranges can be prepared a day or two in advance; once cooled, simply cover and chill in the fridge for 1–2 days, bringing up to room temperature just before using.

Preheat the oven to 180°C/350°F/Gas 4 and grease your cake tin.

Place the whole oranges in a saucepan of simmering water and boil gently for 45–60 minutes, or until very soft. Remove the pan from the heat and leave the oranges to cool in the water. Drain the oranges and roughly chop, discarding the pips.

Add 450g of chopped orange (save any extra for eating!) to a food processor and blend to a purée. Add the sugar, eggs and ground almonds and blitz once more until smooth. Spoon the batter into the cake tin then sprinkle over the flaked almonds.

Bake in the oven for 25 minutes, then cover lightly with foil and bake for a further 25–35 minutes, or until cooked through (a skewer inserted in the middle should come out clean). Remove from the oven and set aside to cool.

Meanwhile, to make the basil cream, heat the basil, sugar and 50ml water in a saucepan until boiling, then simmer for 2 minutes. Blend in a small food processor until smooth, then pass through a fine sieve. Set aside to cool.

Whisk the double cream and vanilla seeds together in a bowl until soft peaks form, then fold in the basil syrup.

Serve the cake as soon as you like, with a generous dollop of basil cream.

Serves 8

You'll need a 23cm springform cake tin

for the cake
3 oranges
225g caster sugar
6 eggs
250g ground almonds
30g flaked almonds

for the basil cream
50g basil leaves, very
    finely chopped
50g caster sugar
150ml double cream
1 vanilla pod, split, seeds
    scraped out (and reserved)

Pastiera di Grano

by Antonio Carluccio

It wouldn't be Easter in Naples without the sweet aromatic tart known as Pastiera di Grano, filled with chewy grains (symbolic of new life), creamy ricotta and candied peel. You can soak the whole wheat a day in advance, or buy cans of cooked wheat, called Grano Cotto per Pastiera, from some Italian delis and online (page 341).

If you're using whole wheat, place the grains in a large bowl, add cold water to cover, put it in the fridge and let it soak for 24 hours, changing the water several times. Drain, then place the wheat in a pan with the milk and lemon zest. Simmer for 3–4 hours over a low heat.

When the grain is tender, add the ground cinnamon, vanilla sugar and orange zest. Remove from the heat, cool, cover and place in the fridge until the next day.

Make the pastry by working together the sugar, butter and egg yolks until smooth, then add the flour and stir to make a smooth dough. Set aside in a cool place for at least one hour.

Preheat the oven to 190°C/375°F/Gas 5.

To continue making the filling, remove the soaked whole wheat from the fridge. Or if you are using the canned cooked wheat, add it to the lemon and orange zest, the ground cinnamon and vanilla sugar.

Beat the ricotta in a large mixing bowl with the egg yolks and the orange water. Add the candied peel and the flavoured grain to the mixture. Beat the egg whites in a separate bowl until stiff, then gradually add the sugar a little at a time until it is all incorporated, and the peaks are light and fluffy. Fold the whites gently into the ricotta mix using a large metal spoon.

Butter the flan tin. Roll two-thirds of the pastry out into a circle that will cover the base of the tin, as well as the sides. Press this pastry into the flan tin, covering the bottom and sides with an equal thickness. Pour in the filling. Roll out the remaining pastry to a circle, then cut it into long strips to form a lattice pattern on top of the tart. Press the ends of the strips against the dough on the sides of the tin, and fold the edge of the crust over the ends of the lattice strips. Press firmly to seal.

Bake in the oven for about 45 minutes or until the cake is golden brown on top and a skewer inserted in the centre comes out clean. Cover with kitchen foil if it is browning too quickly. Allow to cool, then dust with icing sugar.

Serves 6–8

You'll need a 23cm flan tin

for the filling
100g whole wheat grain for soaking, or ½ a 440g can Grano Cotto, drained and rinsed
250ml whole milk (if you are soaking your own wheat)
½ lemon, zest only
½ tsp ground cinnamon
1 tsp vanilla sugar
½ orange, zest only
150g ricotta cheese
2 large eggs, separated
65ml orange flower water
75g candied peel, finely chopped
115g caster sugar
butter, for greasing
icing sugar, for dusting

for the pastry
150g caster sugar
150g butter, cold and cubed
4 large egg yolks
300g plain flour

Peach and raspberry mini pavlovas

by James Martin

Super sweet and fresh, these fruity pavlovas are ideal for summer parties – though you may find it difficult to stop at just one!

For the pavlovas, preheat the oven to 140°C/275°F/Gas 1.

Place the egg whites into a clean bowl and whisk until soft peaks form. Add the sugar, a spoonful at a time, while whisking continuously. Whisk until all of the sugar is incorporated and stiff peaks form. Gently fold in the cornflour and vinegar.

Line a baking tray with parchment paper and place 6 large spoonfuls of pavlova mix onto the tray, in small rounds with a small hollow in the middle. Bake in the oven for 10–12 minutes, or until crisp but not coloured, then turn the oven off and leave for 2–3 hours (or preferably overnight).

For the topping, preheat the oven to 170°C/325°F/Gas 3.

Place 150g of the sugar into a heavy-based saucepan with 50ml water and dissolve over a low heat, stirring occasionally. When the sugar syrup is completely clear, increase the heat and cook for 4–5 minutes, or until the mixture changes colour to a light caramel. Remove from the heat and carefully stir in the orange peach juice (be careful, it will splutter). Set aside to cool.

Use a mini blowtorch to blacken the peach skins, or hold your peaches, one at a time, with a pair of metal tongs over a gas flame until the skin is black, then use a clean cloth to wipe the skins away. Brush the peeled fruit liberally with the soft butter, using a pastry brush. Sprinkle with the remaining sugar, making sure the peaches are thoroughly coated (alternatively, place the sugar on a plate and roll the peaches in it).

Place the peaches in a small roasting tin and spoon the caramel over. Roast in the oven for about 30 minutes, basting the peaches every 10 minutes with the pan juices, until golden-brown and caramelised. Add the raspberries and almonds to the roasting tin during the final 10 minutes of cooking.

To serve, whip the cream in a bowl until soft peaks form. Place a meringue round onto each serving plate. Spoon the whipped cream on top and place a peach in the centre of each meringue. Spoon the orange caramel sauce around and scatter the raspberries and nuts on top.

Serves 6

for the meringues

5 eggs, whites only
    (150g egg whites)
300g caster sugar
2 tsp cornflour
1 tsp white wine vinegar

for the topping

250g caster sugar
250ml fresh orange peach
    juice, or fresh orange juice
3 ripe peaches, stones
    removed, cut in half
50g butter, softened until
    runny but not melted
150g raspberries
110g whole almonds, out of
    their shells
300ml double cream, to serve

Cherry meringues with rhubarb coulis
by Michel Roux

Who better to teach you the art of meringue making than Michel Roux? This elegant dessert is a delight – sweet, sharp, pink and pretty, and bursting with summer flavour.

Wash the cherries in cold water and remove the stones without cutting the cherries entirely in half (a cherry stoner is useful here). Put them into a dish and set aside.

Put 150g caster sugar and 150ml water into a saucepan with the bay leaves and thyme and place onto a medium heat. As soon as the syrup reaches the boil pour it over the cherries, then leave to cool down for at least 2 hours. (If the cherries are not very ripe, add them to the boiling syrup and poach for 2 minutes, then pour into a bowl to cool.)

To make the meringues, preheat the oven to 100°C/200°F/Gas ½ and line a baking sheet with greaseproof paper.

Beat the egg whites with 90g caster sugar until the mixture forms stiff peaks. Add the icing sugar and continue to beat for 4–6 minutes, or until the meringue mixture is smooth and shiny.

Drain the cherries and dab them lightly on kitchen paper to remove as much syrup as possible. Using a large spoon, fold the cherries lightly into the meringue mixture. Using another large spoon, scoop up about a quarter of the mixture to make a rugby ball shape (a quenelle) and place it onto the lined baking sheet. Repeat the process to make 3 more meringues. Cook in the oven for 2 hours.

Once cooked, remove from the oven and allow to cool slightly before removing from the baking tray, using a palette knife. Transfer to a cooling rack and set aside.

For the coulis, place the rhubarb into a saucepan with the sugar, vanilla and 100ml water. Slowly bring to the boil and cook gently until the rhubarb is soft enough to crush with a spoon.

Remove the vanilla pod, tip the coulis mixture into a processor and blend for 2 minutes. Once smooth, sieve the coulis into a bowl (adding a little cold water to thin the sauce, if necessary) and leave to cool.

Place the meringue onto a plate and spoon the rhubarb coulis around the edge. Serve immediately.

Serves 4

for the cherry meringues
300g ripe cherries
240g caster sugar
2 bay leaves
2 sprigs thyme
3 egg whites, at room temperature
90g icing sugar, sieved

for the rhubarb coulis
250g tender young rhubarb stalks, cut into small chunks
100g caster sugar
1 vanilla pod, split lengthways

Red wine soufflé

by Will Holland

Will brings a modern British approach to the classic soufflé. The full-bodied flavours from the wine are balanced beautifully by a mixed berry and mint salad, served alongside.

To make the base, place the cornflour in a mixing bowl and gradually stir in the wine. Transfer to a saucepan and bring to the boil, stirring continuously. Boil for 1 minute then remove the pan from the heat.

Place the sugar in a small pan with a splash of water and boil until it reaches 121°C/250°F, or until it becomes syrupy (take care not to burn the sugar).

Pour the syrup over the cornflour and wine mixture, allow to cool, then transfer to a food processor or blender and blitz until smooth. Chill until ready to use.

For the soufflé, preheat the oven to 180°C/350°F/Gas 4. Butter the ramekins and dust the insides with caster sugar. Whisk the egg whites until they hold soft peaks, then gradually add the sugar and continue whisking until the mixture is glossy.

Place the cold base in a mixing bowl and whisk in half the egg whites. Fold in the rest, ensuring everything is thoroughly amalgamated – the mixture should be one consistency and colour.

Fill the ramekins with the soufflé mix and bake for 8 minutes.

Meanwhile, toss the berries with the sugar and mint leaves and leave to macerate for a couple of minutes.

To serve, spoon the berry salad into 4 small dishes, and top with a spoonful of crème fraîche and a few leaves of basil cress. Place the soufflé alongside and serve immediately.

Serves 4

You'll need four 7.5cm wide and 4cm high ramekins

for the base
4 tsp cornflour
250ml full-bodied red wine (the bigger the better, try Rioja, Shiraz or Bordeaux)
100g caster sugar

for the soufflé
butter, for greasing
caster sugar, for dusting
3 eggs, whites only
30g caster sugar
4 tbsp base (see above)

for the garnish
250g mixed summer berries (strawberries, blueberries, blackberries, raspberries and redcurrants)
2 tbsp caster sugar
2 tsp mint leaves, finely sliced
4 tbsp crème fraîche, to garnish
1 tbsp basil cress (or torn basil leaves), to garnish

Tip: Be certain your soufflé base is cooled to room temperature or below before you fold it into the egg white. A base that is too warm will deflate egg whites. As long as your kitchen is not too warm, the soufflé can sit at room temperature for up to half an hour before you bake.

Victoria sandwich

by James Martin

Layered with cream, jam and fresh raspberries, this is a perennial classic and so simple to bake. Best served with a proper cup of tea.

Preheat the oven to 180°C/350°F/Gas 4. Grease and line the sandwich tins.

Mix the butter, sugar and vanilla essence in a bowl or food processor until well combined.

Slowly beat in the eggs one by one. Fold in the sifted flour and carefully pour the mixture into the prepared tins.

Bake for 20–25 minutes until golden-brown and springy when pressed. Test by pushing a skewer into the centre of the cakes. If the skewer comes out clean, the cakes are ready.

Turn the cakes out onto a wire rack and leave to cool.

Spread one cake with the raspberry jam, followed by the fresh raspberries covered with a layer of whipped cream. Place the other cake on top. Dust finely with icing sugar to finish.

Serves 6–8

You'll need two 20cm sandwich tins

oil, for greasing
200g butter (see tip below)
200g caster sugar
½ tsp vanilla essence
4 eggs (see tip below)
200g self-raising flour, sifted
½ jar raspberry jam
175ml double cream, whipped
250g raspberries
2–3 tbsp icing sugar

Tip: With every recipe, make sure your ingredients are ready before you start. When making a light sponge, eggs should be at room temperature. If they are too cold it will be harder for air to be whisked in, which makes it more likely that the mixture will curdle or separate. For a creamed sponge, the butter should be soft, so take it out of the fridge an hour or so in advance.

Apple croustade with Armagnac custard

by Nick Nairn

Delicate pastry on caramelised apple topped with a rich Armagnac custard. This French-style dessert is so simple to rustle up – like a tart tatin the right way up.

Preheat the oven to 200°C/400°F/Gas 6.

Heat a large frying pan or tarte tatin dish until hot. Sprinkle the caster sugar in an even layer. As you heat the sugar, the edges and bottom will melt first and start browning. With a wooden spatula, gently push the melted sugar toward the centre, to encourage the still-solid sugar to begin caramelising. Once the sugar begins to turn a deep amber colour, add the butter and cook for a further 2–3 minutes.

Remove the pan from the heat and stir in the dried cranberries, sultanas and raisins. Carefully stir in the apple until completely coated in the caramel mixture. Return the pan to the heat and cook for a further 3–4 minutes. Set aside.

Mix the filo pastry strips, cinnamon, clementine zest and lemon zest in a large mixing bowl until the zest and spices coat the pastry, then stir in the clarified butter until it coats the pastry.

Scrunch the coated strips of filo pastry in your hands and place them on top of the caramel mixture in the pan. Transfer the pan to the oven and bake for 10–15 minutes, or until the filo is crispy and golden-brown.

Meanwhile, for the Armagnac custard, whisk the egg yolks and sugar in a bowl until well combined. Heat the milk, cream and Armagnac in a saucepan until just boiling. Remove the pan from the heat, then slowly whisk the warm cream mixture into the egg mixture. Return to the saucepan and cook over a gentle heat for 2–3 minutes, or until the custard is thick enough to coat the back of a spoon.

Serve the croustade in wedges with a generous dollop of custard.

....

Tip: When peeling the apples, be sure to put them in some water with a squeeze of lemon juice so that they don't go brown.

Serves 6

You'll need a 24cm ovenproof frying pan or tarte tatin dish

for the croustade
125g caster sugar
75g butter
50g dried cranberries
50g sultanas
50g raisins
1kg dessert apples, such as Cox's Orange Pippin, peeled, cored and quartered (see tip below)
100g filo pastry, cut into 5cm-wide strips
½ tsp ground cinnamon
1 clementine or small orange, zest only
1 lemon, zest only
75g clarified butter (see tip, page 298)

for the Armagnac custard
4 egg yolks
40g caster sugar
150ml whole milk
150ml double cream
2–3 tbsp Armagnac

Boozy prune tiramisu

by James Martin

*A bit of a store-cupboard wonder. Depending on how extravagant you're feeling,
this rich creamy trifle will indulge a dinner party, or just the two of you...*

For the tiramisu, heat the prunes and brandy in a saucepan until the brandy ignites.
Remove the pan from the heat, cover and set aside to cool. Transfer to a bowl and
chill in the fridge for at least 1 hour.

Meanwhile, whisk the egg yolks and sugar in a bowl until pale and thickened. Gently
beat in the mascarpone until well combined.

In a separate bowl, whisk the egg whites until firm peaks form. Fold into the
mascarpone mixture and set aside to chill in the fridge.

For the praline, line a baking tray with greaseproof paper.

Cook the sugar in a frying pan over a high heat until it has completely melted and
turned golden-brown. Add the chopped hazelnuts and stir until they are coated in the
melted sugar, then pour the mixture onto the prepared baking tray. Set aside until the
mixture has hardened then cover with a sheet of cling film and break into small pieces
using a toffee hammer or rolling pin. Transfer the praline pieces to a food processor
and blitz to fine crumbs.

Dip the sponge fingers into the coffee then lay them in the bottom of a wide
straight-sided serving dish. Spoon over half the brandy prunes, then spread over
half the mascarpone mixture. Repeat with one more layer of each, finishing with the
remaining mascarpone. Sprinkle over the praline. Serve straightaway or place in the
fridge and chill until needed.

Serves 2–4

for the tiramisu
250g good-quality prunes,
    halved, stones removed
75ml brandy
3 eggs, separated
75g caster sugar
250g mascarpone cheese
200g sponge fingers
250ml strong black
    coffee, cooled

for the praline
75g caster sugar
50g chopped hazelnuts
    (see tip below)

....

Tip: You can roast the hazelnuts to intensify their
flavour and loosen their skins. Rub the nuts in a
clean tea towel to remove the skins.

Spiced roasted pineapple

by Michel Roux

Michel's pineapple pud is the ideal finish to a spicy Asian dinner. The coconut rum ice cream (page 322) is a tasty addition, or serve with vanilla ice cream instead.

Place all the syrup ingredients into a saucepan. Slowly bring to the boil over a gentle heat, stirring occasionally. Now simmer over a medium heat to reduce by three-quarters, until it makes a thick syrup. Set aside.

Preheat the oven to 180°C/350°F/Gas 4.

Using a serrated knife, cut a 3cm slice from the top of the pineapple, removing the leaves, and a 2cm slice from the base to enable the pineapple to stand upright. Now working from top to bottom and following the curve of the fruit, remove the peel.

To remove the little black 'eyes', and create an attractive finish at the same time, cut a spiral groove, 5mm deep, around the entire fruit.

Stud the flesh evenly all over with the cloves.

Heat the oil in an oval pan (or one that will take the whole fruit) until very hot, then add the pineapple and lightly colour all over. Transfer the pineapple to a roasting dish, standing it upright. Baste the pineapple with the reduced syrup and roast in the oven for 35–40 minutes, depending on the ripeness of the fruit. Baste every 5 minutes or so with the syrup, keeping the fruit upright.

Leave the roasted pineapple to stand for 10–15 minutes before serving, basting from time to time with the syrup. To serve, lie the pineapple on its side and cut into slices about 1cm thick. Arrange in a serving dish, retaining the star anise for decoration, and serve just warm with ice cream alongside.

Serves 4

1 ripe pineapple, about
   1.8kg (see tip below)
16 cloves
50ml groundnut oil
vanilla or coconut rum
   ice cream, to serve

for the syrup
1 litre water
400g light brown sugar
100g caster sugar
16 dried Sichuan
   peppercorns, crushed
4g quatre épices (a mixture
   of pepper, cloves, nutmeg
   and ginger)
6 star anise

....

Tip: Pineapples wil not ripen further once picked, but unlike most fruits, the colour is not a guide to ripeness. A gold pineapple (from Hawaii) can be just as ripe as a green one (from Central America). To pick the perfect pineapple, sniff the bottom of the fruit – it should smell strongly and sweetly of pineapple. And give one of the small green tufts on top a pull – if it's ripe, it should come out easily.

Jam roly poly

by James Martin

James's gently stodgy pud is delicious with lashings of homemade vanilla custard. The roly poly is steamed first, which keeps the pastry light and fluffy, then finished in the oven for a lovely crisp, golden crust.

Butter and lightly flour a large sheet of baking parchment (about 40 x 30cm), and sit it on a bigger sheet of kitchen foil. Put a steamer on to simmer.

Place the flour, sugar, suet and lemon zest into a bowl and mix thoroughly. Make a well in the centre of the mixture then gradually add enough water (125ml or so) to make a soft dough. Knead lightly until smooth.

Turn the dough onto a well-floured work surface and roll into a rectangle about 1cm thick. Spread the jam generously all over the pastry, leaving a 2cm border around the edges. Dab a little water along the short side then roll the dough towards you to make a thick cylinder (you can use a spatula to help here). Fold the ends underneath to prevent the jam from escaping.

With the long join underneath, lay the roly poly in the centre of the greaseproof paper. Fold over the long paper and foil edges to seal, leaving enough space above the pudding to allow it to rise. Squeeze the paper ends together tightly to seal them.

Lay the parcel in the steamer over the simmering water, cover and steam for 1 hour. While the roly poly is steaming, preheat the oven to 200°C/400°F/Gas 6.

Remove the pudding from the steamer and place on a baking tray in the preheated oven. Bake for 15 minutes, or until browned. Serve straight away, in thick slices, with custard and any extra jam.

Serves 4–6

You'll need a steamer

butter, for greasing
275 self-raising flour
40g caster sugar
110g (Atora) shredded
    suet (vegetarians may
    substitute vegetarian suet)
1 lemon, zest only
5 tbsp warm strawberry jam
    (to make your own, see
    page 18)
vanilla custard, to serve

Vanilla custard

Place the egg yolks and sugar in a bowl and whisk until well blended.

Combine the milk, cream and vanilla pod in a saucepan and bring to the boil. Immediately reduce the heat and simmer for 1 minute.

Pour the milk onto the egg mixture and whisk in. Return the mixture to the saucepan and stir over a low heat until the custard has thickened enough to coat the back of the spoon. Remove and discard the vanilla pod.

Pour the custard into a jug and serve at once.

Serves 4–6

4 egg yolks
40g caster sugar
150ml whole milk
150ml double cream
1 vanilla pod

Caramelised rice pudding with spiced plum compôte

by Matt Tebbutt

The ultimate nursery pud! The plum compôte spices things up nicely, but you can serve this with any seasonal fruits in abundance, or you could simply top the pudding with a dollop of strawberry jam, if you prefer.

Preheat the oven to 180°C/350°F/Gas 4. Grease the pudding basin with butter.

Place the milk and cream in a saucepan with the vanilla pod and bring to the boil. Take the pan off the heat and remove the vanilla pod. Add the rice and sugar and stir until well combined. Pour the mixture into the pudding basin. Sprinkle over the grated nutmeg, to taste, and dot with knobs of butter.

Place in the oven and bake for about 15 minutes, then reduce the temperature to 150°C/300°F/Gas 2 and bake for a further hour. Sprinkle over the demerara sugar and bake for a further 15 minutes, or until the sugar has caramelised and is golden-brown.

Meanwhile, for the spiced plum compôte, heat a frying pan, add the butter and plums and sauté for 1–2 minutes, or until the plums are just beginning to soften. Add the sugar, cinnamon and star anise and fry for a further 2–3 minutes, or until completely tender. Remove the cinnamon stick and star anise before serving. Keep warm until needed.

If your rice pudding is a little too stiff at the end of the cooking process, adding a little extra cream will return it to the unctuous, creamy texture desire.

Serve at room temperature or warm, with the compôte spooned over the top.

Tip: The Victoria plum, with its yellow flesh and red/purple skin, is the most popular variety grown in Britain and can be found in shops from August to mid-September. Raw from the tree, the fruit can be a bit tart, so leave to ripen in a warm room, or use plums that are just on the firm side of ripe to simmer into compôte or bake in a pie.

Serves 4–6

You'll need a 1 litre pudding basin

for the rice pudding
450ml whole milk
450ml double cream
1 vanilla pod, split
150g short grain or
    pudding rice
75g caster sugar
freshly grated nutmeg,
    to taste
25g butter, plus extra
    for greasing
3 tbsp demerara sugar

for the spiced plum compôte
25g butter
350g Victoria plums, stones
    removed, quartered
    (see tip below)
40g soft light brown sugar
1 cinnamon stick, broken
    in half
3 star anise, lightly crushed

Sticky toffee apple pudding

by James Martin

A variation on the classic sticky toffee pudding, featuring apples instead of dates and topped with a boozy caramel sauce. The result is every bit as indulgent, gooey and moreish as the original, and perfect for chilly autumn nights.

Preheat the oven to 190°C/375°F/Gas 5 and grease and flour your baking tin.

Melt 25g of the butter in a saucepan and add the apples, sugar and 50ml water. Cook over a gentle heat until just steaming, then cover with a lid and cook for 3–4 minutes, or until thick and fluffy. Remove the lid and beat well to remove any lumps. Add the Calvados and mix until well combined.

Beat 90g butter and the soft brown sugar in a large mixing bowl until light and fluffy. Add the golden syrup, eggs and vanilla extract and mix until well combined. Fold in the self-raising flour.

Meanwhile, add the bicarbonate of soda to the apple purée and mix well, then stir this quickly into the cake mixture. Pour into the cake tin and gently tap the sides of the tin to settle.

Melt the remaining 25g butter in a saucepan. Arrange the finely sliced apples over the top of the cake in a circles, then brush with melted butter and sprinkle over a little extra soft brown sugar. Bake for 40–45 minutes. Allow to cool slightly before turning out.

For the Calvados caramel sauce, place the sugar and butter into a small saucepan and cook until melted and well combined. Pour in the double cream and Calvados. Simmer gently for 3–4 minutes until just thickened.

Cut the warm cake into slices and serve with a dollop of ice cream and a good drizzle of caramel sauce.

Serves 6–8

You'll need a 23cm springform tin

for the pudding

140g butter, softened at room temperature, plus extra for greasing
300g Bramley apples, peeled, cored and roughly chopped
75g caster sugar
2 tbsp Calvados (apple brandy)
175g light soft brown sugar, plus extra for sprinkling
3 tbsp golden syrup
2 eggs
1 tsp vanilla extract
200g self-raising flour, plus 2 tbsp for dusting
1 tsp bicarbonate of soda
1 dessert apple, such as Cox's Orange Pippin, cored and finely sliced
500g vanilla ice cream, to serve

for the Calvados caramel sauce

110g dark soft brown sugar
110g butter
175ml double cream
2 tbsp Calvados

Chestnut and pear millefeuilles

by Matt Tebbutt

Layers of loveliness, made easy with ready-made puff pastry. Matt shows how a few simple ingredients can create an impressive dinner party dessert.

Dust the work surface with icing sugar and roll out the pastry as thin as you can get it, without stretching the pastry (about 3mm). Cut into 12 equal rectangles, about 12cm x 6cm, trimming the edges straight.

Preheat the oven to 190°C/375°F/Gas 5.

Place the pastry rectangles onto a baking sheet and place another baking sheet on top (this is to keep the top of the pastry flat and even as the puff pastry cooks). Transfer to the oven and bake for about 10–15 minutes, or until the pastry has risen and is golden brown. Remove from the oven, remove the uppermost baking tray and set aside to cool.

Sprinkle 2½ tablespoons of the icing sugar onto a plate. Dredge the pear slices in the icing sugar. Heat a griddle pan over a medium heat until hot, then cook the sugared pear slices for 1–2 minutes on each side, or until golden-brown griddle marks appear on the pears. (You may need to do this in batches.)

Place the double cream, rum and the remaining half tablespoon of icing sugar into a bowl and whisk until firm peaks form when the whisk is removed. Whisk in the chestnut purée, then fold in the chopped chestnuts.

For the caramel, gently heat the sugar in a non-stick pan until the sugar is dissolved and has caramelised. Continue to cook for 4–5 minutes, or until the mixture is dark golden-brown. Remove from the heat and whisk in half of the double cream.

In a separate bowl, whisk the remaining double cream until firm peaks form when the whisk is lifted up. Pour in the caramel mixture and fold together.

To assemble the millefeuilles, spread a thin layer of chestnut cream onto 4 of the puff pastry rectangles. Top each with a few pear slices. Place another piece of puff pastry on top of each millefeuille. Spread another layer of chestnut cream onto the puff pastry, then top with a few more slices of pear. Finish each millefeuille with a third puff pastry rectangle. Dust with icing sugar.

To serve, spoon the caramel sauce onto 4 serving plates and place 1 millefeuille in the centre of each plate.

Serves 4

You'll need 2 baking trays

500g ready-roll all-butter puff pastry
3 tbsp icing sugar, plus extra for dusting
2 small ripe pears, cores removed, cut into thin slices lengthways
110ml double cream
1 tbsp dark rum
250g canned sweetened chestnut purée
110g cooked chestnuts, finely chopped

for the caramel
200g caster sugar
400ml double cream

Coconut rum ice cream

by Michel Roux

Easy to make, ridiculously easy to eat. Leave out the rum if you're making this for kids.

Heat the milk, coconut milk and two thirds of the sugar in a heavy-based saucepan and slowly bring to the boil.

Meanwhile, whisk the egg yolks and remaining sugar together in a heatproof bowl. Continue to whisk until the mixture becomes pale and has a light ribbon consistency.

Pour the boiling milk onto the egg yolks, whisking continuously, then pour the mixture back into the saucepan.

Cook over a low heat, stirring with a wooden spatula or spoon; do not let it boil or it will curdle. The custard is ready when it has thickened slightly – just enough to lightly coat the back of the spatula. When you run your finger through, it should leave a clear trace. Immediately take off the heat and pour into a bowl.

Stir in the desiccated coconut and double cream. Leave to cool, stirring occasionally to prevent a skin forming, then add the rum.

Pour the cool mixture through a fine sieve before churning in an ice cream maker for about 20 minutes, until the ice cream is firm but still creamy. Transfer the ice cream to a chilled freezerproof container and keep it in the freezer until ready to serve.

Serves 4

You'll need an ice cream maker

1 litre whole milk
50ml coconut milk
200g sugar
10 egg yolks
160g desiccated coconut
100ml double cream
75ml dark rum

....

Tip: Don't overfill your ice cream maker! Three-quarters full yields the best results. If you fill the bowl up to the top, the ice cream won't aerate properly. Homemade ice creams keep well in the freezer for up to a week (after this time they start to lose their flavour and creamy texture).

Classic rich chocolate sauce

by Michel Roux

Pour lashings of this warm chocolate sauce over vanilla ice cream, profiteroles, cakes, meringues and puds.

Set a heatproof bowl over a pan of gently simmering water, being careful not to allow the base of the bowl to touch the water. Add the chocolate and melt slowly, stirring occasionally, until very smooth. Remove the bowl from the heat.

Bring the milk, cream and sugar to the boil in a saucepan over a medium heat, whisking continuously.

Pour the boiling cream mixture over the melted chocolate, whisking continuously until the mixture is smooth and well combined. Return the sauce to the pan and heat until just simmering, stirring continuously. Allow to bubble over the heat for a few seconds, then turn off the heat and whisk in the butter, a cube at a time, until the sauce is smooth and glossy and all the butter has melted.

Strain the chocolate sauce through a fine sieve, then serve immediately.

Serves 4

200g good-quality dark chocolate, minimum 70 per cent cocoa solids, chopped
175ml whole milk
2 tbsp double cream
30g caster sugar
30g butter, cut into cubes

....

Tip: Always make sure the chocolate and other ingredients added are the same temperature when combined, otherwise the chocolate will seize up and go lumpy.

Chocolate fondant pots

by John Campbell

John's hot chocolate pots come with a sprinkling of caramelised hazelnuts, a seductive coffee sabayon mousse and luxurious orange foam – and that's before you get to the pudding's meltingly soft interior. The beauty of this dish is that it can all be prepared in the morning, and then you just need 8 minutes in the oven for the fondant to cook. On the live show, the Saturday Kitchen *fan oven broke down and failed to cook the fondant, but barring electrical disaster (and with a little practice) your results should be flawless!*

For the orange foam, heat the orange juice and sugar in a saucepan until the sugar melts and the mixture is syrupy. Pour into a bowl and stir in the yoghurt and milk until smooth and creamy. Pour the mixture into an espuma gun and charge with 2 gas chargers. Keep in the fridge until needed.

For the coffee sabayon mousse, whisk the egg yolks and sugar together in a bowl set over a pan of simmering water, making sure the surface of the water does not touch the bowl. Continue to whisk until the mixture thickens. Remove the bowl from the water and add the coffee mixture, Camp coffee (with its beautiful liquorice note) and softened gelatine. Stir until well combined. When the mixture cools to a luke warm temperature, fold in the semi whipped cream, rewhip slightly to aerate, then divide the mixture among 4 coffee cups.

For the caramelised hazelnuts, preheat the oven to 180°C/350°F/Gas 4.

Scatter the hazelnuts onto a baking tray and roast in the oven for 7–10 minutes, or until golden-brown. Meanwhile, heat the caster sugar, lemon juice and 50ml water in a frying pan until the mixture turns a golden colour.

Remove the pan from the heat and stir in the warm roasted hazelnuts. Pour the mixture immediately onto baking paper or a silicone mat. Set aside to harden.

For the chocolate fondant pots, grease 4 ramekins. Melt the chocolate and butter together in a bowl set over a pan of gently simmering water.

Meanwhile, whisk the egg whites in a bowl, then gradually whisk in the sugar until the whites reach soft peaks (when the whisk is removed).

Carefully fold the chocolate mixture and flour into the egg white mixture. Spoon the mixture into the 4 ramekins and bake in the oven for 6–8 minutes. Remove from the oven and set aside to rest for 2 minutes.

Smash the hazelnut praline into small pieces, using a rolling pin. Place a chocolate pot onto each of 4 serving plates and scatter the hazelnut pieces on top. Place a cup of coffee mousse alongside, squirt the orange foam on top and dust with cocoa powder.

Serves 4

You'll need a cream whipper/espuma gun (with 2 gas charges), four 9cm ramekins, and 4 coffee cups

for the orange foam
300ml orange juice, sieved
150g sugar
300g natural yoghurt
125ml whole milk

for the coffee sabayon mousse
3 egg yolks
100g caster sugar
½ tsp instant coffee mixed with 2 tsp water
10ml Camp coffee (labelled Camp Chicory and Coffee Essence)
1 sheet gelatine leaf, soaked in water until softened
250ml double cream, soft whipped
1 tbsp cocoa powder, to serve

for the caramelised hazelnuts
50g whole hazelnuts
150g caster sugar
½ lemon, juiced

for the chocolate pot
320g dark chocolate, broken into pieces
50g butter
6 egg whites
70g caster sugar
20g plain flour

Mango 'egg' with toasted brioche

by Andrew Turner

Andrew's dessert is for keen kitchen scientists. It employs a spherificaton technique introduced by Ferran Adrià at the famous el Bulli restaurant. The 'egg' is mango purée with added calcium: added to a water bath prepared with alginate it becomes gel like. A spoonful of yoghurt (the 'white) is added, and once immersed in the alginate bath you get a 'poached egg' with a very realistic-looking yolk that oozes when you puncture it!

The day before

To prepare the alginate bath, blend the bottled mineral water and algin powder in a food processor for 5–10 minutes, or until well combined. Strain the mixture through a fine sieve, then pour the strained liquid into a large baking tray a least 5cm deep. Chill in the fridge for 24 hours (this removes the air from the liquid).

Meanwhile, for the brioche, bring the cream, cinnamon, cloves and star anise to the boil in a pan. Remove from the heat and set aside to cool, then discard the cinnamon, cloves and star anise. Whisk the cream into the beaten egg. Add the sugar and whisk again until well combined. Submerge the brioche discs into the egg mixture to soak, then chill, covered, in the fridge overnight.

For the mango 'egg', add the gluco powder to the mango purée. Blend in a food processor until well combined, then transfer to a clean bowl. Cover and chill in the fridge overnight.

Serves 4

You'll need gluco powder and alginate (see page 341)

for the alginate bath
1 litre bottled mineral water
5g alginate or algin powder

for the brioche
100ml whipping cream
1 cinnamon stick
4 cloves
1 star anise
3 eggs, beaten
100g soft brown sugar
4 slices brioche, slices
    cut into discs using
    a 7cm cookie cutter
    (for presentation)
1 tbsp vegetable oil
30g unsalted butter
20g icing sugar

On the day

Using a small spoon or teaspoon, scoop 4 small portions of the chilled mango purée from the mixture and roll into balls, using your hands, or 2 teaspoons.

When all of the mango balls have been prepared, remove the alginate bath from the fridge. Carefully lower the balls of mango purée into the alginate mixture, leave for 30 seconds, or until a skin forms on the outside of the balls, then remove from the liquid using a slotted spoon and transfer to a bowl of water (this will rinse any remaining alginate off the egg).

Using an ice cream scoop or rounded dessert spoon, scoop 4 balls of the yoghurt and carefully lower these into the alginate mixture.

Drain the 'yolks' from the water and return them to the alginate mixture, resting one on top of each ball of Greek-style yoghurt, in the centre to resemble a fried egg. Leave for 30 seconds, or until a skin forms on the 'egg'. Remove from the alginate mixture using a slotted spoon and transfer to a fresh bowl of clean water.

When ready to eat, heat the vegetable oil in a non-stick frying pan over a medium heat. Add the soaked brioche discs to the pan and fry for 2–3 minutes on each side, or until golden-brown on both sides. Add the butter and icing sugar to the pan and continue to cook the brioche until the butter has melted, the icing sugar has dissolved and the brioche discs are caramelised.

To serve, paint a smear of mango purée across the centre of each serving plate. Place one brioche disc into the centre of each plate. Place the 'poached egg' on top of each brioche disc. Garnish with a sprinkling of crackle crystals, if using.

for the mango egg
1g gluco powder, or similar edible calcium ions
150g mango purée (or the flesh of 1 whole mango, chopped, then blended to a smooth purée in a food processor with 30ml water)
50g Greek-style yoghurt
crackle crystals, to serve (optional)

Five-minute desserts

There are times when you need to whip up a pudding out of nowhere, either because of surprise guests, or you suddenly crave something sweet and indulgent at the end of a meal. Here are ten of the best emergency puddings. From Nathan Outlaw's rustic cheesecake to James Martin's simple syllabub, these ideas are quick, easy and combine few ingredients to spectacular effect.

Eton mess
by Mark Sargeant

Mix 400ml whipped cream, 6 crushed, ready-made meringue shells and 800g sliced fresh strawberries. Simple and tasty.

Sugared nuts
by Nathan Outlaw

Bring sugar (175g) and water (125ml) together in a pan and simmer until the mixture begins to turn golden. Remove from the heat. Add a good handful of almonds, pecans, or whatever nut you like, and stir until the sugar begins to crystallise. Lift and cool. These are lovely served with coffee.

Instant berry sorbet
by Jun Tanaka

Freeze some strawberries and raspberries and just before serving blitz in a blender with a squeeze of lemon juice and some stock syrup. You can't get a dessert that's any quicker!

Caramelised bananas
by Mark Sargeant

Bananas make a great quick dessert if you are hosting a barbecue. Once the main food is out of the way and the barbecue is dying down, add some bananas, skin on, and grill for 6–7 minutes each side until the skin turns black. Then carefully peel off the skin with gloves and serve the warm, caramelised banana with ice cream.

Fruit crumble
by Danny Millar

Everybody has some kind of fruit in the house. Make a crumble by rubbing together 50g butter, 110g flour and 55g caster sugar and sprinkle over the fruit. Put in the oven at 180°C/350°F/Gas 4 for 12 minutes and serve with ice cream.

Berry surprise
by Silvena Rowe

Melt 150g white chocolate in a water bath, then slightly cool and add to plain yoghurt, mix and pour over a bowlful of lovely fresh berries. Easy and delicious!

Irresistible cheesecake
by Nathan Outlaw

Crush half a packet of digestive biscuits into crumbs and mix with 50g melted butter. Using your hands, pack the mixture into the base of a 20cm springform cake tin. Combine 300g cream cheese, 100g icing sugar and 250g crème fraîche until creamy and smooth. Add lemon zest or chopped nuts or vanilla essence or whatever else you fancy, then tip onto the biscuit base. Chill until set for a passable rustic cheesecake.

Lemon posset
by Tom Kerridge

This is so very easy to make. You need double cream (about 400ml), sugar (100g) and the juice from 2 lemons. Warm cream and sugar in a large saucepan, stir to dissolve the sugar, then bring to the boil and simmer for 3 minutes without stirring. Remove from the heat, whisk in the lemon juice then pour the mixture into 4 serving glasses. Chill for 3–5 hours until set. A small amount goes great with coffee.

Quick crème brûlée
by Tom Kerridge

Four ingredients – double cream (600ml), sugar (40g), eggs (4) and vanilla (1 pod, split, seeds scraped out) – make the ultimate pud. Bring the cream and vanilla to boiling point. Whisk the eggs and sugar together in a bowl and, still beating, pour the flavoured cream over it. Put the custard back into the pan and cook over a low–medium heat until thickened. Strain the créme through a sieve then pour into 4 ramekins. Leave to cool then chill in the fridge until really cold. Before serving, sprinkle with demerera sugar. Blowtorch or grill for a few minutes to get a crisp crust.

Lemon curd syllabub
by James Martin

Crumble a couple of biscuits into the bottom of 4 tall glasses and moisten with a little white wine. Whip 250ml double cream with 4 tablespoons icing sugar and when the mixture reaches soft peaks, fold in half a glass of white wine and some lemon curd. Spoon the syllabub into the glasses and scatter with more crushed biscuits.

The golden rules for wine & food

We're often asked how we go about choosing wines to partner all the amazing dishes featured on *Saturday Kitchen*. Well, the first thing we do is get our hands dirty. We cook up the dishes, crack open a couple of bottles and go from there. We don't usually see eye-to-eye initially on a wine match. So the process almost always involves what we might politely term a 'lively discussion'. But that's the great thing about wine – the passion it arouses and the different ways of tasting and seeing the same beautiful thing. As for who usually wins – ah, now that would be telling...

When it comes to finding the right wine for any given dish, there's no substitute for eating and drinking the stuff together. For that final decision, to get the wine *just* right for all the intricate flavours, delicate textures and subtle nuances of each dish – that needs knives, forks and a smoking corkscrew.

But in the first instance, a few rules of thumb really help. Here are the golden ones we tend to work by – we hope they work for you too!

Peter Richards and Susie Barrie

Rule one: there are no rules

OK, it may not be the most helpful start, but it stops you taking this whole thing too seriously.

Taste is personal; we're talking shades of grey rather than black and white. Putting wine and food together can be many things – fun, disastrous, delicious, messy, confusing, inspiring – but one thing it shouldn't be is too serious.

Find out what works for you and go from there. And have fun while you're doing it.

Rules two and three: think F and W

The key to good **F**ood and **W**ine matching is to think **F**lavour and **W**eight.

F for Flavour. Think: what are the *dominant* flavours in this dish?

As a general rule, it won't often be 'chicken' or 'pasta', as most wine back labels unhelpfully generalise. Instead, it will be the tikka masala sauce, or the Bolognese. Or the mushrooms, the fruit, the herbs, the chilli, the side order, even (don't tell the chefs) the ketchup!

Find a wine that works with those dominant flavours. For example, with chicken tikka masala, you need a wine that works well with tangy tomato, rich cream and spicy chilli – a zesty but off-dry white or rosé will soothe and stimulate the taste buds while still engaging with the main flavours. It's all about achieving flavour harmony.

W for Weight. By which we mean, how big or heavy the food or dish is. This is different to how flavoursome it is.

To illustrate – rice is heavy but doesn't have much flavour; green peppers are full of flavour but are not especially heavy.

Delicate, 'light' dishes or ingredients, like fresh shellfish, work well with lighter wines (e.g. Muscadet or young Chablis).

Heavier dishes need fuller bodied, more powerful wines – rich mushroom risotto often works better with a red (e.g. Pinot Noir) than a white.

Rule four: if in doubt, stay local

More a starting point for ideas than a hard-and-fast rule this one.

It's often the case that local dishes have evolved side by side with local wines, so there's a natural synergy.

Think Rioja and lamb (or, more wickedly, suckling pig). Truffle risotto and Barolo; Sancerre and goat's cheese (ideally Crottin de Chavignol); *boeuf bourguignon* and red Burgundy; oysters and Muscadet.

It even works further afield – try green-lipped mussels with Kiwi Sauvignon Blanc. Or a tender rib eye steak with Argentine Malbec.

Rule five: keep it sweet

When it comes to the sweet stuff, don't mess around.

The wine needs to be as sweet as, or sweeter than, the dish. Otherwise the wine tastes sour.

Remember too that many so-called savoury dishes have elements of sweetness to them. The rule still holds in this case: if you've got a bit of sweetness in the dish, don't go for a very dry, austere wine – instead choose something with a bit of lushness to it.

Rule six: don't be afraid to throw in the towel

Some food just isn't made to go with wine.

Artichokes. Rhubarb yoghurt. Vindaloo.

Don't bash your head against a brick wall in the cause of wine. There are loads of other fun drinks to enjoy with food – tea, coffee, beer, cocktails, vodka, juice. Hell, even water works sometimes.

Rule seven: enjoy your favourites

Some of ours include:

- Fish and chips from the paper with decadent champagne
- Roast lamb with Rioja Reserva
- Curry with a juicy rosé
- Hard cheese with mature, nutty Chardonnay
- Bangers and mash with a hearty red
- Sushi and Riesling
- Charcuterie with Beaujolais
- Fresh nuts with ice-cold, bone-dry Fino sherry
- Ginger and toffee sponge with a heady, luscious Rutherglen Muscat

What's in season

By cooking with the seasons, you will always enjoy local ingredients at their best and get to appreciate nature's classic flavour marriages throughout the year. Here are some foodie highlights to look out for, as suggested by the *Saturday Kitchen* chefs, plus a selection of recipes to try month by month.

Spring

Make the most of: 'Fresh peas and broad beans' (Gennaro Contaldo). 'Beautiful spring lamb' (Daniel Galmiche). 'The first crop of Jersey Royals in March, cooked simply with fresh mint and served with melting butter' (Shaun Rankin). 'Wild garlic in April' (Jun Tanaka). 'English asparagus – such a short season, but so amazing!' (Adam Byatt). 'Young rhubarb, just blanched, served with a scoop of vanilla ice cream' (Nick Nairn).

March
Potato salad with pancetta and calamari by Shaun Rankin (page 174)
Mini stargazey pies by Tristan Welch (page 272)
Pasta con sarde by Arthur Potts Dawson (page 81)

April
Asparagus with hollandaise by James Martin (page 52)
Salted pollock with asparagus, wild garlic and morels by Michael Caines (page 120)
Kipper cakes with tartare sauce by James Martin (page 34)

May
Malaccan black pepper crab by Rick Stein (page 119)
Roast poussin with morels, broad beans and spätzle by Jun Tanaka (page 134)
Lamb sweetbreads and liver with spring onion and samphire by Richard Corrigan (page 140)

Summer

Make the most of: 'The freshness of beautiful watercress and green beans as an accompaniment to local fish such as pollock, red mullet and Dover sole' (Shaun Rankin). 'Summer tomatoes, so full of flavour' (Tana Ramsay). 'Wild samphire' (Galton Blackiston). 'Hedgerow blackberries in a crumble or jam' (Henry Dimbleby). 'Al fresco lunches where you put platters out and everyone helps themselves' (Mark Sargeant).

June
Mackerel, tomato and samphire salad by Nathan Outlaw (page 166)
Octopus, chorizo and oregano (page 130) with orange, herb and edible flower salad
by Silvena Rowe (page 162)
A classic cherry clafoutis by Matt Tebbutt (page 300)

July
Artichokes à la barigoule by Clare Smyth (page 58)
Home-smoked mackerel with beetroot and horseradish by Lawrence Keogh (page 121)
Peach and raspberry mini pavlovas by James Martin (page 307)

August
Aubergine 'parmigiana' with roasted tomato by Gennaro Contaldo (page 110)
Easy stuffed peppers by James Martin (page 58)
Gurnard with broad bean, spinach and mint stew by Cass Titcombe (page 84)

Autumn

Make the most of: 'The harvest season, for its glut of hearty root vegetables' (Michael Caines). 'This is the time to go foraging for wild mushrooms: look out for puffballs and ceps' (Galton Blackiston). 'Get your braises and slow cooked meats on' (Tom Kerridge). 'Enjoy the game season with all those big strong earthy flavours, which work brilliantly with Indian food' (Vivek Singh).

September
Tandoori grey mullet with cep salad by Atul Kochhar (page 95)
Warm salad of mushroom, beetroot and pan-fried pigeon by James Martin (page 175)
Mixed game pithivier (page 138) with hot and sour cabbage (page 137) by Paul Rankin

October
Roasted pumpkin soup by Tom Kitchin (page 180)
Roast brill with scorched lettuce by Glynn Purnell (page 85)
Sticky toffee apple pudding by James Martin (page 319)

November
Duck confit with lentils by Daniel Galmiche (page 239)
A hearty roast pheasant lunch by Michael Caines (page 244)
Wagyu beef with beetroot, kale and sautéed potatoes by Galton Blackiston (page 284)

Winter

Make the most of: 'Cooking mussels in the cold winter months when they are at their best' (Rick Stein). 'There's so much beautiful shellfish and seafood on offer at this time of year, and great citrus too' (Bjorn van der Horst). 'Enjoy vibrant veg such as beetroot and flavoursome produce like celeriac and cauliflower. On the more extravagant side it's also the time for black truffles and some excellent venison' (Shaun Rankin).

December

Roast cod with winter ratatouille by Galton Blackiston (page 266)
Salad of roast suckling pig and oysters by Richard Corrigan (page 172)
Chestnut and pear millefeuilles by Matt Tebbutt (page 320)

January

Sea bream with fennel and orange by Jason Atherton (page 268)
Clams, smoked bacon and cider broth by Mark Sargeant (page 91)
Apple croustade with Armagnac custard by Nick Nairn (page 312)

February

Tagliatelle with mussels by Gennaro Contaldo (page 78)
Classic beef and ale pie by James Martin (page 145)
Crêpes with orange butter sauce by Michel Roux (page 298)

How to shop

Most of the ingredients used in this book can be bought from any good supermarket. For the few products that are a little harder to track down, online shopping is ideal.

Asian food

www.mountfuji.co.uk Our favourite one-stop shop for all things Japanese.

www.natco-online.com Shop for Indian spices, chutneys, curry mixes and more.

www.theasiancookshop.co.uk Browse their excellent range of Indian, Chinese, Thai, Japanese and other Asian foods.

www.spicesofindia.co.uk The best spices are available online. Buy them in the smallest possible quantities because spices are fragile and don't keep well at all.

Edible flowers

www.firstleaf.co.uk The edible flower season runs from April to September, when you can buy a range of beautiful fresh edible flowers, as well as decorative leaf garnishes.

Fresh and gourmet ingredients

www.campbellsmeat.com 'A superior selection of Scottish meat and fish.' **Nick Nairn**

www.finestfoodsathome.com A fine dining range that supplies many Michelin starred restaurants in London and the south of England, now doing home delivery.

www.finefoodspecialist.co.uk Quality ingredients at competitive prices: look out for dried mushrooms, micro herbs, wagyu beef, and more.

www.foodinthecity.com 'Reliable, speedy delivery and good quality ingredients.' **Antonio Carluccio**

www.glenarmorganicsalmon.com 'The smoked salmon is unbeatable, and handy for throwing in salads, pasta dishes and scrambled eggs.' **Danny Millar**

www.kingsfinefood.co.uk 'Great for caviar.' **Michel Roux**

www.natoora.co.uk 'Stocks the freshest European seasonal vegetables and wonderful charcuterie.' **Henry Harris**

www.melburyandappleton.co.uk Carefully sourced products from artisan producers: luxury items alongside great everyday essentials.

www.riverford.co.uk 'We use their veg on Street Kitchen and it is incredible.'
Jun Tanaka

www.sanpietroapettine.com 'A truffle lovers delight! Try the fresh truffles and the truffle oil.' **Gennaro Contaldo**

Kitchen kit

www.creamsupplies.co.uk All the kit a keen kitchen scientist will need, including sous vide equipment and espuma guns.

www.hotsmoked.co.uk If you're interested in hot and cold food smoking (page 121), Hot Smoked has a great range of equipment and a selection of woods, which impart different flavours during the smoking process.

www.infusions4chefs.co.uk Ingredients and apparatus for molecular gastronomy-style dishes. Get your alginate, gluco powder, vacuum packers and plenty more here.

Mediterranean food

www.purespain.co.uk For hard-to-find Spanish products: everything from wood-roasted piquillo peppers to chorizo, tapenade and cheese.

www.delicioso.co.uk Excellent authentic Spanish ingredients, flavoured oils and even cooking pans. Get your pimientos de Padrón (page 64) here.

www.nifeislife.com, www.valvonacrolla.co.uk and www.luigismailorder.com If you're cooking Italian, you'll find the best Italian delis north of the Alps online.

www.turkishsupermarket.co.uk Authentic Turkish produce, from olives to beer to Turkish Delight. Try the Gaziantep pepper: Rick Stein's favourite spicy chilli paste.

'Buying fantastic local produce will make all the difference to your cooking; visiting your local butcher, greengrocer, fishmonger or farmers' market is a good place to start.'

Tom Kitchin

'Try handpicking fish and seafood at the fish markets. Go as early as possible. It's not just shopping, it's an experience!'

Bjorn van der Horst

'You may think supermarkets are the devil's shop, but realistically we all have to use them and if you shop cleverly and well they will get you all you need.'

Mark Sargeant

'I love scouring organic markets or finding great ingredients at my favourite Chinese grocers.'

Ken Hom

'Have a look at www.slowfood. org.uk/forgotten-foods for some ingredients that we should all be using more of, supporting our farmers and making sure these products don't disappear.'

Richard Corrigan

'All farmers' markets deserve our help and we should visit, buy and encourage them.'

Michel Roux Jr

'There are so many great farmers' markets in the UK. There are also some great family butchers online: www.colinmrobinson. com in Skipton do amazing lamb and, for really good meat and black pudding, check out www. laverstokepark.co.uk, an organic/ biodynamic farm in Hampshire.'

James Martin

Index

Page numbers in *italic* refer to the illustrations

acorn squash
    roast pumpkin soup **180, 181**
aioli **64**
ale
    classic beef and ale pie **145**
almonds
    breast of lamb with apricots and
      almonds **280, 281**
    orange and almond cake with
      basil cream **302, 303**
anchovies
    cavatelli with broccoli and colatura **227**
an Anglo-Indian brunch **36–7**
apples
    apple and fennel raita **49**
    apple croustade with Armagnac custard **312,**
    313
    chutney **233**
    hot and sour cabbage **137**
    pork schnitzel with fried egg and apple **282,**
    283
    sticky toffee apple pudding **319**
apricots
    breast of lamb with apricots and
      almonds **280, 281**
    sweet potato tagine **186, 187**
Armagnac custard **312**
artichokes
    artichokes à la barigoule **58**
    spinach, chorizo and artichoke pizza **200**
    wild sea trout, sorrel and peas **128, 129**
Asian-style pasta **98**
asparagus
    asparagus with hollandaise sauce **52, 53**
    salted pollock with asparagus, wild garlic
      and morels **120**
    scallop mousse with asparagus **261**
Atherton, Jason **17**
    a fancy fry-up **22**
    sea bream with fennel and orange **268**
aubergines
    aubergine 'parmigiana' with roasted
      tomato **110, 111**
    spiced aubergine **54, 55**
autumn, seasonal food **338**
avocados
    Mexican hearts of palm salad **161**
    vuelve a la vida **23**

bacon
    Asian-style pasta **98**
    braised chicory **244–5**
    clams, smoked bacon and cider broth **91**
    a fancy fry-up **22**
    Gruyère and bacon soufflé suissesse **265**
    gurnard with broad bean, spinach
      and mint stew **84**
    lagane in a borlotti bean and guanciale
      soup **226**

mackerel, tomato and samphire
    salad **166, 167**
mini stargazey pies **272–3, 272**
mixed game pithivier **138, 139**
pea, broad bean and bacon salad **150, 151**
a quick coq au vin **204, 205**
tattie scones and a big breakfast **27**
a waffly good breakfast **28, 29**
see also pancetta
bananas, caramelised **328**
basil
    basil cream **302**
    pesto **45**
beans
    lagane in a borlotti bean and guanciale
      soup **226**
    Malaccan black pepper crab with black beans,
      ginger and curry leaves **118, 119**
    octopus, cannellini beans and smoked
      ricotta **66, 67**
    sausage, pumpkin and sage casserole **210,**
    211
béarnaise sauce **209**
béchamel sauce **229**
beef
    an Anglo-Indian brunch **36–7**
    beef in oyster sauce **104, 105**
    beef slices with Oloroso sherry **102, 103**
    beef stroganoff **293**
    classic beef and ale pie **145**
    a classic lasagne **228, 229**
    a modern steak and chips **290–2, 291**
    Mum's hotpot with vinegar onions **252–3**
    spicy stuffed meatballs **213**
    steak, fat chips and béarnaise sauce **209**
    tagliatelle with Bolognese ragu **212**
    the ultimate cottage pie **286–8, 287**
    wagyu beef with beetroot, kale
      and sautéed potatoes **284–5, 285**
beer
    classic beef and ale pie **145**
beetroot
    beetroot and goat's curd tart **57**
    beetroot-cured salmon **230, 231**
    beetroot gnocchi with butter, sage
      and orange sauce **221**
    beetroot salad **232**
    home-smoked mackerel with beetroot
      and horseradish **121**
    roast cod with winter ratatouille **266, 267**
    wagyu beef with beetroot, kale
      and sautéed potatoes **284–5, 285**
    warm salad of mushroom, beetroot and
      pan-fried pigeon **175**
berries
    berry surprise **328**
    instant berry sorbet **328**
    red wine soufflé **309**
    see also raspberries, strawberries etc

Bertinet, Richard
    fougasse (French flatbread) **42–3**
    three classic dips **45**
besan chips **290–2, 291**
beurre blanc, lemon **266**
biryani parcels, wild mushroom
    and sweetcorn **262, 263–4**
black beans
    Malaccan black pepper crab with black beans,
      ginger and curry leaves **118, 119**
blackberries
    raita **264**
Blackiston, Galton **257**
    crisp shrimp risotto cakes **65**
    Gruyère and bacon soufflé suissesse **265**
    roast cod with winter ratatouille **266, 267**
    tomato and radish salad **153**
    wagyu beef with beetroot, kale
      and sautéed potatoes **284–5, 285**
blueberries
    pork belly with blueberry and chilli
      molasses glaze **144**
Bolognese ragu **212**
boozy prune tiramisu **314**
borlotti beans
    lagane in a borlotti bean and guanciale
      soup **226**
brandy
    boozy prune tiramisu **314**
bread
    chapatis **207**
    croûtons **22**
    flatbread **93**
    fougasse (French flatbread) **42–3**
    Irish potato bread **24, 25**
    naan bread **48**
    panzanella with tuna **164, 165**
    Welsh rarebit **26**
brill
    roast brill with scorched lettuce **85**
brioche
    mango 'egg' with toasted brioche **326–7**
broad beans
    gurnard with broad bean, spinach and
      mint stew **84**
    pea, broad bean and bacon salad **150, 151**
    quinoa and broad bean salad **154, 155**
    roast poussin with morels, broad beans
      and spätzle **134, 135**
    spoots with diced veg, chorizo
      and sautéed squid **274**
broccoli
    an Anglo-Indian brunch **36–7**
    cavatelli with broccoli and colatura **227**
    spicy vegetable salad with a curry-soy
      vinaigrette **156**
bulgar wheat salad **168**
butter
    béarnaise sauce **209**

clarified butter **298**
green butter sauce **24**
hollandaise sauce **52, 53**
lemon and parsley butter **134**
lemon beurre blanc **266**
orange butter sauce **298**
buttermilk crumpets **18,** *19*
butternut squash
    an Anglo-Indian brunch **36–7**
    pollock, squid and mussel stew **126–7**
    roast cod with winter ratatouille **266, 267**
    roast salmon, gnocchi and chestnut **115**
Byatt, Adam
    classic mash **214**
    the ultimate cottage pie **286–8, 287**

cabbage, hot and sour **137**
Caines, Michael **109**
    a hearty roast pheasant lunch **244–5**
    herb-crusted roast leg of lamb **142, 143**
    roasted root veg **137**
    salted pollock with asparagus, wild garlic
        and morels **120**
cakes
    orange and almond cake
        with basil cream **302, 303**
    Victoria sandwich **310, 311**
calamari *see* squid
Calvados caramel sauce **319**
Campbell, John
    chocolate fondant pots **324, 325**
candied peel
    pastiera di Grano **304, 305**
cannellini beans
    octopus, cannellini beans and smoked
        ricotta **66, 67**
    sausage, pumpkin and sage
        casserole **210, 211**
Cantonese-style fish with spicy tofu **90**
capers
    green butter sauce **24**
    panzanella with tuna **164, 165**
    tartare sauce **34, 35**
    tuna tapenade **45**
caramel
    Calvados caramel sauce **319**
    caramelised bananas **328**
    caramelised hazelnuts **324**
    caramelised rice pudding with spiced
        plum compôte **318**
    caramelised walnuts **244–5**
    chestnut and pear millefeuilles **320, 321**
    praline **314**
    quick crème brûlée **329**
    sticky toffee apple pudding **319**
Carluccio, Antonio
    pastiera di Grano **304, 305**
carrots
    chilled soup of carrot, pink grapefruit
        and hazelnuts **258, 259**
    classic beef and ale pie **145**
    roast cod with winter ratatouille **266, 267**
    roasted root veg **137**
    the ultimate cottage pie **286–8, 287**
cashew nuts

spicy chicken, cucumber and cashew
    nut salad **170, 171**
cauliflower
    spicy vegetable salad with a curry-soy
        vinaigrette **156**
cavatelli with broccoli and colatura **227**
celeriac mash **241**
celery
    creamy celery and walnut salad **158, 159**
cep salad, tandoori grey mullet with **94, 95**
chanterelle mushrooms
    a fancy fry-up **22**
chapatis **207**
chasseur sauce **238**
cheese
    aubergine 'parmigiana' with roasted
        tomato **110, 111**
    beetroot and goat's curd tart **57**
    creamy celery and walnut salad **158, 159**
    dauphinoise and Taleggio pithivier **112, 113**
    Gruyère and bacon soufflé suissesse **265**
    minted pea and feta salad **160**
    octopus, cannellini beans and smoked
        ricotta **66, 67**
    penne with halloumi and cherry tomatoes **80**
    pesto **45**
    roasted vegetable pizza **201**
    a simple Margherita with rocket **200**
    spicy stuffed meatballs **213**
    spinach, chorizo and artichoke pizza **200**
    Welsh rarebit **26**
    whipped feta, yoghurt and cumin salad **160**
cheesecake, irresistible **329**
cherries
    cherry cream **300**
    cherry meringues with rhubarb coulis **308**
    a classic cherry clafoutis **300, 301**
chestnuts
    chestnut and pear millefeuilles **320, 321**
    roast salmon, gnocchi and chestnut **115**
    scallops with leek and chestnut **260**
chicken
    amazing brined roast chicken **236–8, 237**
    chicken on crispy noodles **96, 97**
    chicken terrine with herbs **234, 235**
    chicken with chorizo, peppers
        and sage **132, 133**
    crispy chicken with braised chicory
        and fennel salad **169**
    lemon and honey spatchcock chicken **131**
    malai murg tikka (chicken cream tikka) **193**
    murg adraki (ginger chicken) **275**
    nasi goreng with lime and sugar barbecued
        chicken **190–2, 191**
    a quick coq au vin **204, 205**
    sesame chicken kebabs and mango
        salsa **68, 69**
    spiced chicken dumpling soup **188, 189**
    spicy chicken, cucumber and cashew
        nut salad **170, 171**
    Thai roast chicken with pak choi
        and sesame noodles **136**
    see also poussins
chicken livers
    rabbit and rosemary terrine with chutney **233**

chickpea flour
    a modern steak and chips **290–2, 291**
chickpeas
    chickpea and courgette curry **182**
    chickpea and olive oil dip **45**
chicory
    braised chicory **244–5**
    crispy chicken with braised chicory
        and fennel salad **169**
chillies
    an Anglo-Indian brunch **36–7**
    beef slices with Oloroso sherry **102, 103**
    green pea and potato cakes **46**
    mango salsa **69**
    nasi goreng with lime and sugar barbecued
        chicken **190–2, 191**
    panzanella with tuna **164, 165**
    pasta con sarde **81**
    spatchcocked poussin with a chimichurri
        sauce **276, 277**
    stir-fried chilli pork **99**
    tomato and onion seed chutney **49**
    veal cutlet with a burnt chilli courgette
        pickle **279**
    vuelve a la vida **23**
chimichurri sauce, spatchcocked poussin
    with **276,** *277*
Chinese pork potsticker dumplings **246–7,** *246*
chips
    herby chips **50, 51**
    a modern steak and chips **290–2, 291**
    patatas fritas **50**
    steak, fat chips and béarnaise sauce **209**
chocolate
    berry surprise **328**
    chocolate fondant pots **324, 325**
    classic rich chocolate sauce **323**
chorizo
    chicken with chorizo, peppers
        and sage **132, 133**
    chorizo in red wine **71**
    octopus, chorizo and oregano **130**
    prawns with chorizo **70, 71**
    quick-smoked salmon paella **88, 89**
    spinach, chorizo and artichoke pizza **200**
    spoots with diced veg, chorizo
        and sautéed squid **274**
chutney **233, 275**
    tomato and onion seed chutney **49**
cider
    clams, smoked bacon and cider broth **91**
clafoutis, a classic cherry **300,** *301*
clams
    clams, smoked bacon and cider broth **91**
    fish stew with Sardinian fregola **82, 83**
    quick-smoked salmon paella **88, 89**
    spoots with diced veg, chorizo
        and sautéed squid **274**
clarified butter **298**
coconut, creamed
    Thai roast chicken with pak choi
        and sesame noodles **136**
coconut milk
    chickpea and courgette curry **182**
    coconut rum ice cream **322**

spiced chicken dumpling soup **188, 189**
cod
   langoustine and cod puff pastry pie **203**
   roast cod with winter ratatouille **266, 267**
coffee sabayon mousse **324**
colatura (anchovy sauce), cavatelli
   with broccoli and **227**
Contaldo, Gennaro
   aubergine 'parmigiana' with roasted
      tomato **110, 111**
   basic pasta dough **224**
   beetroot gnocchi with butter, sage
      and orange sauce **221**
   fennel, radish and pepper salad **150**
   griddled swordfish with mint and
      marjoram **86, 87**
   herby chips **50, 51**
   tagliatelle with mussels **78, 79**
   walnut-crusted pork **100**
Coorg pork stir-fry **248**
coq au vin **204,** *205*
Corrigan, Richard **149**
   lamb sweetbreads and liver with spring onions
      and samphire **140**
   salad of roast suckling pig and
      oysters **172, 173**
cottage pie, the ultimate **286–8,** *287*
country captain shepherd's pie **249–50,** *251*
courgettes
   chickpea and courgette curry **182**
   sole-in-a-bag with courgettes
      and black olives **269, 270–1**
   veal cutlet with a burnt chilli courgette
      pickle **279**
couscous
   couscous with pistachio and pomegranate **156**
   lemon couscous **185**
   okra curry, couscous and flatbread **92–3**
   rabbit with Moroccan-style couscous
      and calamari **278**
crab
   haddock 'ceviche' with crab salad **116, 117**
   Malaccan black pepper crab with black beans,
      ginger and curry leaves **118, 119**
crackling **172**
cream
   basil cream **302**
   caramelised rice pudding with spiced
      plum compôte **318**
   cherry cream **300**
   chestnut and pear millefeuilles **320, 321**
   coffee sabayon mousse **324**
   Eton mess **328**
   lemon curd syllabub **329**
   lemon posset **329**
   quick crème brûlée **329**
cream cheese
   irresistible cheesecake **329**
   smoked mackerel pâté **232**
   spicy stuffed meatballs **213**
crème brûlée **329**
crêpes with orange butter sauce **298,** *299*
croûtons **22**
crumble, fruit **328**
crumpets, buttermilk **18,** *19*

cucumber
   cucumber and mint raita **48**
   fennel, radish and pepper salad **150**
   pickled cucumber salad **122**
   spicy chicken, cucumber and cashew
      nut salad **170, 171**
   a splendid spud (with lobster) **114**
   yoghurt and cucumber dip **208**
curry
   Asian-style pasta **98**
   chickpea and courgette curry **182**
   lamb Madras with chapatis **206–7**
   Malaccan black pepper crab with black beans,
      ginger and curry leaves **118, 119**
   murg adraki (ginger chicken) **275**
   okra curry, couscous and flatbread **92–3**
   pandhi curry (Coorg pork stir-fry) **248**
   sag aloo **46, 47**
   sheek kevaab (lamb kebabs) **194, 195**
   spicy vegetable salad with a curry-soy
      vinaigrette **156**
   wild mushroom and sweetcorn biryani
      parcels **262, 263–4**
custard
   Armagnac custard **312**
   vanilla custard **316**

dauphinoise and Taleggio pithivier **112,** *113*
Demetre, Anthony
   chilled soup of carrot, pink grapefruit
      and hazelnuts **258, 259**
   lemon and honey spatchcock chicken **131**
   quinoa and broad bean salad **154, 155**
Dimbleby, Henry
   fresh herb salad **152**
   spicy stuffed meatballs **213**
dips
   apple and fennel raita **49**
   chickpea and olive oil dip **45**
   cucumber and mint raita **48**
   dipping sauce **246–7**
   pesto **45**
   tuna tapenade **45**
   yoghurt and cucumber dip **208**
dressings
   lemon dressing **150**
   orange dressing **268**
duck
   duck confit with flageolet ragout
      and celeriac mash **241**
   duck confit with lentils **239–40**
dumplings
   Chinese pork potsticker dumplings **246–7,**
      246
   spiced chicken dumpling soup **188, 189**

eggs
   easy egg fried rice **185**
   a fancy fry-up **22**
   mini stargazey pies **272–3, 272**
   pancetta-baked eggs **30, 31**
   perfect poached eggs **21**
   pork schnitzel with fried egg
      and apple **282, 283**
   salmon, eggs and Irish potato bread **24, 25**

tattie scones and a big breakfast **27**
   a very slow omelette **20**
   a waffly good breakfast **28, 29**
equipment **12–13**
Eton mess **328**

a fancy fry-up **22**
fat
   duck confit with lentils **239–40**
fennel
   apple and fennel raita **49**
   crispy chicken with braised chicory
      and fennel salad **169**
   fennel and onion salad **268**
   fennel, radish and pepper salad **150**
   pasta con sarde **81**
fish
   fish stew with Sardinian fregola **82, 83**
   spiced fish tagine **184**
   steamed Cantonese-style fish with
      spicy tofu **90**
   see also salmon, smoked mackerel
fish cakes
   kipper cakes with tartare sauce **34, 35**
flageolet beans
   duck confit with flageolet ragout
      and celeriac mash **241**
flatbread **93**
   fougasse (French flatbread) **42–3**
flowers
   orange, herb and edible flower salad **162, 163**
fougasse (French flatbread) **42–3**
fragrant pilau rice **183**
fregola
   fish stew with Sardinian fregola **82, 83**
French beans
   spicy vegetable salad with a curry-soy
      vinaigrette **156**
French flatbread **42–3**
fritters, prawn and spring onion **62,** *63*
fruit
   berry surprise **328**
   fruit crumble **328**
   see also apples, strawberries etc
fry-up, fancy **22**

Galmiche, Daniel
   duck confit with lentils **239–40**
game
   mixed game pithivier **138, 139**
garlic
   aioli **64**
   roasted root veg **137**
   see also wild garlic
Gillies, Stuart
   beetroot and goat's curd tart **57**
   creamy celery and walnut salad **158, 159**
   spatchcocked poussin with a chimichurri
      sauce **276, 277**
ginger
   murg adraki (ginger chicken) **275**
gnocchi
   beetroot gnocchi with butter,
      sage and orange sauce **221**
   marjoram gnocchi **220**

roast salmon, gnocchi and chestnut 115
goat's cheese
    beetroot and goat's curd tart 57
goose fat
    duck confit with lentils 239–40
Granger, Bill
    a quick coq au vin 204, 205
    spiced chicken dumpling soup 188, 189
    spicy chicken, cucumber and cashew nut
        salad 170, 171
    stir-fried chilli pork 99
grapefruit
    burnt chilli courgette pickle 279
    chilled soup of carrot, pink grapefruit
        and hazelnuts 258, 259
gravlax 230, 231
green butter sauce 24
green pea and potato cakes 46
green peppercorn sauce 138
grey mullet
    tandoori grey mullet with cep salad 94, 95
Gruyère and bacon soufflé suissesse 265
guanciale (fatty bacon)
    lagane in a borlotti bean and guanciale
        soup 226
gurnard with broad bean, spinach
    and mint stew 84

haddock
    haddock 'ceviche' with crab salad 116, 117
ham
    chicken terrine with herbs 234, 235
    rabbit with Moroccan-style couscous
        and calamari 278
Hansen, Anna
    a modern steak and chips 290–2, 291
Harris, Henry
    tomato, mint and crème fraîche salad 157
    wild sea trout, sorrel and peas 128, 129
Hartnett, Angela
    chicken with chorizo, peppers
        and sage 132, 133
    spiced aubergine 54, 55
hay
    lamb cooked on hay with potato
        boulangère 141
Hay, Donna
    minted pea and feta salad 160
    pancetta-baked eggs 30, 31
hazelnuts
    caramelised hazelnuts 324
    chilled soup of carrot, pink grapefruit
        and hazelnuts 258, 259
    praline 314
hearts of palm salad 161
herbs
    fresh herb salad 152
    herb-crusted roast leg of lamb 142, 143
    herby chips 50, 51
Holland, Will
    red wine soufflé 309
    sag aloo 46, 47
hollandaise sauce
    asparagus with hollandaise sauce 52, 53
    a waffly good breakfast 28, 29

Hom, Ken 77
    Asian-style pasta 98
    beef in oyster sauce 104, 105
    chicken on crispy noodles 96, 97
    Chinese pork potsticker dumplings 246–7,
        246
    crispy pork belly 196, 197
    easy egg fried rice 185
    spicy vegetable salad with a curry-soy
        vinaigrette 156
    steamed Cantonese-style fish
        with spicy tofu 90
honey
    lemon and honey spatchcock chicken 131
horseradish
    home-smoked mackerel with beetroot
        and horseradish 121
hot and sour cabbage 137
hotpot with vinegar onions 252–3

ice cream, coconut rum 322
Indian-style chip and dip 48–9
Indian-style shallot salad 153
ingredients 10–12
Irish potato bread 24, 25

Jaffrey, Madhur
    an Anglo-Indian brunch 36–7
jam
    jam roly poly 316, 316
    a speedy strawberry jam 18, 19
jhal faraizi 36–7

kale
    wagyu beef with beetroot, kale
        and sautéed potatoes 284–5, 285
karhai broccoli 36–7
kebabs
    malai murg tikka (chicken cream tikka) 193
    sesame chicken kebabs and mango
        salsa 68, 69
    sheek kevaab (lamb kebabs) 194, 195
Keller, Thomas
    amazing brined roast chicken 236–8, 237
    a very slow omelette 20
Keogh, Lawrence
    beef stroganoff 293
    deep-fried whiting in oatmeal 202
    home smoked mackerel with beetroot
        and horseradish 121
    tart potato salad 159
    tattie scones and a big breakfast 27
Kerridge, Tom
    lemon posset 329
    pork schnitzel with fried egg and apple 282,
        283
    quick crème brûlée 329
Kime, Tom
    couscous with pistachio and pomegranate 156
    spiced fish tagine 184
kipper cakes with tartare sauce 34, 35
Kitchin, Tom 179
    lamb cooked on hay with potato
        boulangère 141
    roast pumpkin soup 180, 181

spoots with diced veg, chorizo
    and sautéed squid 274
Kochhar, Atul
    murg adraki (ginger chicken) 275
    tandoori grey mullet with cep salad 94, 95
    wild mushroom and sweetcorn biryani
        parcels 262, 263–4

lagane in a borlotti bean and guanciale
    soup 226
lamb
    breast of lamb with apricots
        and almonds 280, 281
    country captain shepherd's pie 249–50, 251
    herb-crusted roast leg of lamb 142, 143
    homemade lamb sausages in prosciutto 208
    lamb cooked on hay with potato
        boulangère 141
    lamb Madras with chapatis 206–7
    sheek kevaab (lamb kebabs) 194, 195
    spicy lamb meatballs 72, 73
    sticky chops 101
lamb sweetbreads and liver with spring onions
    and samphire 140
langoustine and cod puff pastry pie 203
lasagne, classic 228, 229
leeks
    roast brill with scorched lettuce 85
    roasted root veg 137
    scallops with leek and chestnut 260
    the ultimate cottage pie 286–8, 287
lemon
    lemon and honey spatchcock chicken 131
    lemon and parsley butter 134
    lemon beurre blanc 266
    lemon couscous 185
    lemon curd syllabub 329
    lemon dressing 150
    lemon posset 329
lemon sole
    sole-in-a-bag with courgettes and black
        olives 269, 270–1
lentils, duck confit with 239–40
lettuce
    fresh green salad 152
    roast brill with scorched lettuce 85
    whipped feta, yoghurt and cumin salad 160
limes
    haddock 'ceviche' with crab salad 116, 117
    nasi goreng with lime and sugar barbecued
        chicken 190–2, 191
    Thai roast chicken with pak choi and sesame
        noodles 136
    vuelve a la vida 23
liver
    lamb sweetbreads and liver with spring onions
        and samphire 140
lobster
    a splendid spud (with lobster) 114

mackerel
    home-smoked mackerel with beetroot
        and horseradish 121
    mackerel pasty with pickled cucumber
        salad 122, 123

mackerel, tomato and samphire
salad **166, 167**
Malaccan black pepper crab with black beans,
ginger and curry leaves *118*, **119**
malai murg tikka (chicken cream tikka) **193**
mangoes
mango 'egg' with toasted brioche **326–7**
mango salsa **69**
maple syrup-glazed potato salad with pancetta
and calamari **174**
marjoram
griddled swordfish with mint and
marjoram **86, 87**
marjoram gnocchi **220**
Martin, James **9**
asparagus with hollandaise sauce **52, 53**
boozy prune tiramisu **314**
buttermilk crumpets **18, 19**
chickpea and courgette curry **182**
classic beef and ale pie **145**
crispy chicken with braised chicory
and fennel salad **169**
duck confit with flageolet ragout
and celeriac mash **241**
easy stuffed peppers **58**
fragrant pilau rice **183**
jam roly poly **316, 316**
kipper cakes with tartare sauce **34, 35**
lamb Madras with chapatis **206–7**
langoustine and cod puff pastry pie **203**
lemon couscous **185**
lemon curd syllabub **329**
orange and almond cake with
basil cream **302, 303**
perfect poached eggs **21**
potato tart with sardines
and tomatoes **124, 125**
a quick salmon terrine **59**
Saturday night pizzas **198–201, 199**
slow-roasted tomatoes **56**
a speedy strawberry jam **18, 19**
steak, fat chips and béarnaise sauce **209**
sticky chops **101**
sticky toffee apple pudding **319**
sweet potato tagine **186, 187**
tagliatelle with Bolognese ragu **212**
Victoria sandwich **310, 311**
a waffly good breakfast **28, 29**
warm salad of mushroom, beetroot
and pan-fried pigeon **175**
Welsh rarebit **26**
masala mash **215**
mascarpone cheese
boozy prune tiramisu **314**
mash **214–15**
mayonnaise **166**
aioli **64**
creamy celery and walnut salad **158, 159**
Mazzei, Francesco
fresh pasta, southern Italian-style **225–7**
octopus, cannellini beans and smoked
ricotta **66, 67**
meatballs
spicy lamb meatballs **72, 73**
spicy stuffed meatballs **213**

meringues
cherry meringues with rhubarb coulis **308**
Eton mess **328**
peach and raspberry mini pavlovas **306, 307**
Mexican hearts of palm salad **161**
milk
caramelised rice pudding **318**
Millar, Danny
fruit crumble **328**
millefeuilles, chestnut and pear **320, *321***
mini stargazey pies **272–3, 272**
mint
cucumber and mint raita **48**
griddled swordfish with mint
and marjoram **86, 87**
minted pea and feta salad **160**
tomato, mint and crème fraîche salad **157**
a modern steak and chips **290–2, *291***
molasses
blueberry **144**
pomegranate **292**
morels
roast poussin with morels, broad beans
and spätzle **134, 135**
salted pollock with asparagus, wild garlic
and morels **120**
mousses
coffee sabayon mousse **324**
scallop mousse with asparagus **261**
Mum's hotpot with vinegar onions **252–3**
murg adraki (ginger chicken) **275**
mushrooms
artichokes à la barigoule **58**
beef stroganoff **293**
chasseur sauce **238**
dauphinoise and Taleggio pithivier **112, 113**
a fancy fry-up **22**
a hearty roast pheasant lunch **244–5**
Mum's hotpot with vinegar onions **252–3**
a quick coq au vin **204, 205**
roast poussin with morels, broad beans
and spätzle **134, 135**
salted pollock with asparagus, wild garlic
and morels **120**
tandoori grey mullet with cep salad **94, 95**
tattie scones and a big breakfast **27**
veal blanquette **242, 243**
warm salad of mushroom, beetroot
and pan-fried pigeon **175**
white wine sauce **120**
wild mushroom and sweetcorn biryani
parcels **262, 263–4**
mussels
fish stew with Sardinian fregola **82, 83**
pollock, squid and mussel stew **126–7**
tagliatelle with mussels **78, 79**
mustard sauce **272–3**

naan bread **48**
Nairn, Nick
apple croustade with Armagnac
custard **312, 313**
haddock 'ceviche' with crab salad **116, 117**
sesame chicken kebabs and mango
salsa **68, 69**

a splendid spud (with lobster) **114**
nasi goreng with lime and sugar barbecued
chicken **190–2, *191***
noodles
chicken on crispy noodles **96, 97**
roast poussin with morels, broad beans
and spätzle **134, 135**
spicy chicken, cucumber and cashew nut
salad **170, 171**
Thai roast chicken with pak choi
and sesame noodles **136**
nuts
sugared nuts **328**
see also almonds, walnuts etc

oatmeal, deep-fried whiting in **202**
octopus
octopus, cannellini beans and smoked
ricotta **66, 67**
octopus, chorizo and oregano **130**
okra curry, couscous and flatbread **92–3**
olive oil mash **214**
olives
orange, herb and edible flower salad **162, 163**
quinoa and broad bean salad **154, 155**
sole-in-a-bag with courgettes and black
olives **269, 270–1**
sweet potato tagine **186, 187**
tuna tapenade **45**
omelette, very slow **20**
onion seeds
tomato and onion seed chutney **49**
onions
an Anglo-Indian brunch **36–7**
classic beef and ale pie **145**
easy stuffed peppers **58**
fennel and onion salad **268**
maple syrup-glazed potato salad
with pancetta and calamari **174**
Mum's hotpot with vinegar onions **252–3**
roasted root veg **137**
spiced aubergine **54, 55**
the ultimate cottage pie **286–8, 287**
wild mushroom and sweetcorn biryani
parcels **262, 263–4**
orange juice
peach and raspberry mini pavlovas **306, 307**
vuelve a la vida **23**
oranges
beetroot gnocchi with butter, sage
and orange sauce **221**
crêpes with orange butter sauce **298, 299**
crispy chicken with braised chicory
and fennel salad **169**
orange and almond cake with
basil cream **302, 303**
orange foam **324**
orange, herb and edible flower
salad **162, 163**
sea bream with fennel and orange **268**
Outlaw, Nathan
irresistible cheesecake **329**
mackerel, tomato and samphire
salad **166, 167**
pollock, squid and mussel stew **126–7**

smorgasbord of smoked fish 230–2, 231
sugared nuts 328
oyster sauce, beef in 104, 105
oysters
  deep-fried oysters 232
  salad of roast suckling pig
    and oysters 172, 173

Padrón peppers 64
paella, quick-smoked salmon 88, 89
pak choi
  spiced chicken dumpling soup 188, 189
  Thai roast chicken with pak choi and sesame
    noodles 136
palm hearts
  Mexican hearts of palm salad 161
pancetta
  a classic lasagne 228, 229
  maple syrup-glazed potato salad
    with pancetta and calamari 174
  pancetta-baked eggs 30, 31
  rabbit with Moroccan-style couscous
    and calamari 278
  tagliatelle with Bolognese ragu 212
  see also bacon
pandhi curry (Coorg pork stir-fry) 248
panzanella with tuna 164, 165
Parma ham
  rabbit with Moroccan-style couscous
    and calamari 278
parsley
  lemon and parsley butter 134
parsnips
  roast cod with winter ratatouille 266, 267
pasta
  Asian-style pasta 98
  basic pasta dough 224
  cavatelli with broccoli and colatura 227
  a classic lasagne 228, 229
  eggless pasta dough 225
  fish stew with Sardinian fregola 82, 83
  lagane in a borlotti bean and guanciale
    soup 226
  pasta con sarde 81
  penne with halloumi and cherry tomatoes 80
  tagliatelle with Bolognese ragu 212
  tagliatelle with mussels 78, 79
pastiera di Grano 304, 305
pastries
  apple croustade with Armagnac
    custard 312, 313
  chestnut and pear millefeuilles 320, 321
  wild mushroom and sweetcorn biryani
    parcels 262, 263–4
  see also pies
pastry, rough puff 203
patatas fritas 50
pâté, smoked mackerel 232
pavlovas, peach and raspberry mini 306, 307
peach and raspberry mini pavlovas 306, 307
peanuts
  green pea and potato cakes 46
  spicy sticky ribs with sweet shallots
    and peanuts 289
pears

chestnut and pear millefeuilles 320, 321
peas
  crisp shrimp risotto cakes 65
  green pea and potato cakes 46
  langoustine and cod puff pastry pie 203
  minted pea and feta salad 160
  pea, broad bean and bacon salad 150, 151
  spicy vegetable salad with a curry-soy
    vinaigrette 156
  wild sea trout, sorrel and peas 128, 129
penne with halloumi and cherry tomatoes 80
peppercorns
  green peppercorn sauce 138
peppers
  Asian-style pasta 98
  beef slices with Oloroso sherry 102, 103
  chicken with chorizo, peppers
    and sage 132, 133
  easy stuffed peppers 58
  fennel, radish and pepper salad 150
  panzanella with tuna 164, 165
  pimientos de Padron 64
  roasted vegetable pizza 201
pesto 45
pheasant
  a hearty roast pheasant lunch 244–5
pickle, burnt chilli courgette 279
pickled cucumber salad 122
pies
  classic beef and ale pie 145
  country captain shepherd's pie 249–50, 251
  dauphinoise and Taleggio pithivier 112, 113
  langoustine and cod puff pastry pie 203
  mackerel pasty with pickled cucumber
    salad 122, 123
  mini stargazey pies 272–3, 272
  mixed game pithivier 138, 139
  Mum's hotpot with vinegar onions 252–3
  see also pastries
pigeon
  warm salad of mushroom, beetroot
    and pan-fried pigeon 175
pilau rice 183, 293
pimientos de Padron 64
pine nuts
  pesto 45
pineapple, spiced roasted 315
piquillo peppers
  beef slices with Oloroso sherry 102, 103
  panzanella with tuna 164, 165
pistachio nuts
  couscous with pistachio
    and pomegranate 156
pithivier
  dauphinoise and Taleggio pithivier 112, 113
  mixed game pithivier 138, 139
Pizarro, José
  beef slices with Oloroso sherry 102, 103
  olive oil mash 214
  patatas fritas 50
  spicy lamb meatballs 72, 73
pizzas
  basic pizza dough 198
  roasted vegetable pizza 201
  a simple Margherita with rocket 200

spinach, chorizo and artichoke pizza 200
plaice
  spiced fish tagine 184
plums
  spiced plum compôte 318
polenta
  creamy wet polenta 215
  a modern steak and chips 290–2, 291
pollock
  pollock, squid and mussel stew 126–7
  salted pollock with asparagus, wild garlic
    and morels 120
pomegranate
  couscous with pistachio and pomegranate 156
  pomegranate molasses 292
pork
  chicken terrine with herbs 234, 235
  Chinese pork potsticker dumplings 246–7,
    246
  crackling 172
  crispy pork belly 196, 197
  pandhi curry (Coorg pork stir-fry) 248
  pork belly with blueberry and chilli molasses
    glaze 144
  pork schnitzel with fried egg
    and apple 282, 283
  rabbit and rosemary terrine with chutney 233
  salad of roast suckling pig
    and oysters 172, 173
  spicy sticky ribs with sweet shallots
    and peanuts 289
  spicy stuffed meatballs 213
  stir-fried chilli pork 99
  walnut-crusted pork 100
posset, lemon 329
potatoes
  an Anglo-Indian brunch 36–7
  beetroot gnocchi with butter, sage
    and orange sauce 221
  classic mash 214
  country captain shepherd's pie 249–50, 251
  dauphinoise and Taleggio pithivier 112, 113
  duck confit with flageolet ragout
    and celeriac mash 241
  green pea and potato cakes 46
  gurnard with broad bean, spinach
    and mint stew 84
  herby chips 50, 51
  Irish potato bread 24, 25
  kipper cakes with tartare sauce 34, 35
  lamb cooked on hay with potato
    boulangère 141
  lamb sweetbreads and liver with spring onions
    and samphire 140
  maple syrup-glazed potato salad with
    pancetta and calamari 174
  marjoram gnocchi 220
  masala mash 215
  Mum's hotpot with vinegar onions 252–3
  olive oil mash 214
  patatas fritas 50
  potato tart with sardines
    and tomatoes 124, 125
  sag aloo 46, 47
  a splendid spud (with lobster) 114

steak, fat chips and béarnaise sauce **209**
tart potato salad **159**
tattie scones **27**
the ultimate cottage pie **286–8, 287**
wagyu beef with beetroot, kale and sautéed
  potatoes **284–5, 285**
Potts Dawson, Arthur
  pasta con sarde **81**
poussins
  roast poussin with morels, broad beans
    and spätzle **134, 135**
  spatchcocked poussin with a chimichurri
    sauce **276, 277**
praline **314**
prawns
  fish stew with Sardinian fregola **82, 83**
  prawn and spring onion fritters **62, 63**
  prawns with chorizo **70, 71**
  shellfish stock **126**
  vuelve a la vida **23**
prosciutto, homemade lamb sausages in **208**
prunes
  boozy prune tiramisu **314**
pumpkin
  roast pumpkin soup **180, 181**
  sausage, pumpkin and sage casserole **210,
    211**
Purnell, Glynn
  roast brill with scorched lettuce **85**

quail eggs
  mini stargazey pies **272–3, 272**
quince purée **244**
quinoa and broad bean salad **154, *155***

rabbit
  rabbit and rosemary terrine with chutney **233**
  rabbit with Moroccan-style couscous
    and calamari **278**
radishes
  artichokes à la barigoule **58**
  fennel, radish and pepper salad **150**
  Mexican hearts of palm salad **161**
  tomato and radish salad **153**
raita **264**
  apple and fennel raita **49**
  cucumber and mint raita **48**
Ramsay, Tana
  homemade lamb sausages in
    prosciutto **208**
  pea, broad bean and bacon salad **150, 151**
Randall, Theo
  a classic lasagne **228, 229**
Rankin, Paul
  hot and sour cabbage **137**
  mixed game pithivier **138, 139**
  spicy sticky ribs with sweet shallots and
    peanuts **289**
Rankin, Shaun
  maple syrup-glazed potato salad with
    pancetta and calamari **174**
  rabbit with Moroccan-style couscous
    and calamari **278**
rarebit, Welsh **26**
ras-el-hanout **184**

raspberries
  instant berry sorbet **328**
  peach and raspberry mini pavlovas **306, 307**
  Victoria sandwich **310, 311**
ratatouille
  roast cod with winter ratatouille **266, 267**
razor clams
  spoots with diced veg, chorizo
    and sautéed squid **274**
red cabbage
  hot and sour cabbage **137**
red mullet
  fish stew with Sardinian fregola **82, 83**
red wine soufflé **309**
Reynaud, Stéphane
  rabbit and rosemary terrine with chutney **233**
  scallops with leek and chestnut **260**
rhubarb coulis **308**
rice
  caramelised rice pudding with spiced
    plum compôte **318**
  crisp shrimp risotto cakes **65**
  easy egg fried rice **185**
  fragrant pilau rice **183**
  nasi goreng with lime and sugar barbecued
    chicken **190–2, 191**
  pilau rice **293**
  quick-smoked salmon paella **88, 89**
  stir-fried chilli pork **99**
  wild mushroom and sweetcorn biryani
    parcels **262, 263–4**
ricotta cheese
  octopus, cannellini beans and smoked
    ricotta **66, 67**
  pastiera di Grano **304, 305**
risotto cakes, crisp shrimp **65**
rocket, a simple Margherita with **200**
roly poly, jam **316, *316***
root veg, roasted **137**
rough puff pastry **203**
Roux, Alain
  scallop mousse with asparagus **261**
Roux, Michel **297**
  cherry meringues with rhubarb coulis **308**
  chicken terrine with herbs **234, 235**
  classic rich chocolate sauce **323**
  coconut rum ice cream **322**
  crêpes with orange butter sauce **298, 299**
  spiced roasted pineapple **315**
Roux, Michel Jr
  veal blanquette **242, 243**
Rowe, Silvena
  berry surprise **328**
  octopus, chorizo and oregano **130**
  orange, herb and edible flower salad **162, 163**
  pork belly with blueberry and chilli
    molasses glaze **144**
  whipped feta, yoghurt and cumin salad **160**
rum
  coconut rum ice cream **322**

saffron sauce **126–7**
sag aloo **46, *47***
salads
  beetroot salad **232**

braised chicory and fennel salad **169**
bulgar wheat salad **168**
cep salad **94, 95**
crab salad **116, 117**
creamy celery and walnut salad **158, 159**
fennel and onion salad **268**
fennel, radish and pepper salad **150**
fresh green salad **152**
fresh herb salad **152**
Indian-style shallot salad **153**
mackerel, tomato and samphire
  salad **166, 167**
maple syrup-glazed potato salad
  with pancetta and calamari **174**
Mexican hearts of palm salad **161**
orange, herb and edible flower salad **162, 163**
panzanella with tuna **164, 165**
pea, broad bean and bacon salad **150, 151**
pickled cucumber salad **122**
quinoa and broad bean salad **154, 155**
salad of roast suckling pig
  and oysters **172, 173**
spicy chicken, cucumber and cashew nut
  salad **170, 171**
spicy vegetable salad with a curry-soy
  vinaigrette **156**
a splendid spud (with lobster) **114**
tart potato salad **159**
tomato and radish salad **153**
tomato, mint and crème fraîche salad **157**
warm salad of mushroom, beetroot
  and pan-fried pigeon **175**
watercress salad **122**
whipped feta, yoghurt and cumin salad **160**
salmon
  beetroot-cured salmon **230, 231**
  a quick salmon terrine **59**
  quick-smoked salmon paella **88, 89**
  roast salmon, gnocchi and chestnut **115**
  salmon, eggs and Irish potato bread **24, 25**
salsa, mango **69**
salted pollock with asparagus, wild garlic
  and morels **120**
samphire
  lamb sweetbreads and liver with spring
    onions and samphire **140**
  mackerel, tomato and samphire
    salad **166, 167**
sardines
  mini stargazey pies **272–3, 272**
  pasta con sarde **81**
  potato tart with sardines and
    tomatoes **124, 125**
Sardinian fregola, fish stew with **82, *83***
Sargeant, Mark **41**
  caramelised bananas **328**
  chorizo tapas **71**
  clams, smoked bacon and cider broth **91**
  Eton mess **328**
  mackerel pasty with pickled cucumber
    salad **122, 123**
  quick-smoked salmon paella **88, 89**
sauces
  Armagnac custard **312**
  béarnaise sauce **209**

béchamel sauce **229**
Bolognese ragu **212**
Calvados caramel sauce **319**
chasseur sauce **238**
chimichurri sauce **276**
classic rich chocolate sauce **323**
dipping sauce **246–7**
green butter sauce **24**
green peppercorn sauce **138**
hollandaise sauce **52, 53**
mustard sauce **272–3**
orange butter sauce **298**
saffron sauce **126–7**
tartare sauce **34, 35**
tomato sauce **202**
vanilla custard **316**
white wine sauce **120**
sausage meat
   mixed game pithivier **138, 139**
sausages
   homemade lamb sausages in
     prosciutto **208**
   sausage, pumpkin and sage
     casserole **210, 211**
   see also chorizo
scallops
   scallop mousse with asparagus **261**
   scallops with leek and chestnut **260**
scones, tattie **27**
sea bream with fennel and orange **268**
sea trout
   wild sea trout, sorrel and peas **128, 129**
seasonal food **336–9**
semolina
   eggless pasta dough **225**
sesame chicken kebabs and mango salsa **68, 69**
shallots
   fried shallots **207**
   Indian-style shallot salad **153**
   shallot rings **284**
   spicy sticky ribs with sweet shallots
     and peanuts **289**
sheek kevaab (lamb kebabs) **194, 195**
shellfish stock **126**
shepherd's pie, country captain **249–50, *251***
sherry
   beef slices with Oloroso sherry **102, 103**
shrimps
   crisp shrimp risotto cakes **65**
   see also prawns
Singh, Vivek
   apple and fennel raita **49**
   green pea and potato cakes **46**
   masala mash **215**
   pandhi curry (Coorg pork stir-fry) **248**
   tomato and onion seed chutney **49**
smoked haddock
   haddock 'ceviche' with crab salad **116, 117**
smoked mackerel
   home-smoked mackerel with beetroot
     and horseradish **121**
   smoked mackerel pâté **232**
smoked salmon
   a quick salmon terrine **59**
   quick-smoked salmon paella **88, 89**

smorgasbord of smoked fish **230–2, *231***
Smyth, Clare
   artichokes à la barigoule **58**
sole-in-a-bag with courgettes and black
   olives **269, *270–1***
sorbet, instant berry **328**
sorrel
   wild sea trout, sorrel and peas **128, 129**
soufflés
   Gruyère and bacon soufflé suissesse **265**
   red wine soufflé **309**
soups
   chilled soup of carrot, pink grapefruit
     and hazelnuts **258, 259**
   clams, smoked bacon and cider broth **91**
   lagane in a borlotti bean and guanciale
     soup **226**
   roast pumpkin soup **180, 181**
   spiced chicken dumpling soup **188, 189**
soy sauce
   curry-soy vinaigrette **156**
spatchcocked poussin with a chimichurri
   sauce **276, *277***
spätzle
   roast poussin with morels, broad beans
     and spätzle **134, 135**
spiced aubergine **54, 55**
spiced chicken dumpling soup **188, *189***
spiced fish tagine **184**
spiced roasted pineapple **315**
spicy chicken, cucumber and cashew nut
   salad *170, 171*
spicy lamb meatballs **72, *73***
spicy sticky ribs with sweet shallots and
   peanuts **289**
spicy stuffed meatballs **213**
spicy vegetable salad with a curry-soy
   vinaigrette **156**
spinach
   country captain shepherd's pie **249–50, 251**
   gurnard with broad bean, spinach
     and mint stew **84**
   Mexican hearts of palm salad **161**
   minted pea and feta salad **160**
   sag aloo **46, 47**
   spinach, chorizo and artichoke pizza **200**
spoots with diced veg, chorizo and sautéed
   squid **274**
spring, seasonal food **336**
spring greens
   dauphinoise and Taleggio pithivier **112, 113**
spring onions
   lamb sweetbreads and liver with spring
     onions and samphire **140**
   prawn and spring onion fritters **62, 63**
squash
   an Anglo-Indian brunch **36–7**
   pollock, squid and mussel stew **126–7**
   roast cod with winter ratatouille **266, 267**
   roast pumpkin soup **180, 181**
   roast salmon, gnocchi and chestnut **115**
squid
   fish stew with Sardinian fregola **82, 83**
   maple syrup-glazed potato salad with
     pancetta and calamari **174**

pollock, squid and mussel stew **126–7**
rabbit with Moroccan-style couscous
   and calamari **278**
spoots with diced veg, chorizo and sautéed
   squid **274**
stargazey pies **272–3, *272***
steak, fat chips and béarnaise sauce **209**
steamed puddings
   jam roly poly **316, 316**
Stein, Rick
   aioli **64**
   Malaccan black pepper crab with black beans,
     ginger and curry leaves **118, 119**
   nasi goreng with lime and sugar barbecued
     chicken **190–2, 191**
   pimientos de Padron **64**
   prawn and spring onion fritters **62, 63**
stews
   artichokes à la barigoule **58**
   beef stroganoff **293**
   fish stew with Sardinian fregola **82, 83**
   gurnard with broad bean, spinach
     and mint stew **84**
   Mum's hotpot with vinegar onions **252–3**
   pollock, squid and mussel stew **126–7**
   a quick coq au vin **204, 205**
   sausage, pumpkin and sage
     casserole **210, 211**
   spiced aubergine **54, 55**
   spiced fish tagine **184**
   sweet potato tagine **186, 187**
   veal blanquette **242, 243**
sticky chops **101**
sticky toffee apple pudding **319**
stock
   shellfish **126**
   tomato **166**
Stovell, Fernando
   Mexican hearts of palm salad **161**
   vuelve a la vida **23**
strawberries
   Eton mess **328**
   instant berry sorbet **328**
   a speedy strawberry jam **18, 19**
suckling pig
   salad of roast suckling pig
     and oysters **172, 173**
suet puddings
   jam roly poly **316, 316**
sugared nuts **328**
summer, seasonal food **337**
swede
   roast cod with winter ratatouille **266, 267**
sweet potato tagine **186, *187***
sweetbreads
   lamb sweetbreads and liver with spring onions
     and samphire **140**
sweetcorn
   wild mushroom and sweetcorn biryani
     parcels **262, 263–4**
swordfish
   griddled swordfish with mint
     and marjoram **86, 87**
syllabub, lemon curd **329**
tagines

spiced fish tagine **184**
sweet potato tagine **186, 187**
tagliatelle
  tagliatelle with Bolognese ragu **212**
  tagliatelle with mussels **78, 79**
Tanaka, Jun
  breast of lamb with apricots and
    almonds **280, 281**
  bulgar wheat salad **168**
  instant berry sorbet **328**
  roast poussin with morels, broad beans
    and spätzle **134, 135**
tandoori grey mullet with cep salad **94, 95**
Tanner, James
  Thai roast chicken with pak choi
    and sesame noodles **136**
tapas, chorizo **71**
tapenade, tuna **45**
tart potato salad **159**
tartare sauce **34, 35**
tarts
  beetroot and goat's curd tart **57**
  pastiera di Grano **304, 305**
  potato tart with sardines
    and tomatoes **124, 125**
tattie scones and a big breakfast **27**
Tebbutt, Matt
  caramelised rice pudding with spiced
    plum compôte **318**
  chestnut and pear millefeuilles **320, 321**
  a classic cherry clafoutis **300, 301**
  dauphinoise and Taleggio pithivier **112, 113**
  fresh green salad **152**
  okra curry, couscous and flatbread **92–3**
  penne with halloumi and cherry tomatoes **80**
  sausage, pumpkin and sage
    casserole **210, 211**
terrines
  chicken terrine with herbs **234, 235**
  a quick salmon terrine **59**
  rabbit and rosemary terrine with chutney **233**
Thai roast chicken with pak choi and sesame
  noodles **136**
tiger prawns
  vuelve a la vida **23**
tiramisu, boozy prune **314**
Titcombe, Cass
  gurnard with broad bean, spinach
    and mint stew **84**
toast
  Welsh rarebit **26**
Todiwala, Cyrus
  country captain shepherd's pie **249–50, 251**
  cucumber and mint raita **48**
  Indian-style shallot salad **153**
  malai murg tikka (chicken cream tikka) **193**
  naan bread **48**
  sheek kevaab (lamb kebabs) **194, 195**
toffee
  sticky toffee apple pudding **319**
tofu
  steamed Cantonese-style fish
    with spicy tofu **90**
tomatoes
  Asian-style pasta **98**

aubergine 'parmigiana' with roasted
  tomato **110, 111**
chutney **233**
a classic lasagne **228, 229**
country captain shepherd's pie **249–50, 251**
duck confit with flageolet ragout
  and celeriac mash **241**
easy stuffed peppers **58**
a fancy fry-up **22**
fennel, radish and pepper salad **150**
lamb Madras with chapatis **206–7**
mackerel, tomato and samphire
  salad **166, 167**
panzanella with tuna **164, 165**
penne with halloumi and cherry
  tomatoes **80**
potato tart with sardines and
  tomatoes **124, 125**
roasted vegetable pizza **201**
sausage, pumpkin and sage
  casserole **210, 211**
a simple Margherita with rocket **200**
slow-roasted tomatoes **56**
spiced aubergine **54, 55**
spicy lamb meatballs **72, 73**
spicy stuffed meatballs **213**
spicy vegetable salad with a curry-soy
  vinaigrette **156**
spinach, chorizo and artichoke pizza **200**
a splendid spud (with lobster) **114**
sticky chops **101**
sweet potato tagine **186, 187**
tagliatelle with mussels **78, 79**
tattie scones and a big breakfast **27**
tomato and onion seed chutney **49**
tomato and radish salad **153**
tomato, mint and crème fraîche salad **157**
tomato sauce **202**
vuelve a la vida **23**
trout see sea trout
tuna
  panzanella with tuna **164, 165**
  tuna tapenade **45**
Turner, Andrew
  mango 'egg' with toasted brioche **326–7**
turnips
  artichokes à la barigoule **58**

vanilla custard **316**
veal
  chicken terrine with herbs **234, 235**
  a classic lasagne **228, 229**
  veal blanquette **242, 243**
  veal cutlet with a burnt chilli
    courgette pickle **279**
vegetables
  roast cod with winter ratatouille **266, 267**
  roasted vegetable pizza **201**
  see also peppers, tomatoes etc
vermouth
  wild sea trout, sorrel and peas **128, 129**
Victoria sandwich **310, 311**
vinaigrette **161**
  curry-soy vinaigrette **156**
vuelve a la vida **23**

a waffly good breakfast **28, 29**
wagyu beef with beetroot, kale and sautéed
  potatoes **284–5, 285**
walnuts
  caramelised walnuts **244–5**
  creamy celery and walnut salad **158, 159**
  walnut-crusted pork **100**
Wareing, Marcus
  Mum's hotpot with vinegar onions **252–3**
water chestnuts
  sesame chicken kebabs and mango
    salsa **68, 69**
watercress
  a modern steak and chips **290–2, 291**
  roast brill with scorched lettuce **85**
  watercress salad **122**
Watt, Nic
  veal cutlet with a burnt chilli courgette
    pickle **279**
Welch, Tristan
  mini stargazey pies **272–3, 272**
Welsh rarebit **26**
wheat grain
  pastiera di Grano **304, 305**
white wine sauce **120**
whiting
  deep-fried whiting in oatmeal **202**
wild garlic
  salted pollock with asparagus, wild garlic
    and morels **120**
wild mushroom and sweetcorn biryani
  parcels *262, 263–4*
Williams, Bryn
  creamy wet polenta **215**
  marjoram gnocchi **220**
  roast salmon, gnocchi and chestnut **115**
  sole-in-a-bag with courgettes
    and black olives **269, 270–1**
wine
  chorizo in red wine **71**
  lemon curd syllabub **329**
  Mum's hotpot with vinegar onions **252–3**
  pasta con sarde **81**
  a quick coq au vin **204, 205**
  red wine soufflé **309**
  scallops with leek and chestnut **260**
  tagliatelle with Bolognese ragu **212**
  the ultimate cottage pie **286–8, 287**
  white wine sauce **120**
  wine and food **332–4**
winter, seasonal food **339**

yoghurt
  apple and fennel raita **49**
  berry surprise **328**
  cucumber and mint raita **48**
  malai murg tikka (chicken cream tikka) **193**
  orange foam **324**
  raita **264**
  whipped feta, yoghurt and cumin salad **160**
  yoghurt and cucumber dip **208**

Acknowledgements

Getting up so early every Saturday to shoot our show continues to be fun, wholly because of the following people. Their considerable efforts have kept Saturday Kitchen on the air, and made it something we can all be very proud of. Heartfelt thanks go to:

The core production team: James Winter (series producer), Andy Clarke (producer), Michaela Bowles, Janet Brinkworth, Claire Paine, Charlotte Johnstone, James Ross, Chris Worthington, Charlie Brades, Jo Birkinshaw, Will Learmonth and all the other Cactus staff who work on the show, including Maureen McPhee and the tireless runners. Simon for the beautiful new set, Dean, Paul and all the builders for finishing the new studio on time.

The incredibly supportive Prolink Television Facilities: the Dugards and all our fabulous crew, the unflappable Silvana for keeping us to time, Jez for keeping us 'lit', Naomi for keeping James fluent, Neil and the gang, including stalwarts on camera – Phil the Fork, Toby and Tom. Our directors Dino, Toby and especially Geri Dowd for tireless eating!

Carla-Maria Lawson, Liam Keelan and everyone at the BBC for their support over the last seven years – and the commission for the next three years!

Everyone at Orion for producing a book that really does justice to the show.

Of course James Martin, our brilliant wine experts Susie Barrie, Susy Atkins, Olly Smith, Peter Richards, Tim Atkin and all the amazing chefs from all over the world whose performances make the show so special and a privilege to work on.

And finally Simon and my beautiful sons for letting me work every Saturday morning.

Amanda Ross

– Amanda Ross, Executive Producer of Saturday Kitchen and co-founder of Cactus TV with her husband Simon